RACE AND THE MODERNIST IMAGINATION

RACE AND THE MODERNIST IMAGINATION

Urmila Seshagiri

Cornell University Press

ITHACA AND LONDON

First published 2010 by Cornell University Press

Printed in the United States of America

Library of Congress Cataloging-in-Publication Data

Seshagiri, Urmila, 1971–
    Race and the modernist imagination / Urmila Seshagiri.
       p. cm.
    Includes bibliographical references and index.
    ISBN 978-0-8014-4821-8 (cloth : alk. paper)
    1. English fiction—20th century—History and criticism.
2. Race in literature.   3. Modernism (Literature)—Great Britain.
I. Title.
    PR888.R34S47 2010
    820.9'3552—dc22   2009041329

Cornell University Press strives to use environmentally responsible suppliers and materials to the fullest extent possible in the publishing of its books. Such materials include vegetable-based, low-VOC inks and acid-free papers that are recycled, totally chlorine-free, or partly composed of nonwood fibers. For further information, visit our website at www.cornellpress.cornell.edu.

Cloth printing   10 9 8 7 6 5 4 3 2 1

For Arjun

CONTENTS

ILLUSTRATIONS

ACKNOWLEDGMENTS

My first thanks go to Janet Lyon, the muse and mentor whose ideas have always illuminated mine. As this book journeyed from genesis to completion, she gave me unstinting personal and intellectual support. Every sentence I have written here is better because of her.

This book would not have been possible without my many teachers. At Oberlin College, David Walker introduced me to the beauty of modernism and Phyllis Gorfain showed me the excitement of scholarly research. At the University of Illinois, I was privileged to learn from Michael Bérubé, Zohreh Sullivan, and Robert Parker, as well as from Jed Esty, whose brilliance continues to guide my work.

I am grateful to the Massachusetts Institute of Technology, where I was welcomed by a circle of scholars and teachers whose work enriched my own. I am especially grateful to Margery Resnick and Steven Strang, who created a place for me in the vibrant, interdisciplinary world of the humanities at the Institute; and I thank the MIT Program in Women's Studies for giving me a room of my own in which to think, read, and write.

My colleagues at the University of Tennessee have supported this book in multiple ways. Allen Carroll, Amy Elias, Tom Haddox, Bob Leggett, Chuck Maland, and John Zomchick read parts of the manuscript and sharpened the book's argument with their questions and critiques. Stan Garner offered sage counsel through some of the rockiest stages of the writing. Heather Hirschfeld, whose friendship sustains and whose scholarly excellence inspires, always made time to discuss the complexities of literary research. I owe a tremendous debt to Lisi Schoenbach, whose knowledge of modernism brought new vitality to this book and whose support and good humor (as well as culinary genius) were crucial for its completion. Joseph

Black patiently read draft after draft and supplied me with numerous first editions of modern works. Thanks to Bethann Bowman for meticulous editorial work and delightful conversations about Virginia Woolf, and to April Hennessey, Courtney Housefield, Hannah McCreery, and Mary Wrenn, who gave generously of their time and enabled me to write.

Colleagues at a number of other institutions have read and discussed portions of this book over the years, and I thank Ian Baucom, Marianne deKoven, Maria diBattista, Jay Dickson, Lynn Garafola, Peter Kalliney, Jesse Matz, Laura Winkiel, Mark Wollaeger, and Rishona Zimring for their ideas, insights, and criticisms. I am especially grateful to Simon Gikandi for conversations that helped me to discover my capabilities as a scholar, writer, and teacher. And I thank Nicolás Wey-Gómez for believing in the spirit of this book long before I could even divine its presence.

This book found a wonderful home at Cornell University Press, and I am grateful to everyone there who worked with me. Thanks to John Ackerman for an enthusiastic initial conversation about the project, and to Susan Specter for the tremendous patience and kindness she showed me through the final stages of writing. Thanks also to Marie Flaherty-Jones for attention to editorial detail. I am deeply indebted to Laura Doyle for many memorable conversations about modernism and race, as well as for an astute reading that brought greater clarity and coherence to this book's claims. I also thank the anonymous reader whose thoughtful suggestions broadened the scope of my key ideas. Most of all, thanks to Peter J. Potter for challenging me to produce my best work and giving me the time to do so.

I had the good fortune to conduct archival research for this book in libraries and museums in the United States and in England, and I would like to thank the curators at the Tate Britain, the staff of the Manuscripts Reading Room in the British Library, Karen V. Kukil at Smith College's Mortimer Rare Book Room, Maria Singer at the Yale Center for British Art, Revinder Chahal at the Victoria and Albert Museum, and Sandra Marques at the Museum of London. The time and resources to conduct my research were enabled by a number of institutions and departments: I am grateful for support from the Paul Mellon Centre for Studies in British Art, the Dean's Fund for Faculty Development at MIT, and the Department of English and the Women's Studies Program at the University of Illinois. The University of Tennessee has provided extremely generous support for this book, and I thank the Department of English, the Hodges Fund for Better English, the Humanities Initiative, and the Office of Research. An especially warm thanks to Judith Welch for help above and beyond on more occasions than I can recall.

My parents, Bala and Girish Seshagiri, taught me to love books and to work with joy. There are no words expressive enough to thank them for their unending support and the faultless example they have set for me. I am profoundly grateful to my brother, Chandran Seshagiri, for his steady belief that I would finish this book, and my sister-in-law, Ilana Brownstein, for our energetic conversations about art. My father-in-law, E. N. Shankar, watched this book unfold in Urbana, Boston, and Knoxville: I thank him for his love and support. And I am overjoyed to be able to thank my ninety-six-year-old grandfather, Krishna Kalyanraman, for his lively interest in my career as a literary scholar, and my eighty-six-year-old grandmother, Rajammal Kalyanraman, for her timeless wisdom and youthful spirit. Finally, thanks to the truly extraordinary friends who cheered me on during the writing: Edwin Tait and Sarita Nori, for ceaseless encouragement during what seemed to be an equally ceaseless process; Lisa Morrison, with whom I had the earliest and most excited conversations about this book; and Jesse Ford, who showered me with affection and enthusiasm as I made my way to the finish line.

My deepest thanks go to my husband, Arjun Shankar, who has lived with this book for many more years than he could have imagined. These pages were written while we mourned the loss of our first baby and then, happily, celebrated the arrival of our daughter, Jaya, and our twin sons, Rama and Krishna. His infinite love and patience have shown me that everything is possible, and it is with great joy that I dedicate this book to him.

Parts of this book have appeared in other forms: "Modernity's (Yellow) Perils: Dr. Fu-Manchu and English Race-Paranoia" first appeared in *Cultural Critique* 62 (January 2006): 162–94, published by University of Minnesota Press; "Orienting Virginia Woolf: Race, Aesthetics, and Politics in *To the Lighthouse*" first appeared in *Modern Fiction Studies* 50, no. 1 (Spring 2004): 58–84, published by Johns Hopkins University Press, copyright © 2004 Purdue Research Foundation; and "Racial Politics, Avant-Garde Poetics: Wyndham Lewis's BLAST and Modernist Form," first appeared in *Modernism*, ed. Astradur Eysteinsson and Vivian Liska, 573–89, published in 2007 by John Benjamins Publishing Company, Amsterdam/Philadelphia, www.benjamins.com. I am grateful to University of Minnesota Press, Johns Hopkins University Press, and John Benjamins for their kind permission to reproduce portions of these essays here.

RACE AND THE
MODERNIST
IMAGINATION

INTRODUCTION

Race and the Modernist Imagination

On a dazzling Covent Garden stage in 1911, the young Russian dancer Vaslav Nijinsky danced the role of the Golden Slave in the Ballets Russes's production of *Schéhérazade*. Clad in only an ornate breastplate and shimmering harem pants, his skin darkened to copper, the now-legendary Nijinsky astonished London audiences with the decisively modern language of his ballet. *Schéhérazade*'s lavish trappings and balletic asymmetry signaled the end of the feminine prettiness that had characterized classical dance through the nineteenth century. Léon Bakst designed exquisite Arabian costumes of billowing jewel-toned silk robes and ingeniously wrapped turbans; Michel Fokine choreographed movements for a vast cast of characters that included eunuchs, odalisques, and Negro and Hindu footmen; and a large orchestra played the sensual melodies and intricate metrical patterns of Nikolai Rimsky-Korsakov's symphonic suite. But it was Nijinsky's gravity-defying performance that held audiences spellbound. As the Golden Slave who dies violently after seducing the Shah's favorite wife, Nijinsky brought a new sexual and racial explicitness to the conventional figure of the ballet prince. At once primitive and classical, masculine and feminine, Eastern and Western, ancient and modern, the Golden Slave was the first of many roles through which Vaslav Nijinsky and Sergei Diaghilev's Ballets Russes would transform the expressive and technical possibilities of traditional Western dance.

We begin with a glance at Diaghilev's Ballets Russes (1909–29) because the dance company's cultural milieux and artistic commitments supply a perfect doorway into this study of race and modernism. The Ballets Russes was one of the most fantastic collaborative enterprises of the modernist era, bringing together visionaries from varied artistic disciplines across Europe.[1]

Figure 1. Costume sketch by Léon Bakst for the Golden Negro, later called the Golden Slave, played by Vaslav Nijinsky in the ballet *Schéhérazade,* 1910. The stylized forms of Middle Eastern and African bodies, the deep colors of Bakst's costumes and sets, and the bold sensuousness of *Schéhérazade*'s modern-Oriental choreography revolutionized the forms of classical ballet. Gouache, watercolor, gold on paper. (Musée des Beaux-Arts, Strasbourg, France. Photo credit: Erich Lessing/Art Resource, New York.)

Figure 2. Costume sketch by Léon Bakst for Cleopatra, played by Ida Rubinstein in the ballet *Cléopâtre,* performed during the 1909 season of the Ballets Russes in Paris. Egyptian murals inspired Bakst's costume sketch, influencing his design for the dancer's veils and jewels as well as for the image of Cleopatra rendered in profile. (Photo Credit: Erich Lessing /Art Resource, New York.)

Figure 3. Pablo Picasso's racially marked cubist costume for the Chinese magician in the ballet *Parade,* 1917. Guillaume Apollinaire praised the ballet for achieving an "alliance of painting and dance, of plastic art and music, which is the clear sign of the approach of a more complete art." (Theatre Archive Champs-Élysées, Paris. Photo Credit: Bridgeman-Giraudon/Art Resource, New York. © 2009 Estate of Pablo Picasso/Artists Rights Society, New York.)

While the startling new dance styles of Nijinsky, Léonide Massine, and Anna Pavlova lit up the stage, the talents behind that stage were equally formidable. With choreography by Michel Fokine and George Balanchine; music by Igor Stravinsky, Claude Debussy, and Maurice Ravel; scripts and libretti by Jean Cocteau; costumes by Léon Bakst, Coco Chanel, and Paul Poiret; and artwork by Pablo Picasso, Henri Matisse, and Natalia Gontchorova, the Ballets Russes launched the careers of many early twentieth-century aesthetic revolutionaries and iconoclasts. Diaghilev's spectacular productions also brought unprecedented visibility to several modernist protomovements: the dreamlike ballet *L'Après-midi d'un faune* (1912) was based on Stéphane Mallarmé's symbolist poem and set to Debussy's impressionist music; Stravinsky's elemental ballet *Le Sacre du printemps* (1913) outraged Paris audiences with its sexualized primitivism; and performers in the cubist piece *Parade* (1917) wore arresting, geometric costumes by Picasso as they danced to a typewriter- and siren-laden score by Erik Satie. Metropolitan audiences expressed their enthusiasm for Diaghilev's dance company in cultural spaces well beyond the opera house and the proscenium stage. Couture from the ateliers of Poiret and Bakst set off an Orientalist craze in Paris and London, where artists and socialites attended fancy-dress parties in opulent costumes akin to those worn in Diaghilev's productions; the jewelers in the house of Cartier designed extravagant necklaces of emeralds and sapphires inspired by *Schéhérazade*'s color schemes; and many private salons, English and French alike, were furnished to imitate the Middle Eastern aesthetic of Ballets Russes productions.[2] As with all of the modernist fiction considered in this book, the performances of the Ballets Russes were part of a metropolitan aesthetic culture that not only blurred the lines between high art and low art, but also rejected the division between art and life.

Most significantly, the Ballets Russes's heady enthusiasm for reinventing dance through perpetually shifting styles and techniques made it a palimpsest for modernism's competing, contradictory racial credos. The dance company's sheer artistic breadth captured the larger cultural climate of modernism, which, in the words of Malcolm Bradbury and James McFarlane, encompassed

the futuristic and the nihilistic, the revolutionary and the conservative, the naturalistic and the symbolistic, the romantic and the classical. It was a celebration of a technological age and a condemnation of it; an excited acceptance of the belief that the old régimes of culture were over, and a deep despairing in the face of that fear; a mixture of convictions that the new forms were escapes from historicism and the pressures of the time with convictions that they were precisely the living expressions of these things. (46)

And in nearly every production that Sergei Diaghilev's Ballets Russes contributed to this extraordinary historical moment, the poetics of racial and cultural difference underscored what was most radical or "modern" about the ballet. Whether the sinuous Indo-Persian and Syrian movements in *Cléopâtre* (1909), the earthy, barbaric Cossack and Tartar dances woven into *Prince Igor* (1909), or the Chinese magician's tricks in *Parade*, dance was liberated from its nineteenth-century academic legacy by newly aestheticized forms of race. The Ballets Russes epitomized the dynamic relationship between racial discourses and the modernist project: this relationship forms the subject of this book.

Race, Modernism, and Modernity

Race and the Modernist Imagination identifies race as a productive element of British modernist form, a central organizing aesthetic category instead of merely a social problem. Surprisingly, while race is readily acknowledged as an artistic and thematic focal point in American modernism and the Harlem Renaissance, as well as in the literature of the "Black Atlantic," its constitutive role in British modernism has received far less critical attention.[3] This is partially due to an axis of postcolonial scholarship that has confined discussions of race in this period to the colonial fictions of Rudyard Kipling, Joseph Conrad, E. M. Forster, George Orwell, Jean Rhys, Joyce Cary, and Graham Greene.[4] It is crucial to recognize, however, that modernism's varied conceptions of race were often unrelated to the sociopolitical concerns raised by colonial contexts. In this book I challenge the assumption that artistic treatments of race in early twentieth-century England were predominantly or univocally imperialist, demonstrating instead that modernism conceived of race as shifting rather than set, disordered rather than hierarchical. Tracing a literary arc that begins with Oscar Wilde's *The Picture of Dorian Gray* (1891) and ends with Virginia Woolf's *Orlando* (1928), I argue that modernism's revolutionary momentum derived from the poetics of racial difference. Modern works that self-consciously abandoned nineteenth-century realism—Joseph Conrad's *Heart of Darkness* (1899), the vorticist review *BLAST* (1914), Ford Madox Ford's *The Good Soldier* (1915), the short fictions of Rebecca West and Katherine Mansfield, and Woolf's *To the Lighthouse* (1927)—achieved their literary radicalism with aestheticized forms of race. An emergent racial aesthetic also invigorated the British avant-garde arts: rival London coteries such as Wyndham Lewis's Rebel Art Centre and Roger Fry's Omega Workshops envisioned modern England's creative mission as a racial mission. And new conceptions of race unsettled the conventions of even popular and nonliterary works on the peripheries of London's modernist culture, such as Sax Rohmer's bestselling Dr. Fu-Manchu thrillers and Vita Sackville-West's travel writing. In this book I recover the common core of race in this spectrum of modernist British literature and art, and, more broadly, establish race as an essential category for understanding the cultural field of modernity.[5]

At the dawn of the twentieth century, imperial London was rife with social, scientific, and political discussions about race. The modern metropolis witnessed polemical debates about colonialism as well as proliferating developments in scientific racism; urban poverty and the rising tide of immigration stirred anxieties about racial degeneration, as did Britain's losses in the Boer War, the campaign for women's suffrage, and the staggering toll of the First World War. But as my introductory discussion of the Ballets Russes suggests, racial discourses in early twentieth-century England also diffused themselves into new, unexpected cultural domains, moving well beyond the scientific and sociopolitical racial axioms that buttressed British colonial authority. While the rise of visual technologies and the mass-produced image during the late nineteenth century contributed to a very specific imperialist "knowledge" of nonwhite races in faraway lands, fresh opportunities for global movement made racial heterogeneity an immediate reality within London and other modern Western cities.[6] The war years saw the formation of lively American and African expatriate communities in London and Paris, while burgeoning trade industries produced urban settlements of Asian, African, and Caribbean merchants and laborers. Wealthy aesthetes flocked to jazz concerts and threw lavish Bohemian-themed parties, and the virtually limitless reach of art collectors and museums sparked unprecedented respect for non-Western art forms in modernism's metropolitan centers. Imaginative divisions between the white self and the nonwhite Other, hard and clear in nineteenth-century England, became marvelously supple in a great deal of modernist work produced in and about these fast-changing urban landscapes. Scholars from Edward Said to Elleke Boehmer have noted the influence of nineteenth-century colonial racism on modern authors, but much of their work has addressed modernist responses to the British Empire's decline.[7] What merits further exploration are modernism's contributions and debts to a growing body of cosmopolitan racial attitudes.

These racial attitudes emerge out of an intriguing reciprocity between concepts of race and concepts of modernity. The complex development of Western racial thought from 1750 to 1900 turned on the surprisingly simple concepts of *continuity* and *discontinuity*. The very idea of race—which in this period described biological, national, religious, linguistic, and character differences—invoked the consistent transfer of traits from one generation to the next.[8] What was lost, gained, or permanently altered in this transfer formed the dominant critical focus of pre- and post-Darwinian scientific racism in Europe and Great Britain. Disruptions in the continuity of racial identity—through miscegenation, geographical displacement, religious conversion, or political upheaval, for example—engendered scientific as well as cultural anxieties about hybridity, contamination, and degeneration. Similar anxieties about transition and loss are inscribed in the broader cultural logic of modernity itself. For well over a century, artists, revolutionaries, social theorists, historians, and cultural critics have defined the modern present through its self-willed break from a past conceived as continuous and coherent. The ever-changing horizon of modernity, in other words, is always distinguished by its radical difference from the allegedly stable historical moment that precedes it. This book finds a deep mutuality between modernity and race, showing that both discourses invest as much in the stability of a consistent past as they do in the exact moment of rupture from that past.

The modernist authors in my study exploited the conceptual affinity between race and modernity as they announced their own breaks from the past. I take my definition of literary modernism from Edward Said, who describes the movement as

> an aesthetic and ideological phenomenon that was a response to the crisis of what could be called *filiation*—linear, biologically grounded process, that which ties children to their parents—which produced the counter-crisis within modernism of affiliation, that is, those creeds, philosophies, and visions re-assembling the world in new non-familial ways. (*Beginnings*, xiii)

Crises of filiation and affiliation were not only keenly felt in the everyday world of the modern metropolis but also found their perfect expression in the racially charged languages of modernism. As authors in early twentieth-century London confronted the erosion of Victorian-era racial codes —what Said calls the "linear, biologically grounded" ties of family, community, nation, and empire—they endowed race with a newly abstract, explicitly aesthetic quality that pervaded their experimental literary techniques. The external particulars of blackness and whiteness, to take the simplest example, served as reliable signs of human character for the Victorians. The moderns, in sharp contrast, transformed the outward signs of race into artistic content notable for its *unreliability*. If modernism's creative energies arose out of profound cultural and historical estrangement, what richer aesthetic resource than the alienation inherent in racial difference?

I argue that race *gives form* to experimental modernism, its immanent narrative patterns of continuity and discontinuity perfectly suited for shaping anew the literary and cultural plots of modern Englishness. Transposing nineteenth-century social concerns about race into a new artistic register, modern authors regarded race as the key to a daring literary horizon that privileged suddenness, autonomy, abstraction, decenteredness, rupture, flux, irresolution, and nonlinearity. Consider Wilde's *The Picture of Dorian Gray*, where a notoriously modern protagonist defies the progression of linear time in London's racial underworlds; Sax Rohmer's Dr. Fu-Manchu tales (1913–17), in which an Oriental mastermind plots to take over modern Western civilization and the "entire white race"; the vorticist manifestoes, fiction, and artwork in *BLAST*, produced to uphold Wyndham Lewis's roaring cry, "The artist of the modern movement is a savage"; and Virginia Woolf's *To the Lighthouse,* where the painter Lily Briscoe achieves her startling "vision" of abstract art through "little Chinese eyes." In these and many other works, what Edward Said terms the "non-familial" world of modern literature comes into artistic being through newly conceived visions of race.

Race and the Modernist Imagination approaches metropolitan modernism through the movement's best-known trait: the self-avowed commitment to literary and cultural renovation. Each artistic moment I map between 1890 and 1930 reflects the spirit of Ezra Pound's incantatory phrase, "Make it new."[9] Race serves as a powerful resource for twentieth-century aesthetic revolution precisely *because* of the unremitting newness that characterizes modernism and modernity alike. Western modernity, to borrow from Fredric Jameson, reinforces its own newness through a "dialectic of the break and the period." Jameson argues that the advent of modernity involves a "twofold movement" wherein

> the foregrounding of continuities, the insistent and unwavering focus on the seamless passage from past to present, slowly turns into a consciousness of a radical break; while at the same time the enforced attention to a break gradually turns the latter into a period in its own right. (*A Singular Modernity,* 24)

Jameson's formulation of modernity absorbs the weight of an enormous philosophical and intellectual discourse devoted to explicating the relationship between traditional past and modern present. This discourse has its roots in the nineteenth century, when the emancipatory ideals of modernity lauded by Enlightenment-era philosophy (that is, the sovereignty of the nation-state, the authority of natural science, the dominance of a free-market economy, and the general triumph of secular reason over faith and tradition) became charged signifiers for atomizing, dehumanizing processes that would eventually fragment and alienate the very culture they promised to perfect. From Karl Marx, whose *The Communist Manifesto* (1848) declared that "All that is solid melts into air," to Marshall Berman, who took Marx's phrase for the title of his 1982 study of modernity's "maelstrom of perpetual disintegration and renewal" (15), theories of modernity consistently rely on overarching concepts of continuity and discontinuity to explain moments of historical rupture.[10] These concepts, I argue, apply with equal force to discourses of race in twentieth-century England. We find striking correspondences between what Janet Lyon calls modernity's "dramatic emphasis on *now*" (*Manifestoes*, 30) and the condition of racial identity, another relationally constituted "now" whose particulars erase *and* make visible the influence of the immediate past.

As they negotiated the mercurial realities of a modern metropolitan "now," the writers I consider in this book—pioneers of experimental fiction, architects of modernist doctrine, and prolific literary critics—assumed an artistic *contrapposto* grounded in the self-conscious cultivation of newness and originality. Wilde's 1891 preface to *The Picture of Dorian Gray*, for example, a document whose flippancy does not undermine the resonance of its postulates, declared that "Diversity of opinion about a work of art shows that the work is new, complex, and vital" (4), while Conrad's 1897 preface to *The Nigger of the "Narcissus"* lauded the "supreme cry of Art for Art itself" (282) as the artist's defense when the "gods" of "Realism, Romanticism, Naturalism, even the unofficial sentimentalism . . . must . . . abandon him" (281). Fifteen years later, just before Britain entered the Great War, Wyndham Lewis's vorticist manifestoes "BLAST years 1837 to 1900" (18) because "We stand for the reality of the Present—not for the Sentimental Future, or the sacripant Past" (7). Virginia Woolf's polemical 1924 essay "Mr. Bennett and Mrs. Brown" announced that "on or about December, 1910, human character changed" (194) and brought about a much-needed literary era of "breaking and falling, crashing and destruction" (209).[11] These artists and their fellow London modernists announced their own historicity in a series of deliberate aesthetic breaks with English literary tradition; and they adapted discourses of race and racial difference to generate artistic forms that would oscillate between permanence and mutability, stability and transience. Joseph Conrad's Charlie Marlow, for example, gazes at the severed heads of Congolese people and recognizes the political emptiness of nineteenth-century imperialism in the same moment that he discovers the artistic plenitude of modern primitivism. James Joyce's Leopold Bloom, the Hungarian-Jewish-Irish Everyman making a day-long odyssey through Dublin, envisions a utopian society whose conglomeration of humanity echoes the vast literary conglomerations of Joyce's novel: "Union of all, jew, moslem and gentile . . . Esperanto the universal language with universal brotherhood. . . . Mixed races and mixed marriage" (399–400). And Virginia Woolf's Orlando, who magically becomes a woman amidst the "strident and multicoloured and barbaric population" (120) of seventeenth-century Constantinople, achieves an elastic racial consciousness that liberates her from the constraints of English patriarchy and historical time. Such instances abound in modern British fiction, suggesting that race underpins experimental modernism's most salient qualities: self-conscious historicity and aesthetic radicalism.

As British modernism brought itself into being by repeatedly proclaiming its unruly arrival in the imperial metropole, the "now-ness" and "newness" of its racial ideas enabled a purposeful rewriting of the Victorian novel. The modernist renovation of novelistic tradition proceeded from a pivotal moment in cultural history when, in Franco Moretti's words,

> the new psychology started to dismantle the unified image of the individual; when the social sciences turned to "synchrony" and "classification," thereby shattering the synthetic perception of history; when youth betrayed itself in its narcissistic desire to last forever; when in ideology after ideology the individual figured simply as a part of the whole. (228)

We are familiar with the cascading literary consequences of these late nineteenth-century shifts. The realist bildungsroman—the coming-of-age story exemplified by Charlotte Brontë's *Jane Eyre* (1847) and Charles Dickens's *Great Expectations* (1861)—metamorphosed into the experimental *Künstlerroman*, the story of artistic development exemplified by Joyce's *The Portrait of the Artist as a Young Man* (1916) and Woolf's *To the Lighthouse*. Accordingly, the marriage plot often remained unfulfilled; modernism's isolated protagonists rarely attained the wedded bliss (and attendant social integration) of their nineteenth-century predecessors. The complex architecture of Victorian morality, famously captured in the novels of George Eliot and Thomas Hardy, gave way to the modern moral indifference of fiction

by Joyce, Katherine Mansfield, and Jean Rhys. Ambiguity and purposeless-
ness thwarted the forward movement of imperial adventure stories, so that
the robust patriotism of H. Rider Haggard, G. A. Henty, and Wilkie Collins
broke down entirely in novels by Conrad and Forster. Finally, panoramic
narratives of capitalist progress such as William Thackeray's *Vanity Fair*
(1848) and Elizabeth Gaskell's *Mary Barton* (1848) were supplanted by novels that betrayed profound ambivalence about ideologies of national development, such as Forster's *Howards End* (1910) and D. H. Lawrence's
Women in Love (1921). The primary literary texts in my study enact each of
the shifts I have outlined here, offering a comprehensive picture of modernism's formal and thematic priorities. Read individually and together,
these texts affirm that modernity's "detotalized totality," as Sartre puts it,
splinters its subjects and its narrative forms alike. The language of race articulates this very process of splintering, offering the moderns a discourse
obsessed with the ever-present possibility of fracture and fragmentation.

Telling the story of British modernism as a story about race offers a necessary counterpoint to the numerous literary histories that describe the
movement's well-known sequence of artistic innovations but consistently
underestimate or elide the role of race in those innovations.[12] Further, tracing an emergent aesthetics of race sheds new light on authors not conventionally read in terms of race: Oscar Wilde, Ford Madox Ford, Katherine
Mansfield, Virginia Woolf. Revisiting the literary accomplishments for
which these writers are famed—Wilde's revisions to the bildungsroman,
Ford's impressionism, Mansfield's narrative indirection, Woolf's psychological realism—I restore the long-obscured role of race in each writer's
explicitly modern aesthetic, and, more broadly, reveal that modernism's
worship of artistic form is inseparable from its investment in the forms
of race. Indeed, discourses about racial purity and hybridity anatomize
modernism's divergent aspirations to formal purity on one hand, and to
heterogeneity and montage on the other. In the elliptical time schemes,
kaleidoscopic narrative patterns, and elaborate psychological landscapes
that comprise modern fiction, race serves as an entry point into artistic
creativity, a set of tropes and plots that rejuvenates British aesthetic tradition, and an encrypted cipher for modernity itself.

Chapter 1 offers a cultural history of scientific racism from 1750 to 1900
and calls attention to the growing aesthetic importance of race in the British
literary tradition. I then take up Oscar Wilde's *The Picture of Dorian Gray* and
Joseph Conrad's *Heart of Darkness,* inaugural modernist novels whose racial
politics reinvent two dominant Victorian literary genres: the bildungsro-

man and the imperial adventure tale. Wilde's eternally youthful Dorian Gray, "artist of modern life" as well as modern art object, stakes his fatal claim to originality in London's fluid, dangerous racial spheres: East End docks, Chinese opium dens, and Jewish theaters. In *Heart of Darkness,* Charlie Marlow's famously "inconclusive" tale about the artist-imperialist Kurtz anticipates the racial ambivalence of a new century. Unable to maintain a psychic or artistic distance between modern Europe and primitive Africa, Marlow endows race with the abstract volatility that characterizes metropolitan modernity itself. Wilde and Conrad reframe nineteenth-century social and imperial conceptions of race in self-consciously aesthetic terms: and their experimental fin-de-siècle works launch a literary movement in which race serves as a crucial site and source of artistic revolution.

Chapter 1 concludes with a discussion of Sax Rohmer's decidedly noncanonical Dr. Fu-Manchu novels, which challenge white Western authority over the public institutions of twentieth-century modernity. In the high-tech race wars of *The Mystery of Dr. Fu-Manchu* (1913), *The Devil-Doctor* (1916), and *The Si-Fan Mysteries* (1917), Anglo-Saxon heroes struggle against Dr. Fu-Manchu, an evil Chinese polymath building a Yellow Empire in the heart of modern London. This Yellow Empire, a despotic amalgam of the systems that distinguish Western modernity, dramatizes what Georg Simmel dubbed the "sovereign powers of society" (324): scientific and medical knowledge, state-regulated military technologies, interconnected channels of global politics, and the abundant resources of the imperial machine. Rohmer's novels unwittingly invert the formulas of imperial-era popular fiction, anticipating the complex figurations of race and modernity in high modernist literature. Urban alienation, dehumanization, and dispossessed masculinity—experimental modernism's signature anxieties—are explicitly portrayed as failures of the white race in Rohmer's bestselling Yellow Peril adventures.

Chapter 2 steps into the brilliant, cacophonous worlds of experimental metropolitan literature and art during the war years, uncovering divergent visions of race in the embattled maturing of English formalism. Formalism grew out of the belief that the art forms of "primitive" non-Western races could revive England's moribund creative spirit; its racial tropes engaged industrial modernity with equal measures of serenity and explosiveness. Apolitical, impersonal abstraction vied with politicized, antibourgeois art in London's coteries and salons; however, virtually all the competing forms of new English art—cabaret performances in the Cave of the Golden Calf (1912–14), art objects from Roger Fry's Omega Workshops (1913–

19), vorticist polemics in Wyndham Lewis's *BLAST* (1914)—appropriated primitive aesthetics from Africa, Oceania, and Asia. Stylized claims to aesthetic originality reverberate through Rebecca West's vorticist tale, "Indissoluble Matrimony" (1914), as well as through Katherine Mansfield's short story, "Je Ne Parle Pas Français" (1918): in these texts, negrophilia and negrophobia celebrate as well as mock the modernist mania to "make it new." The warring factions of London's avant-garde derived their shocking aesthetics from the artistic practices of non-Western races, and the very aesthetics of shock reflected a powerful desire for racial self-assertion. In sum: the avant-garde literature, visual arts, and performing arts that declared themselves "modern British" took their inspiration from the premodern and the not-British.

Ford Madox Ford's 1915 novel *The Good Soldier,* an impressionist work poised between Edwardian tranquility and the anguish of the Great War, stands at the chronological center of this book. Building on my earlier discussion of *BLAST*—where *The Good Soldier* was first excerpted—I read against the prevailing view that Ford's work is anomalous in Wyndham Lewis's aggressive war journal. *The Good Soldier*'s racial politics shed new light on the avant-garde schism between engagement and autonomy. On one hand, the novel's Anglo-American love triangles, colonial liaisons, and transatlantic migrations betray a profound nostalgia for racial stability and national belonging; on the other, the forking paths of John Dowell's "saddest story" lead only to stark racial abstractions. Race remains a blind spot in scholarship about this canonical text of high modernism; however, I demonstrate that Ford depicts the predicament of modern subjectivity as an elementally racial predicament, and that John Dowell's wandering impressions reflect the incoherence of race and nation in a borderless, wartorn world.

In chapter 3 I focus on Virginia Woolf, showing that the most explicitly modern elements of her mature novels owe their modernity to the author's intricate orchestration of racial discourses. Dialogues about Woolf's anti-imperialism have obscured the role of racial difference in her work; however, biographical as well as literary evidence indicates that Woolf relied on race as a site for cultural resistance. This concluding chapter considers the racial politics and poetics of *To the Lighthouse,* Woolf's modernist-feminist reworking of the Victorian bildungsroman, and *Orlando,* the genre-bending text whose androgynous hero/ine leaps nimbly across four centuries of English history. I argue that aesthetic philosophy in *To the Lighthouse* reflects the radical theories about race and abstraction that served as guiding principles for Roger Fry's *Vision and Design* (1920) as well as for the Omega Workshops. *To the Lighthouse* encodes a resolutely modern world-view through Lily Briscoe's "little Chinese eyes," which exile her from the marriage plot and, simultaneously, endow her with powerful artistic vision. Tropes of racial difference create provocative narrative contradictions in the antibiographical biography *Orlando,* which partially destabilizes but ultimately reinstates the myth of an all-powerful white England. I read this work in dialogue with Vita Sackville-West's travelogue *Passenger to Teheran* (1926), revealing that *Orlando*'s jubilant challenges to genre and gender depend on the uncritical Anglocentrism of imperial travel writing. In Woolf's novels, as in modern fiction more broadly, we find deep mutualities between daring new literary plots and richly imagined racial plots.

The advent of Western modernity, as Matei Calinescu has written, "engenders the utopia of a radiant instant of invention" (68). Calinescu's description of a historical phenomenon speaks eloquently to an artistic phenomenon as well: one "radiant instant of invention" succeeded another as modernism unfolded in the early decades of the twentieth century and sought an aesthetic newness appropriate to its era. I map a sequence of radiant instances to demonstrate how consistently modernist authors invoked diverse forms of race as they reinvented British literary tradition. From the last traces of realism at the fin de siècle to the radical narrative experiments of the late 1920s, modernism's quest for originality derived much of its energy from the brilliant aesthetic collisions of metropole and colony, Europe and Africa, Occident and Orient. And although the aesthetics of race in modern literature have not yet received the same critical attention as the lived experience of racial identity, our understanding of modernism should reflect an awareness of race as an elemental artistic force. Modernist writers and artists—all prophets of the new—wove racial discourses into the century's emergent artistic discourses. Their stunning formal accomplishments reveal that the modernist imagination was indeed a racial imagination.

1

RACE AND THE EMERGENCE OF METROPOLITAN MODERNISM

The study of human races began in antiquity and spiraled outwards in an enormous web of social, scientific, and political theories.[1] In the pages that follow, I call my reader's attention to a sequence of key moments in the development of European and British race science between the mid-eighteenth century and the early twentieth century. During these years, the word "race" itself eluded precise definitions, referring at different points to complexion, physiology, religion, language, class, or nationality. The European movement to abolish slavery, which began in the Enlightenment and ended successfully in 1833, should theoretically have deepened European racial sympathies. But abolitionist idealism met with a nineteenth-century cultural backlash that produced violent, enduring views of nonwhite, non-Western peoples. As Jean-Paul Sartre trenchantly observes in his Preface to Frantz Fanon's *The Wretched of the Earth*:

> There is nothing more consistent than a racist humanism since the European has only been able to become a man through creating slaves and monsters. While there was a native population somewhere this imposture was not shown up; in the notion of the human race we found an abstract assumption of universality which served as cover for the most realistic practices. (26)

All manner of "realistic practices" were vindicated by nineteenth-century imperial expansion, best symbolized by the 1884 Berlin Conference that parceled out Africa to western European nations. A huge array of popular, religious, and especially scientific discourses combined to justify the brutal racial asymmetries of a colonized world. New scientific (and pseudoscientific) disciplines—paleontology, embryology, craniometry, craniology, anthropology, taxonomy, archaeology, geology—created seemingly irrefutable empirical criteria to identify and order human beings. And although Charles Darwin's theories of evolution and natural selection radically realigned the coordinates of racial thought in the mid-nineteenth century, earlier ideas about race as the immutable cause of human self-actualization persisted well into the twentieth century. The modernist reordering of the aesthetic universe availed itself of pre- and post-Darwinian racial attitudes, and I therefore reconstruct the history of scientific racism by touching on the ideas most relevant to modernism's multiple visions of racial identity.[2]

Natural history and race science in the eighteenth century in Great Britain and western Europe developed largely within the context of Judeo-Christian creationism.[3] George Stocking explains that

> the pre-Darwinian period in Britain is one in which, after a century in retreat, the biblical tradition reassumed a kind of paradigmatic status. Within this framework, all men were presumed to be descended from one original pair, who had been formed by God as the final act of Creation, and to whom he had revealed the one true religion and certain other fundamental institutions of civilization. (*Victorian Anthropology*, 44)

Theological belief in humanity's common origins translated into the doctrine of scientific monogenism, which argued that all human beings belonged to a single species regardless of their physical differences. The prevailing monogenist view assumed that after the creation and the fall from Paradise, Adam and Eve's descendants settled in different parts of the world and then lost, in varying and racially marked degrees, their moral and physiological prelapsarian perfection. Monogenism reflected the universalizing, egalitarian humanism that drove Enlightenment thought; the dominant eighteenth-century attitude toward race privileged humankind's spiritual unity over its physical variation.[4] But as exploration, trade, and imperial conquest brought Europeans into contact with more and more of the world's peoples, physical variation presented itself in an incredible range of skin color, hair texture, smell, and skull size that demanded scientific explanation. Scientists maintained faith in humanity's original, Edenic perfection, but assigned the various existing races to hierarchical positions that inevitably exalted white bodies and degraded black bodies.[5]

In *Imperial Eyes: Travel Writing and Transculturation*, Mary Louise Pratt characterizes the burgeoning discourse of eighteenth-century natural history as "a rich and multifaceted mirror onto which all Europe could project itself" (34). Compelling evidence of this scientific Eurocentrism appears in the numerous theories that explained the phenomenon of human racial difference by turning to the external factors of climate and environment. Scientists had long promulgated the belief that a racial group's character was a function of temperature, weather patterns, and geological terrain. In *The Complexion of Race: Categories of Difference in Eighteenth-Century British Culture,* Roxann Wheeler describes the English view toward race and climate in the mid-eighteenth century:

> Because of the excessive heat that was believed to enervate the body, mind, and morals, commonplaces about the torrid zone being the home of dark-skinned people who were indolent, lascivious, and subject to tyranny often seemed confirmed when Englishmen confronted social and political life as well as labor arrangements that were alien to them. In the same vein, excessive cold was believed to produce effects similar to hot climates, and the contemptuous descriptions of the physical features and cultural life of the populations from the torrid and arctic zones were largely interchangeable. (24)

Such beliefs assumed that England and western Europe stood as civilization's temperate cradles: the farther one traveled from the British Isles or the Continent, the less civility one would encounter.[6] But dominant Christian attitudes rendered climate-induced racial variances quasi-superficial, since each individual was thought to be redeemable in God's eyes.

The opening of William Blake's 1789 poem "The Little Black Boy" gives us a pithy summation of the monogenist climatic view to race in the eighteenth century:

> My mother bore me in the southern wild,
> And I am black, but O! my soul is white;
> White as an angel is the English child,
> But I am black as if bereav'd of light. (9)

The heat of the "southern wild" may have caused the black skin, but the white soul is the divine right of all of God's creatures. The poem's end idealizes ontological human unity: the black child and the white child reach heaven together and lean against God's benevolent knee. More than one hundred years later, the London avant-garde recuperated climatic theories about race for the revolutionary 1914 war journal *BLAST;* Wyndham Lewis, Ezra Pound, and their supporters scorned the intemperate passions of artists from southern or Mediterranean nations and extolled the cold northern climate that produced English artistic genius. Similarly, in D. H.

Lawrence's *Women in Love,* the modern intellectual Rupert Birkin decides that racial destiny is determined by climate: "The white races, having the arctic north behind them, the vast abstraction of ice and snow, would fulfill a mystery of ice-destructive knowledge, snow-abstract annihilation. Whereas the West Africans, controlled by the burning death-abstraction of the Sahara, had been fulfilled in sun-destruction, the putrescent mystery of sun-rays" (254). Leopold Bloom in Joyce's *Ulysses* attributes his wife Molly's "passionate temperaments" (520) to her birth in Gibraltar, telling Stephen Dedalus that "I for one certainly believe climate accounts for character. . . . All are washed in the blood of the sun" (520–21). And a far less uplifting expression of climatic theory appears in Jean Rhys's *Voyage in the Dark* (1934), where the self-destructive Creole narrator Anna Morgan frames her horrifying cultural displacement as a failure to adjust to England's cold temperatures. Caught in a dehumanizing cycle of alcoholism and prostitution, Anna inhabits an emotional geography haunted by the lingering shadows of eighteenth-century race science: "I wanted to be black, I always wanted to be black. . . . Being black is warm and gay, being white is cold and sad" (31).[7]

The main scientific principle behind the early work of eighteenth-century natural historians was the Great Chain of Being, a long-held and much-contested view of the interrelatedness of all animate and inanimate matter.[8] Nancy Stepan points out that although the Chain "expressed God's plenitude and the harmony of nature, as well as the necessary relation of all things to each other" (6), it also suggested that "the different races of mankind formed a natural scale, with the European on top and the African at the bottom" (8). Indeed, the three titans of eighteenth-century natural history—the Swedish botanist Carl Linnaeus, the French naturalist Auguste Comte de Buffon, and the German anatomist Johann Friedrich Blumenbach—devised taxonomic and classification systems that naturalized white Europe's dominance over other nations and races. Buffon's 1749 *Histoire Naturelle* set forth theories of human race based on climate, food, and way of life. As members of the species dispersed over the earth after the fall from Paradise, Buffon reasoned, they deteriorated physically in accordance with their chosen climate and could hence be racially classified from most to least degenerate. Similarly, in 1758, the tenth edition of Linnaeus's influential *Systema Naturae* argued that six geographically determined "varieties" comprised the species *Homo sapiens,* with the well-mannered, fair-complected "*europaeus*" at the top and the indolent, black-skinned "*afer*" at the bottom. And Blumenbach, widely considered the father of modern anthropology, also concluded that environment was responsible for the races of humankind. His 1776 work *On the Natural Variety of Men* divided *Homo sapiens* into five classes: Caucasian, Mongolian, Ethiopian, American, and Malayan.[9] Although these three scientists (and their contemporaries) diverged in the theoretical particulars of their classification systems, they buttressed the monogenist view of a divinely created single human species characterized by naturally occurring and geographically specific racial differences.

Paradoxically, as the abolitionist movement in Britain gained momentum, culminating in the end of slavery in 1833, the science of race divorced itself firmly from Enlightenment humanism and became more systematically and overtly violent in its approach to non-European, nonwhite peoples.[10] The monogenist explanations of human anatomical differences based on the external influences of environment and climate proved unsatisfactory, and the turn of the nineteenth century brought a surge of new scientific efforts to theorize race. In *The Order of Things,* Michel Foucault distinguishes between eighteenth- and nineteenth-century natural history to explain the new attitudes that shaped European race science after abolition. Foucault characterizes eighteenth-century natural history as a *"description of the visible"* (137), an elaborate process of classification that "require[d] the principle of the smallest possible difference between things" (159). But science in the nineteenth century, Foucault argues, linked the external visible forms of nature to their invisible underpinning systems; the act of ordering the world now involved mapping nature's "hidden architecture" onto "the more obvious signs displayed on the surfaces of bodies" (229). In the changing realm of race science, this meant that physical appearance was taken as direct evidence of a group's innate character and capacity for civilization. Biology, in other words, provided the blueprint for destiny. Nancy Stepan describes how the eighteenth-century belief in the "physical and moral homogeneity of man, despite superficial differences" was supplanted by the nineteenth-century insistence on the "essential heterogeneity of mankind, despite superficial similarities":

> It was a shift from a sense of man as primarily a social being, governed by social laws and standing apart from nature, to a sense of man as primarily a biological being, embedded in nature and governed by biological laws. It was a move away from an eighteenth-century optimism about man, and faith in the adaptability of man's universal "nature", towards a nineteenth century biological pessimism, and a belief in the unchangeability of racial "natures." . . . By the middle of the nineteenth century, everyone was agreed, it seemed, that in essential ways the white race was superior to non-white races. (4)

Many nineteenth-century scientists, in other words, would have denied that Blake's little black boy could possess a white soul or share God's knee with a white child.

In *Staying Power: Black People in Britain since 1504,* Peter Fryer argues that the character of nineteenth-century British race science stemmed from the administrative practices and physical expansion of the British Empire. Declaring that "the golden age of the British Empire was the golden age of British racism too" (165), Fryer claims that the empire's increasing responsibility over foreign bodies led to new and almost invariably violent philosophies about how those bodies should be understood and controlled. He points to two consecutive and racially significant events at the end of the eighteenth century: the initiation of British parliamentary control over the East India Company in 1773, when Warren Hastings was made the first governor-general of Bengal, and the publication in 1774 of Edward Long's vicious work *The History of Jamaica.* Edward Long's three-volume book, based on the author's experiences as a planter and landowner in Jamaica, argued that slavery in the West Indies and in Africa was an absolute necessity because the Negro was mentally, morally, and physiologically unfit to rule himself. *The History of Jamaica* depicts Negroes as monstrous and criminal, scarcely human, and certainly not possessed of redeemable Christian souls. Long's vitriolic and prejudiced writings found a scientific analogue in the work of the British doctor Charles White, whose *Account of the Regular Gradation in Man* (1799) used comparative measurements between the facial angles of animals and humans to "prove" that Negroes were separated from the near-perfect anatomical structure of white Europeans by many unbridgeable degrees.

The unyielding race hatred of Long's *History* and the assumption that race was a quantifiable set of physical traits in White's *Account* heralded a new era of scientific racism. The early nineteenth century witnessed a period of intense debate between the monogenists and their opponents, the polygenists, who espoused the nonbiblical view that different races were in fact completely different and unequal species. Both monogenists and polygenists agreed that the white races were physiologically and morally superior to the dark races; however, they diverged on the exact *cause* and *character* of this racial hierarchy. In the decades leading up to Darwin's theories of evolution, phrenology, the science of the mind, created the main arena for the monogenist-polygenist debate. Starting from the assumption that the mind was the locus and index of human civility, the Victorian phrenologists developed a number of ways to measure, quantify, and evaluate the brain and the skull. As Stephen Jay Gould has persuasively shown, both the monogenists' and the polygenists' impassioned devotion to skull measuring created a broad platform from which nineteenth-century racial prejudices could be affirmed.[11]

In England, the abolitionist and scientist James Cowles Prichard and the surgeon Sir William Lawrence supported the monogenist view of race not only with craniometry but also with the new scientific methods of comparative anatomy, ethnology, zoology, and linguistics. Prichard's *Researches into the Physical History of Man* (1813) and *The Natural History of Man* (1842) and Lawrence's *Lectures on Physiology, Zoology, and the Natural History of Man* (1819) emphasized the distances separating the bodies and characters of Europeans, Negroes, and Asiatics, but ultimately defended the unity of the species (Stepan, 34–38). In contrast, polygenists in North America, Great Britain, and Europe used craniometry to establish that the races of humankind were different biological species. The American physician Samuel Morton, for example, compiled detailed statistics about the cranial capacity of Caucasians, Mongolians and Negroes; his methods ensured that the Caucasian male's skull always indicated the greatest capacity for intelligence and advanced thought. In 1850, the Scottish surgeon Robert Knox published his polygenist study *The Races of Men,* which declared that "Race is everything: literature, science, art, in a word, civilization depend on it" (7). Knox presented a comparative analysis of skulls to prove that the races are locked into a fixed, unchanging hierarchy that keeps the white species necessarily separate from the dark species. The American scientists Josiah Nott and George Gliddon put forth perhaps the most unsubtle of the mid-Victorian ethnological studies: their 1854 *Types of Mankind* offered numerous unflattering comparisons between the heads of apes, Negroes, and Europeans in an exhaustive effort to show that blacks were physiologically closer to animals than they were to whites.

This barrage of racial theories about skull size and biologically determined character extended its influence well beyond what Thomas Carlyle snidely called "the Nigger question." In Paris, George Cuvier's disciple Paul Broca, who founded the Société d'Anthropologie in 1859, applied the racial rhetoric of craniometry to explain the brain structures of the insane and the criminal. Broca's findings, as well as the later findings of the Italian anthropologist Cesare Lombroso, conjoined the intellectual and moral limitations of nonwhite races to mentally unstable and degenerate people in "civilized" European societies. And as Edward Said remarks in *Orientalism,* "Theses of Oriental backwardness, degeneracy, and inequality with the

West most easily associated themselves early in the nineteenth century with ideas about the biological bases of racial inequality. Thus the racial classifications found in Cuvier's *Le Règne animal*, Gobineau's *Essai sur l'inégalité des races humaines*, and Robert Knox's *The Dark Races of Man* found a willing partner in latent Orientalism" (206). The collective body of craniometric scholarship affirmed the idea of the world's nonwhite races as perverse, stupid, criminal, indolent, deviant, and lascivious.[12]

The link between race, civility, and skull size captivated the popular imagination, perhaps best epitomized by the British craze for head measuring.[13] Late Victorian and early modernist fiction reflects this widespread fascination with the racial semiotics of the skull and the head. Conrad's *Heart of Darkness*, for example, registers the view that traveling to the savage, tropical Dark Continent would negatively alter the structure of the head. A doctor tells Marlow before he leaves for the Congo that "'I always ask leave, in the interests of science, to measure the crania of those going out there,'" and uses calipers to get "the dimensions back and front and every way, taking notes carefully" (58). Sir Arthur Conan Doyle's 1901 mystery *The Hound of the Baskervilles* features a Dr. Mortimer who marvels at Sherlock Holmes's skull: "A cast of your skull, sir, until the original is available, would be an ornament to any anthropological museum. . . . I confess that I covet your skull" (9). During the war years, as I will discuss later in this chapter, competing views of race and skull size appear in Sax Rohmer's Fu-Manchu novels, where the criminality as well as the genius of the Chinese villain Dr. Fu-Manchu are attributed to his abnormally large head. And as late as 1934, when the connections between anatomy and character had been weakened by science if not by popular culture, Elizabeth Lackersteen in Orwell's *Burmese Days* draws on the languages of phrenology and craniology to justify her hatred of Burmese natives:

> "They have such hideous-shaped heads! Their skulls kind of slope up behind like a tom-cat's. And then the way their foreheads slant back—it makes them look so *wicked*. I remember reading something in a magazine about the shape of people's heads; it said that a person with a sloping forehead is a *criminal type*." (118–19)

The racial differences evident in skull size were thought to manifest themselves most dangerously in the reproduction of races. As Robert Young's study *Colonial Desire: Hybridity in Theory, Culture and Race* has shown, the many gray areas between "race" and "species" in the mid-nineteenth century were shaped by questions of fertility, hybridity, and miscegenation. Monogenists like James Cowles Prichard believed that human beings of all races could breed with no negative effects. At the other end of the spectrum, Arthur Comte de Gobineau's notorious *Essay on the Inequality of Races* (1853) warned readers that the racial purity of whites, on which civilization itself depended, would be fatally jeopardized by miscegenation: "Such is the lesson of history. It shows us that all civilizations derive from the white race, that none can exist without its help, and that a society is great and brilliant only so far as it preserves the blood of the noble group that created it, provided that this group itself belongs to the most illustrious branch of our species" (210).[14] A number of other hybridity theories bridged the chasm between Prichard's benevolence and Gobineau's doom mongering. Polygenists such as Edward Long, Josiah Nott, and Paul Broca believed that while two different races could breed, the offspring would be infertile and degenerate in varying degrees, and might, therefore, face the danger of extinction. Again, Elizabeth Lackersteen's attitudes toward mixed-race characters in Orwell's *Burmese Days* express the enduring imaginative power of Victorian hybridity theories: "'So thin and weedy and cringing; and they haven't got at all honest faces. I suppose these Eurasians *are* very degenerate? I've heard that half-castes always inherit what's worst in both races'" (123).

The racial hierarchies established by nineteenth-century craniometry and its related fields were accepted so enthusiastically because they complemented the ideologies and hegemonies of the growing British Empire. Three bloody political events at midcentury—the Sepoy Mutiny in India (1857), the U.S. Civil War (1861–65), and the Morant Bay Uprising in Jamaica (1865)—heightened the need to assert white superiority with the putatively unassailable evidence offered by scientists such as Robert Knox and Paul Broca. The U.S. Civil War added to the voluminous writings and vociferous debates about slavery and the Negro's character, but the Sepoy Mutiny and the Morant Bay Uprising brought English racial paranoia and hatred to a pitch that sustained itself for decades. In 1857, Indian soldiers, or sepoys, rose against their British commanding officers and tried to reinstate Hindu and Mughal rule in regions across India. The infamous siege at Kanpur, where the Indian soldiers killed two hundred English women and children, caused tremendous furor in England. The idea of defenseless white women being raped, mutilated, and murdered by "Hindoo savages" stirred equal measures of patriotism and violence, and the British retaliated by killing hundreds of sepoys as well as Indian civilians.[15] Almost seventy years later, the sexual and racial myths of the mutiny would haunt

E. M. Forster's *A Passage to India* (1924), where Adela Quested's accusation that Dr. Aziz raped her provokes the deepest wrath and the loftiest nationalism of the other English characters:

> They had started speaking of "women and children"—that phrase that exempts the male from sanity when it has been repeated a few times. Each felt that all he loved best in the world was at stake, demanded revenge, and was filled with a not unpleasing glow, in which the chilly and half-known features of Miss Quested vanished, and were replaced by all that is sweetest and warmest in private life. (183)

In exalting the nobility of the white civilizers and condemning the barbarity of imperial subjects, the English reactions to the Sepoy Mutiny reinforced the twin racial ideologies that would justify the empire's material practices into the early decades of the twentieth century.

English passions about racial hierarchy rose even higher in the aftermath of the Morant Bay Uprising. In 1865, when a group of black Jamaican peasants rioted to protest unjust labor practices and killed twenty white officials, the British governor, Edward Eyre, declared martial law and launched a campaign of shocking brutality. Over thirty days, Governor Eyre's troops enacted systematic, ruthless violence against the rioters and other native Jamaicans, flogging six hundred of them, executing four hundred, and burning down over a thousand private homes.[16] The governor's decision to "exterminate all the brutes," for which he was never punished, stirred polemical debate in England. The Jamaica Committee, whose members included John Stuart Mill and Charles Darwin, opposed Governor Eyre's suppression of the riot and sought harsh judicial punishment for him. In contrast, the Eyre Defense Committee, led by Thomas Carlyle and John Ruskin, stood behind the Governor and supported his views on controlling dark races with violence.[17] Robert Young comments that following the Sepoy Mutiny and the Jamaica Uprising, "The cultural ideology of race became so dominant that racial superiority, and its attendant virtue of civilization, took over even from economic gain or Christian missionary work as the presiding, justifying idea of the empire" (92). It was therefore in the interest of the empire's moral and physical sovereignty that the human races were imagined in a fixed hierarchy that naturalized the white race's ability and right to rule over their permanently savage, demonic, or childlike imperial subjects.

In the heated climate of the Victorian race debates, Charles Darwin's theories of human evolution and natural selection, published in *On the Origin of Species* (1859) and *The Descent of Man* (1871), irrevocably changed the terrain on which race could be defined.[18] Darwin argued that all of the earth's life forms had evolved gradually from common ancestors, and that the process of natural selection would eliminate physiological features that did not aid a life form's survival; the contest for survival took place between individuals rather than between whole species. Through Darwin's eyes, the relatively static natural world of eighteenth- and early nineteenth-century scientific thought was replaced with a natural world that evolved constantly; the doctrine of creationism became untenable; the concept of "cosmic teleology" lost its authority because evolution rendered fixed end points in nature impossible; and humans beings, regardless of their color and skeletal structure, were all linked by their common descent (Banton, 88). The monogenist-polygenist debates became irrelevant because, as Douglas Lorimer remarks, "Darwin had proved not only that the European was related to the Negro, but that all men were related to the ape" (142).

Despite Darwin's radical moves away from the prevailing nineteenth-century belief in fixed human types, his theories did not immediately transform the biases of race-science in his own lifetime. Ironically, as Nancy Stepan points out, Darwin's evolutionary model of human descent was "compatible with the idea of fixity, antiquity, and hierarchy of human races. Far from dislodging old racial ideas, evolution strengthened them, and provided them with a new scientific vocabulary of struggle and survival" (49). In other words, Darwin's paradigms could be applied to new social models or to existing race theories in order to affirm white European or Anglo-Saxon racial superiority. George Stocking explains that

> Darwinian evolution, evolutionary ethnology, and polygenist race thus interacted to support a raciocultural hierarchy in terms of which civilized men, the highest products of social evolution, were large-brained white men, and only large-brained white men, the highest products of organic evolution, were fully civilized. The assumption of white superiority was certainly not original with Victorian evolutionists; yet the interrelation of the theories of cultural and organic evolution, with their implicit hierarchy of race, gave it a new rationale. (122)

The principles underlying biological evolution were quickly reoriented to meet sociopolitical ends, leading to the tenacious ideas behind social Darwinism. In 1869, Francis Galton published *Hereditary Genius,* a study based on the premise that mental ability and intelligence can be inherited in the same manner as physical traits. Galton praised a science of race hygiene that he named eugenics, a breeding practice that would build a powerful society by eliminating the weak and selecting the strong. Galton's ideas, and the larger body of social Darwinist thought, attracted many adherents as the nineteenth century drew to a close.[19]

In particular, social Darwinism became one of the most powerful weapons of Queen Victoria's empire, which acquired millions of miles of territory and millions of new subjects between 1870 and 1914. In these years, a virtually endless stream of imperial propaganda adopted the vocabulary of social Darwinism to disseminate the values of British monarchism, Christian missionary activity, and imperial authority to an English public.[20] While the forms of this propaganda are wildly varied—children's books glorifying imperial explorers; picture postcards and cigarette cards featuring British monuments and buildings in colonized nations; music hall ditties about the conquest of the dark races; tea tins, biscuit tins, and soap advertisements extolling the empire's resourcefulness; documentary and feature films that replayed military and naval achievements; colonial exhibitions showcasing the empire's impact on the lives of millions at home and abroad —their message could almost always be distilled to one of white superiority in an era of forward technological, social, and biological progress. In 1899, Rudyard Kipling's poem "The White Man's Burden" famously captured imperial ideology's reliance on eugenics and evolution:

> Take up the White Man's burden—
> Send forth the best ye breed—
> Go bind your sons to exile
> To serve your captives' need;
> To wait in heavy harness,
> On fluttered folk and wild—
> Your new-caught, sullen peoples,
> Half-devil and half-child.[21]

But the imperial propaganda machine's ideals were not always borne out by the empire's actual circumstances. If social Darwinism provided the language of racial and cultural progress, it also raised fears of racial and cultural regression. At the fin de siècle, a widespread cultural obsession with racial degeneration counterbalanced the jingoism that promoted imperial racial hierarchies. General Gordon's crushing defeat at Khartoum in 1883 shook British confidence in the empire's invincibility, and reports of murder, torture, and other atrocities in the Belgian Congo reached England in 1897, exposing the imperial mission's deep-rooted hypocrisy. Further, heavy British casualties during the Second Boer War in South Africa (1899–1902) caused panic about the physiological soundness of the nation's men. Anxiety about military and colonial incidents abroad was matched by growing social unease within England. A large body of writing about the metropolitan corruption and poverty resulting from industrialization and immigration—for example, Andrew Mearns's pamphlet *The Bitter Cry of Outcast London* (1883), W. T. Stead's prostitution exposé "The Maiden Tribute of Modern Babylon" (1885), George Gissing's *The Nether World* (1889)—deployed the vocabulary of race and imperialism to sound an alarm about the nation's moral and physical integrity. The proliferation of poor, criminal, or sexually unregenerate white bodies in the imperial metropole incited as much fear as the dark-skinned pagan masses in the empire's subject nations.[22]

Like popular journalism and sociological writings, late Victorian fantasy literature expressed fears of social decay through racially coded metaphors. Robert Louis Stevenson's *Dr. Jekyll and Mr. Hyde* (1886) imagines the monstrous criminal form lurking inside the rational English scientist; Oscar Wilde's *The Picture of Dorian Gray* (1891) brings out the hidden but inexorable decay of a society afflicted with decadence and depravity; Bram Stoker's *Dracula* (1897) creates terror through the alien being who invades London and literally sucks out its lifeblood. And perhaps most powerfully evocative of Darwin, H. G. Wells's *The Time Machine* (1895) narrates the futuristic tale of the beautiful white Eloi who live harmoniously above ground and are threatened by the dark, nocturnal savagery of the underground, underevolved Morlocks. The very culture of fin-de-siècle literature and art inspired the best-known work on social and racial collapse, Max Nordau's *Degeneration* (1895). Nordau's enormous volume railed against the immorality, excessive emotionalism, and hysteria that would inevitably be caused by the fin-de-siècle poets, playwrights, and artists who belonged to "the elements of the race which are most inimical to society" (337). E. M. Forster's novel *Howards End* (1910) would gather together these various different specters of urban disintegration, depicting the contaminating degeneracy of the city's slum dwellers (embodied in the tragic figure of Leonard Bast) as well as the feminizing degeneracy of Oxford-bred aesthetes (embodied in the Schlegels' ineffectual younger brother, Tibby).

On the eve of British literary modernism, then, we can say that dominant British and western European racial discourses reflected a powerful concatenation of evolutionary theory, social Darwinism, and imperial ideology. And while much early twentieth-century literature uncritically reproduced

Victorian attitudes to race, the racial formations of experimental modernism often rewrote the nineteenth century's black and white hegemonies. Loosened from the confines of Victorian science, racial discourses served as mercurial instruments of aesthetic and intellectual revolution. In 1899, Sigmund Freud redirected evolutionary models of race in order to foster a new awareness of human consciousness. Imagining the chain of races as a template for the human psyche, Freud's *Interpretation of Dreams* argued that each individual's movement from infancy to adult consciousness reenacts humanity's development from (dark) savagery to (white) civilization. And in the same year, Conrad's *Heart of Darkness* not only explored the intersection of human consciousness and imperial racial conquest but also hybridized the foundational act of storytelling itself. Conrad's Marlow stands at the crossroads of multiple cultural traditions: "He had sunken cheeks, a yellow complexion, a straight back, an ascetic aspect, and, with his arms dropped, the palms of hands outwards, resembled an idol. . . . With his legs folded before him, he had the pose of a Buddha preaching in European clothes and without a lotus flower" (48–51). Unwhite and pagan, partially Western and partially Eastern, the racial disparities of Marlow's physical appearance displace him from any single historical or literary legacy and symbolize his narrative's resistance to unified, stable perspectives.

In the decades following the publication of *Heart of Darkness,* several modernist artists and intellectuals moved away from linear narratives of racial development, rejecting the concept of ordering human beings by degree of civility in much the same way they rejected the concept of life as a knowable series. In Lawrence's primitivist theories of "blood-consciousness," Wyndham Lewis's and Roger Fry's hortatory writings about the formal virtues of African art, and stories about race and metropolitan modernity by Jean Rhys and Katherine Mansfield, an individual character or artist's multiple racial identities produce multiple chronological, spatial, and perceptual vantage points. The final lines of Joyce's *A Portrait of the Artist as a Young Man* crystallize race as site and source of the modernist imagination, as Stephen Dedalus exiles himself from those institutions that safeguard cultural continuity—"my home, my fatherland, or my church" (208) —and elects instead to "forge in the smithy of my soul the uncreated conscience of my race" (213).[23] Virginia Woolf's *The Waves* (1930), one of the most lyrical reinventions of the English novel, intertwines historically grounded representations of race with timeless racial abstractions to critique the master narratives of British patriarchy and imperialism. Submerged, sculptural visions of race steal through the six soliloquies in *The Waves:* whether the silhouette of the absent imperial hero Percival and the dark Indian bodies he governs, or the stylized forms of Egyptian women and turbaned warriors, Woolf's poetic depiction of modern Englishness reworks the forms of colonial racial hierarchy.

The diverse visions of alterity I have mentioned here show us that race—whether conceived as a closed set of continuous, self-perpetuating identities or as a self-destabilizing phenomenon—serves as a crucial and pervasive aesthetic category for modern authors who sought to "make it new." The rest of this book will follow a sequence of originary moments in the modernist revolution that begins with Wilde and ends with Woolf: and as we will see, the historical and aesthetic self-consciousness that are modernism's signature traits express themselves through the forms and plots of race.

Conrad, Wilde, and Race at the Fin de Siècle

Let us begin our investigation of the relationship between race and modernist revolution by considering Oscar Wilde's *The Picture of Dorian Gray* (1891) and Joseph Conrad's *Heart of Darkness* (1899), two influential fin-de-siècle fictions that transpose social questions about race into a new artistic register. These pivotal novels pose a series of self-conscious challenges to the literary eminences that preceded them, rewriting imperial racial conceptions to inaugurate metropolitan modernism's attention to the *formal* aspects of race. Wilde and Conrad usher in a self-consciously modern literature through texts that adhere to prefatory doctrines about the changing role of the artist and the status of the art object: Wilde's 1891 preface to *Dorian Gray* and Conrad's 1897 preface to *The Nigger of the "Narcissus"* announce a new epoch marked by ongoing declarations and revisions of aesthetic method. *Heart of Darkness* and *The Picture of Dorian Gray* reflect a new cultural obsession with temporality; they trouble the relationship between imperial center and colonial periphery; their narratives feature artist-protagonists who take their place in art of their own creation; and, most importantly, both texts present London as the racially charged fount of modernist experimentation. Wilde and Conrad depict art and modernity as matters of *racial consciousness:* not only the psychological consciousness of individual races but, more generally, the new consciousness or awareness of race as an aesthetic category. And in redirecting the sociopolitical aspects of race toward the domain of art, *The Picture of Dorian Gray* and *Heart of Darkness* establish the *agon* of modernism—art versus life—as elemen-

tally shaped by and inseparable from questions of race and racial difference.

The Picture of Dorian Gray was first printed in Lippincott's Monthly Magazine in 1890 and then revised for publication in book form in 1891. Heart
of Darkness was serialized in Blackwood's Magazine in 1899 and issued by Blackwood's as part of a separate volume of Conrad's fiction in 1902.[24] In creating their most famous works at the nineteenth century's end, Wilde and
Conrad—expatriate writers with differently complex ties to England and
the British Empire—wrote as inheritors of the abundant racial "knowledge"
produced and disseminated by the social, scientific, and cultural machinery of Victorian-era imperialism.[25] Certainly, the canonical status of Wilde's
novel has very little to do with the author's treatment of race, while the
canonical status of Heart of Darkness has come to exclude virtually all else.
But although Dorian Gray's beautiful Mayfair salons seem a world apart
from the corrupt wasteland of Charlie Marlow's Congo, pairing these texts
illustrates a pervasive preoccupation with racial aesthetics that informs modernism's broad-ranging priorities and engagements.

To understand how Wilde and Conrad reconceptualize nineteenth-century racial ideologies, it is helpful to consider Fredric Jameson's seminal
essay "Modernism and Imperialism," which identifies the artistic dilemma
created by the economic and spatial relationships of imperial modernity.
Colonialism, Jameson argues,

> means that a significant structural segment of the economic system as a whole
> is now located elsewhere, beyond the metropolis, outside of the daily life
> and existential experience of the home country, in colonies over the water
> whose own life experience and life world—very different from that of the im-
> perial power—remain unknown and unimaginable for the subjects of the im-
> perial power. . . . Such spatial disjunction has as its immediate consequence
> the inability to grasp the way the system functions as a whole. (50–51)

The spatial disjunction between imperial center and colonial periphery
powerfully influences the quotidian experience of metropolitan existence,
which

> no longer has its meaning, its deeper reason for being, within itself. As artis-
> tic content it will now henceforth always have something missing about it, but
> in the sense of a privation that can never be restored or made whole simply
> by adding back the missing component. . . . It is only that new kind of art
> which reflexively perceives this problem and lives this formal dilemma that
> can be called modernism in the first place. (51)

British modernist style, in Jameson's formulation, compensates for a domestic "privation" caused by the outward expansion of imperial power.[26] In *The Picture of Dorian Gray* and *Heart of Darkness*—as in the flood of modernist literature published in their wake—this privation is most keenly felt and most daringly addressed in the domain of race. Wilde and Conrad alter the structure of literary plots in order to reflect the increasingly unstable *racial* plots of a metropolis in transition. The anxiety that individual and collective racial identities will "always have something missing"—or, to return to the opening terms of this study, anxiety about filiation and affiliation—produces narratives of undoing whose artist-protagonists fail to integrate themselves into any racial, national, or cultural collectivity. In the readings that follow, I map the invention of race as a formal device profoundly suited to literature intent on revolutionizing the traditions it has inherited.

The Picture of Dorian Gray is at once a morality tale, a crypto-queer novel, an undoing of the Victorian bildungsroman, and a dark tour of fin-de-siècle decadence. It is also a text whose very modernity emerges through discourses about race. The conventional reading of Oscar Wilde's succès de scandale—Dorian Gray, doomed to eternal youth through a compact with his own portrait, exiles and eventually kills himself because of his stylized homosexuality—has tended to eclipse the novel's preoccupations with race.[27] But it is crucial to recognize that Dorian's notoriety arises not only out of his excessive, transgressive sexuality but out of an equally transgressive racial identity. Dorian's remaking of life into art depends on a series of racial discontinuities, and his refusal to participate in the bourgeois public world around him takes the form of deadly racial betrayals. And although Wilde's narrator insists that "the canons of good society are, or should be, the same as the canons of art. Form is absolutely essential to it" (111), the very forms of Dorian Gray's artistry violate the racial protocols of upper-class London society at the end of the nineteenth century. His suicide at the novel's end points to the inevitable self-destruction of a racially fragmented, aesthetically autonomous modern subject who cannot be assimilated into the very Victorian master narratives the novel critiques.

Basil Hallward's painting of Dorian Gray effects a tripartite aesthetic shift: this "finest portrait of modern times" (25), as Lord Henry Wotton calls it, reconfigures the identities of artist, art object, and spectator. Dorian himself perfectly models each of these identities: his eternal youth unfolds as a series of originary moments distinguished by aesthetic daring and resistance to the past, and he comes to embody the relationship between the artistic goals of modernism and the social realities of modernity. In Wilde's revision of the realist bildungsroman, Dorian increasingly conceives of himself in aesthetic rather than social terms; and his inventions of self turn as much on the instabilities of racial identity as they do on shifting sexual mores. His racialized self-fashioning is foreshadowed in a seemingly inconsequential speech by Lady Henry Wotton, uttered in the course of a conversation about music:

> "I have simply worshipped pianists. . . . I don't know what it is about them. Perhaps it is that they are foreigners. They all are, ain't they? Even those that are born in England become foreigners after a time, don't they? It is so clever of them, and such a compliment to art. Makes it quite cosmopolitan, doesn't it?" (40–41)

Lady Henry's witticisms describe an aesthetic-racial cycle that powerfully shapes the originality of Dorian's life: artistic expression transfigures the racial character of artists, who then, from their newfound roles as "foreigners," make art itself "quite cosmopolitan." Disjoined from the natural process of aging, Dorian's development over the course of the novel involves perfecting an artistry notable for its increasing foreignness and cosmopolitanism. It is the emergence of Dorian's multifaceted racial identity that I wish to consider here: the mutually constitutive relationship between race and modern aesthetics—although punished by Dorian's alienation and suicide—provides a template for the self-avowed newness that very soon comes to distinguish literary and artistic experiments in the early twentieth century.

I call my reader's attention to three key points in Dorian's life when he reinvents himself by severing all ties with the immediate past: first, the abrupt demise of his affair with Sybil Vane; second, his reading of Lord Henry's "Yellow Book" and attendant cultivation of "wanton luxury and gorgeous splendour" (110); and third, the murder of Basil Hallward and Dorian's subsequent descent into opium addiction. Each crisis marks not only the progressive rupturing of Dorian's own past, but more broadly, the radical discontinuities facing an era that has exhausted its own moral and artistic postulates. The execrable acts that produce these moments of crisis, of course, manifest themselves on Dorian's magical aging portrait, that "visible emblem of conscience" (74) hidden from the world. But at the same time, a deeply racialized metropolitan geography bears *public* witness to Dorian's disintegration. Wilde stages the collapse of Dorian's worlds in multiple, racially distinct spaces: the Jewish-dominated theater district, the exquisite aesthetic hybridity of Dorian's Grosvenor Square residence, the immigrant-filled East End docks. Racially coded spaces outside of London —such as the houses in Algiers and Trouville that Dorian shares with Lord Henry, the Australian outback where Sibyl Vane's brother Jim seeks his fortune, and the African, Asian, and Latin American cultures that furnish Dorian with exotic markers of his modernity—similarly serve as sites of Dorian's gradual undoing. This complex geography operates not to affirm a unified English imperial self but to signify instead the widening fissures of modern racial identity.

The first step in Dorian's catastrophic disintegration—the short-lived love affair with Sibyl Vane—takes the form of a grotesquely racialized fairy tale.[28] With the restlessness of a Baudelairean flâneur, Dorian departs from the upper-class world of Mayfair and moves through "grey, monstrous London" on a "search for beauty" (42). That this aesthetic quest leads Dorian to the unlovely world of the East End speaks to Wilde's realignment of late Victorian-era racial coordinates. In contrast with characters such as Lord Henry's Aunt Agatha, who works in the East End to elevate poor and migrant communities through philanthropy, Dorian searches the ghettoes for "the real secret of life":

> "I don't know what I expected, but I went out and wandered eastward, soon losing my way in a labyrinth of grimy streets and black, grassless squares. About half-past eight I passed by an absurd little theatre, with great flaring gas-jets and gaudy playbills. A hideous Jew, in the most amazing waistcoat I ever beheld in my life, was standing at the entrance, smoking a vile cigar. He had greasy ringlets, and an enormous diamond blazed in the centre of a soiled shirt. 'Have a box, my Lord?' he said, when he saw me, and he took off his hat with an air of gorgeous servility. There was something about him, Harry, that amused me. He was such a monster." (42–43)

Dorian's "grey, monstrous London" has yielded up a servile Jewish "monster": and a racialized structure of feeling frames the love affair that commences once Dorian vanishes into the theater world. Over the sounds of a "dreadful orchestra, presided over by a young Hebrew" (44), Dorian falls in love with Sibyl Vane in the dramatis persona of Juliet and vows (in a series of vicious anti-Semitic slurs) to rescue her from the "horrid old Jew" (45) to whom she is indentured for three years.[29] However, the romance of racial uplift between the actress and the gentleman fails because Dorian's love hovers in the stalled temporality of autonomous art. Although he begins by playing the part of "Prince Charming" in the hopes of rescuing Sibyl from the "vulgar" and "tawdry" (43) theater and the obscurity of her Euston Road origins, Dorian insists on affixing his lover in a permanent present that bears no connection to past or future. His preference for self-conscious artifice over earnest emotion—a foundational aspect of decadent consciousness—leads him to abandon his fiancée at the moment when she renounces art in favor of love. Sibyl's confession that "'I might mimic a passion that I do not feel, but I cannot mimic one that burns me like fire'" meets with Dorian's cruel dismissal, "'Without your art you are nothing'" (70).[30] The ruptured marriage plot propels Dorian back through the racially marked terrain that originally led him to the theater:

> Where he went he hardly knew. He remembered wandering through dimly-lit streets, past gaunt black-shadowed archways and evil-looking houses. Women with hoarse voices and harsh laughter had called after him. Drunkards had reeled by cursing, and chattering to themselves like monstrous apes. He had seen grotesque children huddled upon doorsteps, and heard shrieks and oaths from gloomy courts. (71)

This "monstrous" and "grotesque" East End landscape externalizes Dorian's artistic priorities, which are henceforth indistinguishable from his social priorities. The arresting silhouettes of anonymous, racially degenerate bodies, as well as the "shrieks and oaths" of voices "chattering to themselves," are forerunners of the self-referential, fractured, and racially startling tropes through which high modernism will depart from the consolidating fictions of nineteenth-century realism. Thus, Dorian's first "break" from his personal past—and, by implication, from a broader cultural past—signals the ascendance of a racial aesthetic that decenters and rewrites sociopolitical discourses of race.

Transformed by his odyssey through London's racially troubled worlds, Dorian is horrified and enthralled when his portrait, too, transforms itself in the wake of Sibyl Vane's suicide. The cruelty-marred portrait shows Dorian that his thoughtlessly uttered, temporally impossible wish—"that his own beauty might be untarnished, and the face on the canvas bear the burden of his passions and his sins" (73)—has been granted. Protected by this newly autonomous work of art that magically stills time and liberates him from conventional morality, Dorian renounces the forward-moving bourgeois narratives of marriage and family, devoting himself instead to a perpetually modern existence defined by sensory gratification and beauty. As the "'spectator of [his] own life,'" Dorian celebrates the lost unity of his formerly coherent self, refusing to "conceive the Ego in man as a thing simple, permanent, reliable, and of one essence":

> To him, man was a being with myriad lives and myriad sensations, a complex multiform creature that bore within itself strange legacies of thought and passion, and whose very flesh was tainted with the monstrous maladies of the dead. (111)

Wilde articulates the "myriad lives" and "strange legacies" of his detotalized artist-protagonist along racial lines. Earlier, Lord Henry co-opts Basil Hallward's painting into a cultural narrative of Englishness, assuring the artist that the extraordinary aesthetic of his work—"'one of the greatest things in modern art'" (25)—will "set [him] far above all the young men in England" (8). Now, as the painting demonstrates, in Dorian's words, "'a life of its own'" (91), modern Englishness takes on a dispersed racial character independent of any foregoing ethno-racial cogency. A fresh radicalism distinguishes Basil's painting as it describes the lost racial unity of its "complex multiform" subject: Dorian's darkened and distorted portrait poses an ever-sharpening contrast with the unchanging racial perfection of his own white skin, blue eyes, and golden hair. Dorian accepts this dispersal ("What did it matter what happened to the coloured image on the canvas? He would be safe" [84].) and makes his second "break" from the past by obliterating all thoughts of Sibyl Vane and announcing "'I am a man now. I have new passions, new thoughts, new ideas'" (87). The self-conscious claim to newness that soon becomes modernism's rallying cry signals more than the exchange of a heterosexual marriage plot for the aesthete's sexual ambiguity: it turns Dorian into the emblem of a modern moment delineated by the ever-changing particulars of racial identity.

Having hidden Basil's painting so that no eyes will witness its transmogrification, Dorian now absorbs himself in Lord Henry's notorious "yellow book," a "novel without a plot" (97), whose diktats determine his "conception of the beautiful" (115). It is this phase of Dorian's life that most crucially demands to be revisited for its racial rather than its sexual significance. As a dandy, Dorian becomes an icon in London's elite social neighborhoods, where he strives to "assert the absolute modernity of beauty" through fashion:

> His mode of dressing, and the particular styles that from time to time he affected, had their marked influence on the young exquisites of the Mayfair balls and Pall Mall club windows, who copied him in everything that he did,

and tried to reproduce the accidental charm of his graceful, though to him only half-serious, fopperies. (100)[31]

Despite the veiled homosexuality suggested by his "fopperies" (Regenia Gagnier points out that Dorian's dandyism rejects "the normative image of the gentleman" [52]), Dorian Gray remains socially desirable as long as he confines himself to the *racially homogenous* worlds of Mayfair, Pall Mall, and other stylish areas of London. But when Dorian tires of the accolades he receives for "the wearing of a jewel, or the knotting of a necktie, or the conduct of a cane" and cultivates instead a "new scheme of life" (101), the artistry of his life acquires a racial taint that culminates in near-total social exile. His departures from sealed, continuous racial tradition cause greater cultural panic than his revisions of sexual identity.

Dorian's lengthy phase of decadent aestheticism—which at one level reinvents and pays homage to the art and philosophies of Walter Pater, Joris-Karl Huysman, Theophile Gautier, and James Whistler—achieves its most shocking effects through its willful embrace of non-Western culture.[32] Pondering the source of the corrupt tendencies that now dominate his life, Dorian realizes, crucially, that "one had ancestors in literature, as well as in one's own race, nearer perhaps in type and temperament, many of them, and certainly with an influence of which one was more absolutely conscious" (113). Here is the filiative-affiliative matrix that distinguishes modernism from its Victorian heritage. By relocating his racial consciousness from the linear ties of familial genealogy to the domain of literature, Dorian ensures that his personal "past would have little or no place" (102) in the multiracial aesthetics that now determine his relationship to the world around him. He begins to amass beautiful objects from non-Western, premodern cultures: and although he begins by collecting the ritual objects of Catholic communion and studying the creeds of German mysticism, he soon devotes himself to accumulating perfumes, jewels, embroideries, and textiles from India, China, Ceylon, Arabia, Indonesia, Japan, Italy, Hungary, Spain, and Greece. His worship of cosmopolitan and racially hybrid art transforms his Grosvenor Square house into an extravagant and fully global display of ancient, medieval, and modern artistry.[33]

Dorian's indifference to Western cultural tradition is illustrated most pointedly by his discoveries in music:

> At another time he devoted himself entirely to music, and in a long latticed room, with a vermilion-and-gold ceiling and walls of olive-green lacquer, he used to give curious concerts in which mad gypsies tore wild music from lit-

tle zithers, or grave yellow-shawled Tunisians plucked at the strained strings of monstrous lutes, while grinning negroes beat monotonously upon copper drums, and, crouching upon scarlet mats, charmed, or feigned to charm, great hooded snakes and horrible horned adders. The harsh intervals and shrill discords of barbaric music stirred him at times when Schubert's grace, and Chopin's beautiful sorrows, and the mighty harmonies of Beethoven himself, fell unheeded on his ears. He collected together from all parts of the world the strangest instruments that could be found, either in the tombs of dead nations or among the few savage tribes that have survived contact with Western civilization, and loved to touch and try them. (104)

Concert performances by gypsies, Tunisians, and Negroes, as well as instruments from "tribes that have survived contact with Western civilization," call vivid attention to modernism's counterimperial perceptions of race as artistically rather than sociopolitically meaningful: Dorian's love for racially distinct, dissonant, and "barbaric" art foreshadows the avant-garde protomovements that announce aesthetic revolution through the forms of the primitive, the barbarous, and the exotic. Further, as Dorian accelerates his modernity through non-Western artistic forms, he willfully shatters the integrity of his own Englishness. His portrait grows daily more hideous as he moves between the racial heterogeneity of his private world and undesirable racialized spaces in the public arenas of the city. He haunts "dreadful places near Blue Gate Fields" (109), a seedy, immigrant-filled district near the London docks; and rumors abound that he has been seen "brawling with foreign sailors in a low den in the distant parts of Whitechapel" (110), and "'slinking in disguise into the foulest dens in London'" (118). Most significantly, he is "very nearly blackballed at a West End club of which his birth and social position fully entitled him to become a member" (110). Dorian's self-renewing modernity, embodied by the racial coordinates of metropolitan geography and by his objets d'art from wide-ranging, disconnected races and cultures, outrages the "good society" (111) that originally bred him.

This racially diffuse aestheticism ends abruptly when Dorian murders Basil Hallward, who brings about his own death by reproaching Dorian for his social treacheries and unrepentant breaches of racial codes. While Basil's cry, "Dorian, why is your friendship so fatal to young men?" (117) carries an unmistakable suggestion of homosexuality, it also dovetails into a greater fin-de-siècle anxiety about the imperiled racial integrity of the imperial center. Insinuating that intimacy with Dorian leads to the fracturing of Englishness itself, Basil confronts the young aesthete with the disruptions that his companionship has wrought in the lives of formerly respectable Londoners, men and women alike: aristocrats, gentlemen, dukes, lords, members of the Guard, Lord Henry Wotton's sister, and Lady Gwendolen whose children are no longer allowed to live with her. These ruined lives, like the collection of art objects in Dorian's mansion, affirm Lady Henry's earlier claim that artists "become foreigners." Indeed, Basil begs Dorian to repent so that his sins become "'white as snow'" (123), a startlingly apt Biblical metaphor for the purification of contaminated Englishness. Dorian murders Basil to quell the latter's knowledge of the alien character of his life, stabbing him mercilessly after the painter sees the transmogrified canvas that now depicts Dorian's "monstrous" (121) racial baseness. And in fact the murder itself is bookended by artifacts of cultural alterity: Dorian lights Basil's path to the painting with a Moorish lamp "made of dull silver inlaid with arabesques of burnished steel, and studded with coarse turquoises" (124), and the morning after the murder, loses himself in the pleasures of an edition of Gautier's poetry bound in Japanese paper and decorated with pomegranates. In this novel, the beauty and the danger of racial instability are inseparable: the racial fluidity that enables the posture of life as art also jeopardizes the continuity of imperial metropolitan identities.

Race mediates most powerfully between aesthetic beauty and moral sanctity when Dorian makes his third and final "break" from the past: his surrender to opium in the wake of Basil's death. After burning Basil's coat and bag, Dorian perfumes his room with Algerian pastilles and reaches into a hidden drawer in a Florentine cabinet to retrieve

> a small Chinese box of black and gold-dust lacquer, elaborately wrought, the sides patterned with curved waves, and the silken cords hung with round crystals and tasseled in plaited metal threads. He opened it. Inside was a green paste waxy in lustre, the odour curiously heavy and persistent. (141)

As before, beautiful foreign objects at home lead Dorian to unbeautiful foreign spaces in the city: the aesthete-turned-murderer endeavors to purge his memory of past crimes by haunting opium dens in London's East End.[34] These disreputable establishments epitomize the complex temporality that ensues from Dorian's pact with his portrait. Like the hidden and ugly painting, the dens simultaneously conceal and register the troubled morality of the fin de siècle; they promise forgetfulness of the past through the endless present of the opium stupor; and, paradoxically, they also confront Dorian with former crimes he seeks to escape. Consider the scene that greets Dorian when he enters the opium den:

> The door opened quietly, and he went in without saying a word to the squat misshapen figure that flattened itself into the shadow as he passed. . . . Dorian winced, and looked around at the grotesque things that lay in such fantastic postures on the ragged mattresses. The twisted limbs, the gaping mouths, the staring lustreless eyes, fascinated him. (144–45)

On one level, the spectacle of Chinese, Malaysian, and "half-caste" (145) bodies participates in a negative Orientalism that—as the next section on Sax Rohmer's Fu-Manchu tales will demonstrate—belongs to late nineteenth-century metropolitan anxiety about a growing "Yellow Peril." But if we look ahead to the breakaway gestures of high modernism, these time-frozen figures also allegorize the chronological paralysis that halts the maturation of Dorian and other modern artist-protagonists. Further, Dorian's fascination with the "misshapen" forms and "fantastic postures" of foreign bodies represents a first step toward the radical, racialized formalism that will soon be developed in the fictions of Joseph Conrad, Ford Madox Ford, and Virginia Woolf, and in the artwork of Roger Fry, Wyndham Lewis, and Henri Gaudier-Brzeska.

Inside the opium den, Dorian is forced to acknowledge two repressed sexual encounters from his past that have now resurfaced as *racial* encounters. The ruined lives of a young Englishman and a no-longer-young Malaysian woman testify to the racial chaos engendered by the stylized modernity of Dorian's life. Dorian first meets Adrian Singleton, a former comrade whose "dreadful end" (117) Basil Hallward had lamented:

> "You here, Adrian?" muttered Dorian.
> "Where else should I be?" he answered, listlessly. "None of the chaps will speak to me now."
> "I thought you had left England." . . .
> "I don't care," he added with a sigh. "As long as one has this stuff, one doesn't want friends. I think I have had too many friends." (144)

Adrian Singleton comes to his "dreadful end" in the racial underworld of the Chinese opium den, the sole social space available to him after his English friends and family have shunned him. Equating patronage of the opium den with a departure from England itself, Singleton capitulates to the isolation suggested by his surname and exchanges human companionship for the ravages of an illegal foreign substance. Dorian, unnerved to discover his accountability in "the ruin of that young life" (146), is further discomfited when he is accosted by a second former intimate, an unnamed foreign woman who has led the desperate life of a quayside prostitute after a long-ago dalliance with Dorian.[35] Despite the abjection and degeneration suggested by this character's "crooked smile, like a Malay crease," "sodden eyes," "greedy fingers," and "hideous laugh" (145), and despite the brevity of her appearance in the text, she performs a crucial narrative role. The Malay woman betrays the secret of Dorian's youthfulness to James Vane, who has been hunting "Prince Charming" ever since Sibyl's suicide. "'Why, man, it's nigh on eighteen years since Prince Charming made me what I am,'" the prostitute cries to James after his quarry has fled the opium den (148). Her next words persuade James that the beautiful youth who seems too young to have been his sister's lover is indeed Dorian Gray:

> "He is the worst one that comes here. They say he has sold himself to the devil for a pretty face. It's nigh on eighteen years since I met him. He hasn't changed much since then. I have though," she added, with a sickly leer.
> "You swear this?"
> "I swear it," came in hoarse echo from her flat mouth. (148)

The Malaysian prostitute is the only character in the novel who pronounces the terms of Dorian's fatal pact and uncovers the mysterious source of his beauty. The English characters who suspect the truth about Dorian's abominations die before they can verify or disclose it: Dorian kills Basil Hallward as soon as the latter sees the altered painting; Alan Campbell, who destroys Basil's corpse, commits suicide; and James Vane is accidentally shot soon after receiving the Malaysian woman's information. The expressive capabilities of these nineteenth-century Englishmen—the artist, the scientist, and the colonial—are insufficient to describe the racial striations that divide Dorian against himself. The source of the aesthete's racially marked modernité receives its sole articulation as a "hoarse echo" from the "flat mouth" of an anonymous, degraded foreign woman whose own place in the metropolis is so tenuous that she has to beg for money for a single night's lodging.

By the novel's end, the twin bulwarks of the Victorian bildungsroman— the smooth forward progress of imperial life-narratives and the aesthetic transparency of realism—have been destabilized by the accumulated weight of Dorian's racial acts: flânerie rather than philanthropy in the East End, love in the Euston Road, brawls in Whitechapel, miscegenation with the Malay woman, the passionate accumulation of Orientalia, the preference for Gypsy and Negro music over Schubert and Beethoven, the addiction to opium. Unable any longer to occupy the permanent present of youthfulness and craving a self-consolidation rendered impossible by his racial consciousness, Dorian tries to unify the fractured pieces of his identity by killing his portrait:

> He looked round, and saw the knife that had stabbed Basil Hallward. He had cleaned it many times, till there was no stain left upon it. It was bright, and glistened. As it had killed the painter, so it would kill the painter's work, and all that that meant. It would kill the past, and when that was dead he would be free. It would kill this monstrous soul-life, and without its hideous warnings, he would be at peace. He seized the thing, and stabbed the painting with it. (169)

But Dorian succeeds only in restoring the cultural protocols that his life has violated. When his servants enter their master's chamber, they discover a "splendid" portrait looking exactly as it did when Basil Hallward first painted it, and beneath it, a "withered, wrinkled" (170) human body marked by the passage of time. Although Wilde capitulates to Victorian moral doctrine by ending his unrepentant protagonist's life and by restoring stasis to the autonomous art object, it is crucial to recognize that the novel has unmoored the concept of race from prevailing nineteenth-century sociopolitical contexts and redirected it into the domains of aesthetic originality. Wilde inscribes this very process of cultural redirection in the two halves of his protagonist's name: "Dorian," a harmonious musical mode that originates in classical Greece, is followed by "Gray," a hybrid modern topos between whiteness and darkness that reveals no ties to any particular cultural lineage. The lacuna that simultaneously separates and connects the culturally stable first name and the ambivalent surname suggests, in miniature, the dialectical break that defines artistic modernism and cultural modernity. And the "picture" of Dorian Gray is the picture of this break, a vision of racial mutability that narrows the distance between art and life.

 Dramatically extending Oscar Wilde's racial gestures in *The Picture of Dorian Gray,* Joseph Conrad's *Heart of Darkness* transforms race into an aesthetic category inseparable from the birth of modern art. In the three decades since Chinua Achebe blasted Conrad for being a "thoroughgoing racist," attention to race in *Heart of Darkness* has eclipsed virtually all other aspects of Conrad's 1899 novella; it is now a scholarly axiom that no element of *Heart of Darkness* stands untouched by troubled racial assumptions.[36] I hope to avoid the longstanding debate about Conrad's racism, calling attention instead to the complex process by which *Heart of Darkness* shifts the terms of art by shifting the terms of race. Poised at the meeting ground of nineteenth-century realism, fin-de-siècle symbolism, and twentieth-century literary impressionism, this novella's proliferating uncertainties foreground the complex status of race for modern art and modern artist alike.[37] Fredric Jameson claims that the play of meaning in Conradian narrative "is assured by the initial fragmentation of the raw material, which allows a relative independence between foreground and background, a kind of coexistence between the radically different and even distinct materials of the narrative moment in question" (*Political Unconscious*, 223). The "raw material" of art and narrative play in *Heart of Darkness*, I argue, takes the form of wide-ranging racial discourses. The "fragmentation" of these discourses not only suggests the racialized terms of modernist formal radicalism, but, more foundationally, establishes that metropolitan modernism henceforth envisions itself through shifting conceptions of race.

The relationship between Mr. Kurtz (the ur-modernist who dies in Africa after breaking away from the accumulated weight of European cultural practices) and Charlie Marlow (the ambivalent apprentice who transports the "unsound method" of Kurtz's modernism back to Europe) heralds the varied racial modes of subsequent aesthetic experimentation. Both characters enter the Belgian Congo as a consequence of their racial exceptionalism. "All Europe contributed to the making of Kurtz," Marlow tells his listeners of the mysterious agent born to a "half-English" mother and a "half-French" father (109). The ambiguous racial, national, and ethnic particulars of Kurtz's ancestry—the unknown "halves" of his parentage—confer an opaque hybridity on Kurtz himself, forecasting the racial disorder that shocks his associates in the Congo. Marlow, more subtly, stands apart from other English "types." The unnamed narrator, whose description of Marlow's racially indeterminate appearance we have touched on earlier, informs us that Marlow is "not typical" (50), and Marlow himself assures the Company doctor who measures his head that he is "not in the least typical" (59). In the context of nineteenth-century racial typology, these repeated mentions of Marlow's atypicality separate him from the metropolitan racial aggregate of London or Brussels.[38] Although Marlow is thought to be "a piece of good fortune for the Company" (59), just as Kurtz is thought to be "of the greatest importance to the Company" (73), these hybrid, atypical, and genealogically inconclusive characters succeed less as agents of the nineteenth-century ivory trade than as agents of a distinctly modern racial chaos. Conrad's artist-protagonists transform empire's well-worn racial tropes into newly dynamic sites where they investigate the problems of modernity, rewrite the conventions of realist art, and reinvent the symbolic significance of colonial racial categories.

This process of reinvention is readily visible in Kurtz's artwork. Whether the oil painting Kurtz leaves in the Central Station, the pamphlet he authors for the International Society for the Suppression of Savage Customs, or the heads of Congolese tribesmen mounted on stakes in front of his Inner Station house, the disintegrating artist-imperialist finds his principal medium in visual and linguistic discourses of race. The modernity of these varied artworks emerges through a complex racial parataxis, an aesthetic strategy that, to borrow from Theodor Adorno, refers to "artificial disturbances that evade the logical hierarchy of a subordinating syntax" (131). Kurtz's paratactic gestures reveal not only his evasions of the empire's "subordinating syntax," but more significantly, a desire to reinvent race as a series of "artificial disturbances." By denaturalizing the hereditarian, hierarchical Victorian-era conceptions of race that buttress Europe's presence in the Congo, Kurtz unveils two truths untenable in the domain of colonial modernity. His varied works of art suggest, first, that racial integrity—physiological or psychological—is a cultural fiction; and second, that modern aesthetic sensibilities will be elementally informed by the disintegrations, disjunctions, and discontinuities of race. Marlow conjoins the twin truths of Kurtz's tortured oeuvre as he spins a racially conflicted narrative that renounces Victorian-era literary and imperial conventions. Kurtz's paratactic racial aesthetics, in other words, give rise to the race consciousness of Marlow's tale, producing the novel's stunning double helix of racially marked aesthetics.

Marlow first encounters Kurtz's artwork when he discovers an oil painting in the tent of the brickmaker of the Central Station:

> "Then I noticed a small sketch in oils, on a panel, representing a woman, draped and blindfolded, carrying a lighted torch. The background was sombre—almost black. The movement of the woman was stately, and the effect of the torchlight on the face was sinister." (76)

On one hand, the painting overturns the classical Western iconography of a blindfolded and impartial Lady Justice and critiques the "sinister" blindness of Europe's civilizing mission in Africa. But it is the ambiguous race of the woman in the painting—she appears neither definitively black nor definitively white—that surfaces in Marlow's subsequent descriptions of Kurtz's racial instability and eventual demise. The "draped" and "stately" aspect of the woman in the painting reappears in Kurtz's privileged African mistress, who walks the riverbank "draped in striped and fringed cloths" (124) with "something ominous and stately in her deliberate progress" (125). Further, the draped figure progressing through darkness also presages Kurtz's own dangerous progress through the Congo where he becomes "a shadow darker than the shadow of the night, and draped nobly in the folds of a gorgeous eloquence" (142). The painting's racial and spatiotemporal indeterminacies fuse white Europe and black Africa, a fusion that torments Marlow when he speaks with Kurtz's fair-haired, cultivated Belgian Intended and hears in her voice "the ripple of the river, the soughing of the trees swayed by the wind, the murmurs of wild crowds, the faint ring of incomprehensible words cried from afar, the whisper of a voice speaking from beyond the threshold of an eternal darkness" (145). And when the Intended implores Marlow to tell her Kurtz's last words, Marlow sees "a tragic and familiar Shade, resembling in this gesture another one, tragic also, and bedecked with powerless charms, stretching bare brown arms over the glitter of the infernal stream, the stream of darkness" (146).[39] Kurtz's chiaroscuro painting suggests the multilayered racial modes that constitute the modern subject, looking ahead to the cubist, vorticist, and futurist works that would depict a single figure through simultaneous, competing, and racially coded perspectives.

The indeterminate racial poetics of the little oil painting take on menacing explicitness in Kurtz's notorious pamphlet for the International Society for the Suppression of Savage Customs. Although the pamphlet begins by deifying the racial wholeness of "we whites" who bring boundless good to the Dark Continent's "savages," Marlow's stammering description of this "beautiful piece of writing" (110) captures Kurtz's growing knowledge of race as a series of discontinuous identities:

> It was eloquent, vibrating with eloquence, but too high-strung, I think. Seventeen pages of close writing he had found time for! But this must have been before his—let us say—nerves, went wrong, and caused him to preside at certain midnight dances ending with unspeakable rites, which—as far as I reluctantly gathered from what I heard at various times—were offered up to him—do you understand?—to Mr Kurtz himself. (110)

Fluid sentences about the pamphlet's "eloquent" imperial commitments splinter into half-complete phrases when Marlow mentions African rites and dances, a narrative enactment of Kurtz's own splintering European racial and cultural affiliations. Race and art are inextricably, jarringly linked in Kurtz's famous scrawl, "Exterminate all the brutes!" which destroys the pamphlet's literal and metaphorical integrity:

> There were no practical hints to interrupt the magic current of phrases, unless a kind of note at the foot of the last page, scrawled evidently much later, in an unsteady hand, may be regarded as the exposition of a method. It was very simple, and at the end of that moving appeal to every altruistic sentiment it blazed at you, luminous and terrifying, like a flash of lightning in a serene sky: "Exterminate all the brutes!" (110)

In Kurtz's "unsteady hand," a "luminous and terrifying" rhetorical abruption cuts across the pamphlet's final page, embodying the racial unsteadiness that underpins modernism's future aesthetic disjunctions. The pamphlet's "exposition of a method" delineates the modernist aesthetic strategies that resist imperial subject making and that characterize the mature fictions of Forster, Woolf, and Rhys. The forcefulness of "Exterminate all the brutes!" also reverberates in the avant-garde manifestoes produced during the war years, those startling documents that would sever ties to a cultural past by proclaiming their authors' racial exceptionality and artistic originality. After Kurtz's death, Marlow further perpetuates the pamphlet's aesthetic discontinuity when he gives the pamphlet to a Company bureaucrat "with the postscriptum torn off" (140), creating an illusory wholeness for the document that barely masks Kurtz's disintegration and anticipates the jagged totality of the modernist movement.

The pamphlet's suggestion that Kurtz has abandoned his role as a Company agent and assumed instead the posture of a modern artist is affirmed by the display of African heads outside his house in the Inner Station. The race-maddened artist treats the corpses of the Congolese people as resources for artistic expression, a gruesome literalizing of Fredric Jameson's claim that meaning is produced by the "fragmentation of the raw material." Kurtz's palisade of black heads marks his irreversible departure from imperial protocols and predicts the shock tactics of the early twentieth-century avant-garde, which, in Peter Bürger's apt definition, involve "killing the 'life' of the material, that is, in tearing it out of its functional context that gives it meaning" (*Theory of the Avant-Garde*, 70). Gazing at Kurtz's house through field glasses from the deck of his steamer, Marlow assumes that he sees "half-a-dozen slim posts . . . with their upper ends ornamented with round carved balls" (113). He subsequently realizes that

These round knobs were not ornamental but symbolic; they were expressive and puzzling, striking and disturbing. . . . They would have been even more impressive, those heads on the stakes, if their faces had not been turned to the house. Only one, the first I had made out, was facing my way. I was not so shocked as you may think. The start back I had given was really nothing but a movement of surprise. I had expected to see a knob of wood there, you know. I returned deliberately to the first I had seen—and there it was, black, dried, sunken, with closed eyelids,—a head that seemed to sleep at the top of that pole, and, with the shrunken dry lips showing a narrow white line of the teeth, was smiling too, smiling continuously at some endless and jocose dream of that eternal slumber. (120)

Marlow has to look at the heads twice through his field glasses before identifying them correctly, a "double take" that enacts the "discovery" of primitive art that galvanized avant-garde artists in London and Paris. Like Dorian Gray finding aesthetic fascination in the paralyzed Asian bodies in the opium den, Marlow understands the black heads outside Kurtz's house as part of a modern visual economy that displaces the longstanding racial hierarchies of empire. (Indeed, Marlow's own description of the grove of death—where "Black shapes" and "bundles of acute angles" lie "scattered in every pose of contorted collapse" [65–66]—reflects a primitivist geometry grounded in the newfound aesthetic provocations of race.) Further, Marlow's insistent statement, "I want you clearly to understand that there was nothing exactly profitable in these heads being there" (121), reinforces the counterimperial nature of Kurtz's display of heads. Against the prevailing character of nineteenth-century imperial exhibitions—exemplified in *Heart of Darkness* by the brickmaker's tent in the Central Station, where "native mats covered the clay walls; a collection of spears, assegais, shields, knives, was hung up in trophies" (75)—Kurtz's rebel heads do not advance the empire's historical or anthropological knowledge of the Congo.[40] The heads have no use-value: they neither contribute to the efficiency of the "work" in Africa nor add to the Company's profits, and they cannot be exported back to Europe. Severed from the bodies of Congolese people, the "shrunken" heads testify to the most brutal kind of racial discontinuity and grotesquely illustrate the concluding maxim in Oscar Wilde's preface to *The Picture of Dorian Gray*, "All art is quite useless" (4). Inward facing, formally arresting, and wholly resistant to the forces of social convention, the "expressive and puzzling, striking and disturbing" aspect of the heads on stakes announces a modernism whose attention to interiority and consciousness finds original—and frequently violent—expression in the language of race.[41]

While Marlow responds to the artistic import of Kurtz's display of African heads, the Company manager who accompanies him to the Inner Station interprets them as a sign of Kurtz's capitulation to the very "savage customs" his presence was intended to suppress. The manager's condemnation of Kurtz as a man whose "method is unsound" (126) prompts Marlow to affiliate himself for the first time with the racially multivalent Kurtz:

> "Do you," said I, looking at the shore, "call it 'unsound method'?" "Without doubt," he exclaimed, hotly. "Don't you?" . . . It seemed to me I had never breathed an atmosphere so vile, and I turned mentally to Kurtz for relief—positively for relief. "Nevertheless, I think Mr Kurtz is a remarkable man," I said with emphasis. He started, dropped on me a cold heavy glance, said very quietly, "He *was*," and turned his back on me. My hour of favour was over; I found myself lumped along with Kurtz as a partisan of methods for which the time was not ripe: I was unsound! Ah! but it was something to have at least a choice of nightmares. (126–27)

As a "partisan of methods for which the time was not ripe," Marlow now joins Kurtz as a prescient modernist. This moment marks Marlow's self-willed break from the "vile" atmosphere of nineteenth-century European imperialism and its attending myths of cultural coherence. As a consequence of this break, Marlow too becomes the practitioner of an art whose problematic cultural stance as well as its originality depend on its racial engagements. And in facing his "choice of nightmares," Marlow has to decide whether he will uphold the imperial fiction of a unified and sovereign racial self by defending Kurtz's reputation in Europe, or whether he should unmask this fiction by describing Kurtz's racially fragmented existence in the Congo. Versions of Marlow's nightmares torment subsequent modernist artists, who similarly devise new art forms to compensate for the disintegrations of race, nation, and culture: Yeats imagines an apocalyptic world "vexed to nightmare by a rocking cradle"; Joyce's Stephen Dedalus, forging "the uncreated conscience of my race," experiences history as "a nightmare from which I cannot awake"; Forster's Mrs. Moore cannot distinguish between "vision or nightmare" on her sojourn into the Marabar Caves.[42] Marlow, of course, "can't choose" (111) either nightmare and finds himself enmeshed in a narrative that refuses to settle into a unitary cultural vantage point as it simultaneously protects and betrays Kurtz. And this narrative, the unnamed narrator tells us, inspires a "faint uneasiness" as it "seemed to shape itself without human lips in the heavy night-air of the river" (80): Marlow's tale, like Basil Hallward's painting of Dorian

(handwritten in left margin: positive? (But))

Gray, breaks free of the artist's control and hovers in discomfiting autonomy on the periphery of the imperial metropole.

If Kurtz's aesthetics emerge through paratactic gestures that look ahead
to high modernism's racial preoccupations, Marlow's story ruptures precisely at the points when his own racial multiplicity clashes with the perceptual limitations of an audience that still conceives of race in hierarchical
social terms. I conclude this opening discussion of emergent modernism's
racial turn by examining a sequence of moments when Marlow breaks away
from his tale's forward progress to address his listeners aboard the *Nellie*.
Oscillating between rhetorical gestures of completeness and incomplete-
ness as he spins the tale of Kurtz's death in the Congo, Marlow struggles
against the inflexible racial prejudices of listeners who admonish him, "Try
to be civil, Marlow" (89). In his first direct challenge to his listeners, Marlow demands, famously, "Do you see him? Do you see the story? Do you
see anything?" (79), queries that on one hand reflect his awe of Kurtz,
whose own gaze is "wide enough to embrace the whole universe" (138) and
who makes others "see things" (117), but that, on the other hand, more
broadly evoke Joseph Conrad's authorial ambition "before all, to make you
see" (preface, 235). Greeted only by baffled silence from the Englishmen
aboard the *Nellie*, Marlow answers his own questions with a self-referentiality
that becomes modernism's signature gesture: "No, it is impossible; it is impossible to convey the life-sensation of any given epoch of one's existence,
—that which makes its truth, its meaning—its subtle and penetrating
essence. It is impossible" (79). His thrice-repeated word "impossible" pinpoints a cultural (and, hence, a narrative) stalemate that results from in-
commensurate racial attitudes: the "penetrating essence" of Marlow's story
lies in an *anti-essential* vision of race that repeatedly discomfits his "civil"
listeners. His increasingly abstract figurations of race remove him from an
imperial community in which he no longer has a fixed place.

The "impossible" ideal of a stable, transmissible, and racially unified imperial identity is thrown into relief by two subsequent and intertwined digressions. These innermost moments of Marlow's tale rebuke Victorian
myths of cultural continuity, widening the impasse separating Marlow from
his audience of imperial Everymen—the Accountant, the Lawyer, the Di-
rector of Companies, and the unnamed narrator—and establishing that
the task of representing modernity's broken promises is the task of reinventing race.[43] On the journey to the Inner Station, when a violent attack
on Marlow's steamer costs him his black helmsman, Marlow worries that
Kurtz, too, has already died and that they will never meet. This "extreme

disappointment," Marlow tells his audience, produced "a startling extravagance of emotion, even such as I had noticed in the howling sorrow of these savages in the bush" (106). When the men dismiss his emotional identification with black African "savages," Marlow snaps, "Why do you sigh in that beastly way, somebody? Absurd? Well, absurd. Good Lord!" (107). His audience's resistance to the transposition of racial consciousness renders futile the very act of storytelling:

> "Absurd!" he cried. "This is the worst of trying to tell. . . . Here you all are, each moored with two good addresses, like a hulk with two anchors, a butcher round one corner, a policeman round another, excellent appetites, and temperature normal—you hear—normal from year's end to year's end. And you say, Absurd! Absurd be—exploded! Absurd!" (107)

A near-identical digression bursts out of Marlow when he describes Kurtz's "high seat amongst the devils of the land" (108), a more extreme racial transposition in which Kurtz has willingly subsumed his whiteness into the lived forms of Congolese culture:

> "You can't understand. How could you?—with solid pavement under your feet, surrounded by kind neighbours ready to cheer you or to fall on you, stepping delicately between the butcher and the policeman, in the holy terror of scandal and gallows and lunatic asylums—how can you imagine what particular region of the first ages a man's untrammeled feet may take him into by the way of solitude—utter solitude without a policeman—by the way of silence—utter silence, where no warning voice of a kind neighbour can be heard whispering of public opinion?" (108–9)

The plot ceases to move in these moments, trapped in a narrative stasis produced by the mutual racial incomprehension of teller and listener. Scholars have long noted that Marlow condemns hegemonic social systems that repress difference: desirable addresses; butchers and policemen; the gallows and the asylum; public respectability; temperate climates, appetites, and bodies.[44] More significantly for our purposes, however, Marlow's detailed tirades expose the hollow center of imperial racial knowledge itself. The imperial metropole's protective structures do not seal Marlow's English psyche against the emotions of "savage" African people; no boundaries immanent to whiteness keep Kurtz away from the "powers of darkness" (108). By disjoining conceptions of race from geography, climate, and physiology—the exact sites of scientific racism's epistemic violence—Marlow forces the men aboard the *Nellie* to confront the incoherence of *all* racial identities. Marlow's six iterations of the word "absurd" and his cry, "Absurd be—exploded!" (a rhetorical cousin of "Exterminate all the brutes!") issue a clarion call to destroy the Victorian racial attitudes that threaten to silence his modern tale. The terms of his art demand a foundational reconfiguration of the terms of race.

One final outburst from Marlow cements his fidelity to Kurtz's "method" and looks ahead to the racialized future of modernist aesthetics. On his midnight pursuit of Kurtz through the jungle that surrounds the Inner Station, Marlow realizes that

> "I had to deal with a being to whom I could not appeal in the name of anything high or low. I had, even like the niggers, to invoke him—himself—his own exalted and incredible degradation. There was nothing either above or below him, and I knew it. He had kicked himself loose of the earth. Confound the man! he had kicked the very earth to pieces. He was alone, and I before him did not know whether I stood on the ground or floated in the air. I've been telling you what we said—repeating the phrases we pronounced,—but what's the good? They were common everyday words,—the familiar, vague sounds exchanged on every waking day of life. But what of that?" (132)

This passage illuminates the racial deracination that produces the startling aesthetic commitments of Conrad's modern artists. Powerless "even like the niggers," Marlow literally wonders if he "stood on the ground or floated in the air" as he gazes on Kurtz, who has "kicked himself loose of the earth" and abandoned his ties to any continuous identity defined by race or nation. Living among the Congolese with "nothing either above or below him," Kurtz shatters the dominant plots of Victorian imperial culture: narratives of progress, imperial adventure tales, and the racial "Chain of Being" that justifies colonial praxis. His self-willed exile, like Dorian Gray's, also collapses the forward movement of the bildungsroman and the integrative promises of the marriage plot. Marlow, enraged by his failure to convey Kurtz's astonishing metamorphosis to his listeners, lashes out at the meaninglessness that has descended on "common everyday words," those most basic units of meaning compromised by the racial possibilities that hemorrhage in the Congo and on the Thames. The sudden emptiness of "familiar, vague sounds" initiates a defamiliarized, antimimetic language that will soon jangle through the works of Gertrude Stein, T. S. Eliot, and Mina Loy, authors who experiment with a cacophonous language by turns celebratory and desperate, raucous and numb. Marlow's futile repetition of "the phrases we pronounced" anticipates two crucial instances of inef-

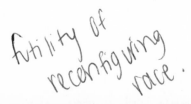

futility of reconfiguring race.

fectual repetition within *Heart of Darkness* itself: Kurtz's dying whisper, "The horror! The horror!" (137), and the last phrases of Marlow's own narrative, "It would have been too dark—too dark altogether . . ." (147).[45] In these closing utterances, repetition does not intensify meaning but, rather, marks its absence. The final words of Conrad's protagonists remain cryptic, stifled by a racial dissonance that lies beyond the purviews of imperial Victorian world order.

Read together, these brief, impassioned digressions crystallize Marlow's "choice of nightmares": his narrative's self-referential utterances, proleptic and analeptic fragments, and obfuscating gestures expose the fractured, unruly nature of race itself. And if Oscar Wilde had suggested this unruliness through Dorian Gray's racial decadence but punished it with a crushing return to Victorian morality, the modernity of Joseph Conrad's fictional universe reflects a new moral indifference toward reconceived ideas about race. Marlow's final lie to Kurtz's Intended—in which he conceals Kurtz's nightmarish racial dissolution by proclaiming that "'The last word he pronounced was—your name'"—turns into an unremarkable banality, a "trifle" for which "the heavens do not fall" (147). The social implications of race recede in the context of its aesthetic implications, and the fragmented racial identities that expel Charlie Marlow and Mr. Kurtz from the totalizing master narratives of European imperialism also give rise to startling and explicitly modern art forms. As Marlow's narrative trails off into an "inconclusive" ellipsis, he remains "apart, indistinct, and silent, in the pose of a meditating Buddha" (147): and this iconic image of an alienated metropolitan artist finds its very modernity—its break from foregoing historical, social, and aesthetic norms—in reimagined domains of racial alterity.

As transitional fictions that enact the opening moments of British modernism, *The Picture of Dorian Gray* and *Heart of Darkness* illuminate a foundational reciprocity between newly conceived aesthetics and new conceptions of race. Chinua Achebe has drawn a famous, troubled parallel between the two texts:

> Africa is to Europe as the picture is to Dorian Gray—a carrier onto whom the master unloads his physical and moral deformities so that he may go forward, erect and immaculate. Consequently Africa is something to be avoided just as the picture has to be hidden away to safeguard the man's jeopardous integrity. Keep away from Africa, or else! Mr. Kurtz of *Heart of Darkness* should have heeded that warning and the prowling horror in his heart would have kept its place, chained to its lair. But he foolishly exposed himself to the wild irresistible allure of the jungle and lo! the darkness found him out. (348)

But if we read Dorian Gray, Mr. Kurtz, and Charlie Marlow as revolutionary artists, rather than "petty European mind[s]" (344), we find in Africa and other non-Western sites not a corrosive force that exposes "physical and moral deformities" but the impetus for a new aesthetic mode. The racial dispersals of metropolitan modernity ensure that Dorian Gray's story does not, as Achebe would have it, progress "erect and immaculate" with the teleological momentum of coming-of-age fictions; and Marlow's fragmented narrative illustrates why modern racial identity would not have "kept its place" in either the colonial center or any of its peripheries. Wilde and Conrad answer the nineteenth century's broken *social* promises of race with a dawning modernist consciousness of the *formal* promises of race. And the racial work begun by these authors evolves to meet the increasingly radical aesthetic commitments of English writers who depart from realist conventions to investigate the problems and promises of twentieth-century modernity. *The Picture of Dorian Gray* and *Heart of Darkness* anticipate what the rest of metropolitan modernism will show us in greater detail: that the forces of modernity produce artists and subjects whose fragmentation and disintegration occur at the site of race, whose rejection of the past is a refusal or inability to attain racial unity, and whose aesthetic impulses require racial tropes, plots, and iconographies.

Modernity's (Yellow) Perils: Dr. Fu-Manchu and English Race Paranoia

When *The Mystery of Dr. Fu-Manchu* was published in London in 1913, Sax Rohmer (1883–1959) catapulted from literary obscurity into astonishing fame that lasted for almost fifty years. Over the decades that witnessed two world wars, the emerging cold war, and rapid scientific and technological change, Rohmer's thirteen novels about a Chinese "devil-doctor" captivated massive readerships in England and America. The central, recurring conflict of these thrillers—Dr. Fu-Manchu's schemes for global domination—rewrote the master narrative of modern England, inverting the British Empire's racial and political hierarchies to imagine a dystopian civilization dominated by evil Orientals.[46] Although the rhetoric of these novels exalts twentieth-century England as a fount of progress, knowledge, and virtue, Dr. Fu-Manchu's near-total appropriation of sociopolitical and technological systems points to the negative capabilities of industrialization and modernization. By paralyzing English heroes and giving a Chinese villain limitless authority over the metropole, Sax Rohmer's novels overturn the tropes of imperial-era popular fiction and echo the complex treatments of urban modernity in the experimental literature of high modernism. Metropolitan alienation and dehumanization—modernism's signature discontents—become, in the Fu-Manchu tales, conditions expressed through an irrefragable racial anxiety. And rather than illustrating imperial Britain's unassailable authority, these best-selling thrillers unwittingly reveal the very emptiness of technocratic utopianism, an emptiness that constitutes the focus of much modernist thought.

The celebrity that began in 1913 with *The Mystery of Dr. Fu-Manchu* and ended in 1959 with *The Emperor Fu-Manchu* rested on Rohmer's imaginative representations of the Yellow Peril.[47] The Fu-Manchu novels—and indeed, Rohmer's entire oeuvre—gained their powerful cultural foothold because of their author's extraordinary market savvy. Born Arthur Henry Ward in Birmingham in 1883, Sax Rohmer came of age during the same years when sensational journalism and mass-produced pulp novels blitzed record numbers of working- and middle-class readers.[48] Although Rohmer's biographers make the lofty claim that "Sax was essentially one with the ancient Great masters of the arts and sciences" (Van Ash and Rohmer, 256–57), a vast paper trail of fiction, drama, and prose indicates that Rohmer's strongest talents lay in deliberately playing to the racial prejudices and desires of white bourgeois audiences. The image of Oriental hordes invading Western nations yielded a malleable literary formula that became the cornerstone of Rohmer's commercial success: the thirteen Fu-Manchu novels sold over twenty million copies during Rohmer's lifetime. *Vanity Fair* magazine called Dr. Fu-Manchu "the most exotic and diabolic of contemporary villains in the annals of crime," and for decades, the imperial propaganda machine, the burgeoning horror-movie industry, and British and U.S. publishing houses reaped material (and ideological) profits by selling Rohmer's Chinese villain to white middle-class audiences.[49] Methuen & Company first published *The Mystery of Fu-Manchu* in 1913 and went on to reprint this title another twenty times; between U.S. and British reprints, this first Fu-Manchu novel alone has seen forty different editions (Van Ash and Rohmer, 297).[50] The Yellow Peril promised to be almost infinitely commodifiable, a set of paranoid race fantasies that audiences eagerly consumed in a variety of genres and guises. In 1923, English audiences flocked to the cinema to be awed by the Stoll Production Company's film *The Mystery of Fu-Manchu*. Stoll plastered London's Underground stations with enormous posters featuring the devil-doctor's malevolent face and boasting that over one hundred thousand Fu-Manchu novels had been sold. Movie studios in Hollywood took over the production of Fu-Manchu feature films in the 1930s, and Rohmer contributed to scripts and screenplays while continuing to write new novels about his despotic Chinese villain.[51] During World War II, he circulated the Fu-Manchu stories through radio broadcasts, and in the 1950s, he helped to create a series of half-hour television shows called *The Adventures of Fu-Manchu*. Rohmer's Chinese doctor has cast a long shadow: not only was Fu-Manchu a progenitor of Flash Gordon's villain Ming the Merciless and James Bond's evil Dr. No, his imprimatur has been stamped on comic books, board games, candies, moustaches, playing cards, cocktails, and rock bands.[52]

Sax Rohmer's Fu-Manchu novels forge an intimate connection between racial identity and the various promises of twentieth-century modernity. In translating the conditions of Western modernity into a battle for racial dominance, Rohmer's fictions give surprising expression to the cultural anxieties and dislocations that high modernist authors negotiate in better-known or canonical texts. This chapter considers the earliest Fu-Manchu stories, which were originally printed as magazine serials in London in 1911 and 1912. During World War I, the stories were collected and issued as full-length novels called *The Mystery of Dr. Fu-Manchu* (1913), *The Devil-Doctor* (1916), and *The Si-Fan Mysteries* (1917). Rohmer designs these tales around a single, unchanging conflict: Dr. Fu-Manchu, an evil Chinese mastermind who has infiltrated modern London, plans to take over the Western world and establish a Yellow Empire.[53] The heroes of the Fu-Manchu novels are Sir Denis Nayland Smith, the intrepid Burmese Commissioner-turned-detective, and his companion Dr. Petrie, the novels' candid narrator, who together fight tirelessly to foil Dr. Fu-Manchu's plans and to stem the tide of Chinese immigrants polluting the modern West with their bodies and belief systems. Adroitly combining the stock gimmicks of English adventure fiction with the lurid, fantastic tropes of occult literature, Rohmer assures his readers at every turn that the world is at the mercy of Dr. Fu-Manchu's unfathomable Oriental villainy and that "if that Satanic genius were not indeed destroyed, then the peace of the world might be threatened anew at any moment!" (*Devil*, 226).

The opening episode of *The Mystery of Dr. Fu-Manchu* sets up the paradigm for all of Nayland Smith and Dr. Petrie's subsequent adventures with Fu-Manchu. Upon learning that Sir Crichton Davy, a pillar of the British Raj, has been mysteriously murdered, Nayland Smith and Petrie rush to his flat in the heart of London and find grisly evidence of Fu-Manchu's machinations. As they discover envelopes containing poisonous letter paper, cap-

ture a never-before-seen species of poisonous centipede, and fight violently
with one of Fu-Manchu's Malaysian thugs, they realize that Fu-Manchu has
struck a blow to the British Empire and vanished without a trace. Horrified that an empire-building colleague has fallen prey to the devil-doctor,
Nayland Smith and Petrie summon the considerable institutional resources
at their disposal: the protection of Scotland Yard, the support of the British
Medical Association, the manpower of His Majesty's Secret Service, and the
knowledge and power offered by the English War Office, the Criminal Investigation Department, the India Office, and the Royal Geographical Society. But no imperial organization can successfully combat Dr. Fu-Manchu,
and Nayland Smith darkly informs Petrie that their enemy wields unlimited control over the modern world:

> "Imagine a person tall, lean and feline, high-shouldered, with a brow like
> Shakespeare and a face like Satan, a close-shaven skull, and long, magnetic
> eyes of the true cat-green. Invest him with all the cruel cunning of an entire
> Eastern race, accumulated in one giant intellect, with all the resources of
> science past and present, with all the resources, if you will, of a wealthy gov-
> ernment—which, however, already has denied all knowledge of his existence.
> Imagine that awful being, and you have a mental picture of Dr. Fu-Manchu,
> the yellow peril incarnate in one man." (15)

Powerless to halt this enemy of "the entire white race" (3), Nayland Smith
and Petrie return to their homes and wait for Fu-Manchu's next attack.

In each subsequent episode, Rohmer introduces a fresh cast of minor
characters who get embroiled in Fu-Manchu's scheme to rule the modern
West. Nayland Smith and Dr. Petrie are repeatedly called to crime scenes
where Fu-Manchu has kidnapped, murdered, or otherwise enacted violence
against upstanding white English citizens. The Chinese doctor always tar-
gets the men who, like his first victim, Sir Crichton Davy, would be most
prized by an imperial nation-state impassioned about its global dominance:
scientists, cartographers, aviators, explorers, engineers, surgeons, and missionaries. Dr. Petrie and Nayland Smith therefore labor not merely to rescue ordinary, innocent English victims but also to safeguard England's
torchbearers from being murdered or absorbed into a Yellow Empire. To
complicate matters, Dr. Petrie falls in love with the beautiful Kâramanèh,
Fu-Manchu's half-caste slave girl with wavering, dangerous loyalties to her
insidious master. As Nayland Smith's imperial authority fails him, and as
Dr. Petrie struggles against his desire for Kâramanèh, the two Englishmen
frequently fall prisoners to Fu-Manchu. Their confrontations with Fu-

Manchu provide a series of cliffhanging moments where readers are led to believe that either Nayland Smith and Petrie will die horrible deaths, or that Fu-Manchu will be vanquished once and for all. Of course, like all heroes of serial fiction, Rohmer's English protagonists escape miraculously from their enemy's clutches at the last minute. Similarly, Fu-Manchu himself always eludes his pursuers, surviving flaming buildings, sinking ships, and bullets shot through his brain.

Clive Bloom's work *Cult Fiction,* one of very few critical studies to consider Rohmer's writing, explains Fu-Manchu's invincibility as a function of his unearthly powers. "The modern world, represented by Nayland Smith," Bloom argues, "is a world essentially haunted by an international mafia with supernatural powers; powers which at once uphold and destabilize reality and whose presence is material yet invisible" (191). Indeed, Rohmer bedecks his novels with the trappings of occult fiction: cats with poisonous claws, fatal siren calls, thinking insects, potions that induce artificial death. But I find that Fu-Manchu's occult mystique only cloaks the far more troubling source of his invincibility: his unlimited command over the systems of daily modern existence in the industrialized West. Supernatural elements in Rohmer's novels entertain and fascinate, but Dr. Fu-Manchu's calculated control over the imperial metropole alerts us to modernity's dystopian possibilities. Neither Englishness nor twentieth-century modernity—the unquestioned ideals of most coeval popular imperial adventure tales—can sustain stable meaning over the course of these narratives.

The semaphores of modernity in these ostensibly patriotic fictions do not describe a Western nation-state made invulnerable through the virtues of reason, scientific knowledge, and the autonomy of the individual. Rather, as suggested by Dr. Petrie's comment that Fu-Manchu has made "living mockeries of our boasted modern security" (*Mystery,* 98), they signal a troubling disjuncture between modern England's estimation of its power and the limits that Fu-Manchu imposes on that power. The Fu-Manchu novels explicitly acknowledge their cultural moment and the exigency of protecting that moment, as when Dr. Petrie is imprisoned by Dr. Fu-Manchu and declares, "It was difficult to believe that we were in modern, up-to-date England; easy to dream that we were the captives of a caliph, in a dungeon in old Baghdad" (*Mystery,* 102); or when he waits outside Fu-Manchu's London laboratory and realizes that "save for the periodical passage of an electrical car, in blazing modernity, this was a fit enough stage for an eerie drama" (*Devil,* 262). As self-conscious fictions of metropolitan modernity, Rohmer's best-selling thrillers offer provocative counterpoints to high modernism's representations of cultural ambivalence and insecurity. The high modernist literature of the teens and twenties is saturated with well-known images of fracture and fragmentation: authors as diverse as T. S. Eliot, Ezra Pound, Ford Madox Ford, James Joyce, Mina Loy, and E. M. Forster all remade literary forms by rejecting a vision of the world seen steadily and whole. Sax Rohmer's works register a similar awareness of a fragmented, discordant world. But unlike many of the modernist authors who sought refuge from modernity's entropy in aesthetically complex explorations of interiority and subjectivity, Rohmer bluntly projects modernity's threats and promises onto the racially threatening figure of Dr. Fu-Manchu. It is through the language of race that the Fu-Manchu novels express, to return to Fredric Jameson, modernity's conflicted and defining "consciousness of a radical break" (*Singular*, 24). In other words, the threatened discontinuities of race in Rohmer's thrillers expose the uneven promises of a culture enthralled with the forward march of technology, knowledge, and progress.

Sir Denis Nayland Smith characterizes Dr. Fu-Manchu as an entity beyond the ken of the modern West:

> "This man, whether a fanatic, or a duly appointed agent, is, unquestionably, the most malign and formidable personality existing in the known world today. He is a linguist who speaks with almost equal facility in any of the civilized languages, and in most of the barbaric. He is an adept in all the arts and sciences which a great university could teach him. He also is an adept in certain obscure arts and sciences which *no* university of today can teach. He has the brains of any three men of genius." (*Mystery*, 14)

This description, which Rohmer repeats with slight variations in all the Fu-Manchu novels, reflects anxiety about individual and collective English agency. Fear of Fu-Manchu's intelligence signals a deeper British unease about what Thomas Richards calls the imperial archive, fin-de-siècle England's "collectively imagined junction of all that was known or was knowable, a fantastic representation of an epistemological master pattern, a virtual focus point for the heterogeneous local knowledge of metropolis and empire" (11). Authors who witnessed twentieth-century modernity emerging from Victorianism's carapace grappled with the imperial archive's decreasing power to organize and contain knowledge: the hallmark anxiety of the modernist canon, manifested as both style and substance, fixates on the dissolution of objective certainties. And while Sax Rohmer's writing shares little or no stylistic affinity with the literature of high modernism, the Fu-Manchu novels share modernism's obsession with England's loss of epistemological supremacy. Despite the bravado and bluster of Rohmer's adventure-novel tropes, the Fu-Manchu novels, like so many modernist texts, ultimately register England's moral, political, and physiological failures.

Of course, Rohmer does not explicitly cast failure as the dominant focus of the Fu-Manchu tales. By modeling the novels on Arthur Conan Doyle's wildly popular Sherlock Holmes mysteries, Rohmer in fact works diligently for the epistemological certainty (and narrative tautness) of Conan Doyle's stories. Rohmer replicates the paradigm of the brilliant detective and his ingenuous companion with almost comic fidelity. The role of Sherlock Holmes is played by Sir Denis Nayland Smith, who labors ceaselessly to save the white race from the devil-doctor. And like Dr. Watson, Rohmer's everyman narrator Dr. Petrie is a London-based middle-class medical practitioner who spends his evenings writing. But whereas Watson's narratives praise Holmes's reason and intellectual breadth, Dr. Petrie's storytelling too often revolves around his own gee-whiz bewilderment and Nayland Smith's braggadocio:

> I had jumped to my feet, for a tall, lean man, with his square-cut, clean-shaven face sun-baked to the hue of coffee, entered and extended both hands with a cry:
> "Good old Petrie! Didn't expect me, I'll swear!"
> It was Nayland Smith—whom I had thought to be in Burma! . . .
> "Petrie, I have travelled from Burma not in the interests of the British Government merely, but in the interests of the entire white race, and I honestly believe—though I pray I may be wrong—that its survival depends largely upon the success of my mission."
> To say that I was perplexed conveys no idea of the mental chaos created by these extraordinary statements, for into my humdrum suburban life Nayland Smith had brought fantasy of the wildest. I did not know what to think, what to believe. (*Mystery*, 1–3)

Not knowing "what to think, what to believe" becomes a recurring, inescapable intellectual condition for Rohmer's protagonists. Despite Rohmer's aspirations to re-create flawlessly plotted mysteries in the Sherlock Holmes tradition, his protagonists lack the antidote for the social and cultural disorder that Fu-Manchu brings to modern London. The national optimism and sense of invulnerability that British institutions typically embody in popular adventure fiction give way here to a grim racial fatalism.

The race paranoia that suffuses the Fu-Manchu novels unfolded in the context of imperial Britain's varied reactions to transformative political events in China at the turn of the century. In 1900, the slaughter of hundreds of English officials in China during the Boxer Uprising portended the collapse of the imperial Christian West's decades-long control over China; the motto of the Boxer rebels was "Preserve the dynasty; destroy the foreigners," a fierce defense of China's native cultural traditions against Western economic and religious interference.[54] China's bloody rebellion further destabilized England's already-shaky confidence about its own strength; the British army's recent heavy losses at the hands of the Boers in South Africa had stirred wide cultural unease about the physical deterioration of white English bodies. Vociferous debates about the British Empire's physiological and ideological soundness saturated the English press, along with moral indignation at the barbarity and cruelty of the Chinese.[55] When Rohmer penned the first of the Fu-Manchu serials in 1911, he declared, "Conditions for launching a Chinese villain on the market were ideal. . . . The Boxer Rebellion had started off rumors of a Yellow Peril which had not yet died down" (Van Ash and Rohmer, 75).[56] Indeed, the Fu-Manchu novels reply directly to the Boxers: just as the Boxers killed Westerners to rid China of unwanted foreign influence, Rohmer's stories describe valiant struggles to expel Fu-Manchu and his Asiatic hordes from England. Filled with gory details about Fu-Manchu's calculated cruelties, the novels capitalize on British prejudice against China's antimodernity and invite readers to shudder at Chinese tortures, like Fu-Manchu's fearsome wire-jackets, which surround the wearer in barbed wire until "the flesh swelled out in knobs through the mesh" (*Devil*, 244); his methods of murder, including death by outsized Cantonese rats described as "'the most ravenous in the world'" (416); and his trained Chinese scorpions, pythons, and hamadryads.

But Rohmer's depictions of a premodern, barbaric, and anti-Western China coexist with textual anxieties about China's very pretensions to modernization. In 1911, when the first Fu-Manchu stories were serialized, sociopolitical revolution in China ended the Manchu dynasty and Confucian social order, which resulted in the founding of Sun Yat-Sen's Chinese Republic in 1912 and eventually led to the formation of Chiang Kai-Shek's Nationalist China in 1928. Fu-Manchu and his hordes, therefore, emblematize not only dynastic China's opposition to the modern Christian West, but also the emergent geopolitical ambitions of a post-1911 China determined to fashion itself as a nation unhindered by the imperial designs of Britain, Germany, France, Austria, Italy, Russia, or Japan.[57] And although the Fu-Manchu stories never explicitly mention the formation of the Republic of China, Nayland Smith and Dr. Petrie's horror at Dr. Fu-Manchu's nascent Yellow Empire dramatizes Britain's growing concern about China's plans to strengthen its global presence. Thus, Dr. Fu-Manchu's multifaceted racial alterity—a confluence of modern political ambition, the "cruel cunning of an entire Eastern race," and Western science and technology—sheds light on the British Empire's vulnerability, undermining the very master narrative of British imperial sovereignty that these novels aim to reinforce.

If Fu-Manchu's threats adumbrate imperial Britain's soon-to-be-lost global control, they also announce the racial atomizing of the empire's metropolitan center. Nayland Smith and Petrie repeatedly despair that London's sanctity—its cultural unity and the racial purity of individual English bodies—has been violated by the arrival of Fu-Manchu and his foreign henchmen. Virtually every episode calls attention to the sordid world of London's migrant Chinese population and its latent dangers of miscegenation and opium addiction. The Chinese characters so vilified in Rohmer's thrillers, of course, bore little resemblance to their real-life counterparts in modern London; English paranoia about immigration was radically disproportionate to the threat posed by the tiny Chinese settlements that had developed after the first Chinese came to London in the 1830s with the British merchant navy.[58] (By 1913, the city's Chinese population barely numbered four hundred, and there were just thirty Chinese shops and restaurants in the Limehouse district of London, which provided the setting for Rohmer's Fu-Manchu novels.[59]) But by exaggerating the threat that Chinese immigrants posed to London's Anglo-Saxon population, Rohmer rewrites the racial politics of British adventure tales. Foreigners in Rohmer's fiction—no longer marginal figures or silent actors in cosmopolitan spectacle—enjoy the textual centrality usually reserved for white English protagonists and empire builders. Because Dr. Fu-Manchu takes up residence in London and utilizes the city's resources for his despotic ends, Rohmer's thrillers replace ideals of England-as-home with fears of England as the source of its own racial and political downfall. Racial conflict becomes the charged locus of Western modernity's internal contradictions.

It is precisely this racializing of modernity's crises that invites us to read the Fu-Manchu thrillers against the more subtle, nuanced racial dialectics of the modernist literary canon. As Rohmer's novels sensationalize an impending Yellow Peril's impact on London and gesture toward the changing face of modern China, they reconfigure experimental modernism's

obsession with fragmented metropolitan existence as well as its concomitant investment in the wholeness of the empire's colonial peripheries.[60]
Reverse colonization in the Fu-Manchu novels provocatively racializes the
metropolitan alienation that characterizes high modernist literature; urban
anomie becomes a function of Western racial inadequacy in the face of a
politically and technologically ascendant East. Perhaps most arrestingly,
Fu-Manchu's unrestricted circulation through the metropole suggests a
racially threatening version of Baudelaire's flâneur. As a corrupt "artist of
modern life" who simultaneously participates in and remains detached
from his surroundings, Fu-Manchu perpetually reinvents the ideological
and material architectures of the present moment for the future Yellow Empire. The totality of modern life—its mosaic of quotidian rituals and its consciousness of the future that awaits—becomes the domain of Fu-Manchu's
despotic, Oriental flânerie. Indeed, Rohmer's Chinese villain symbolizes a
monstrous pastiche of several modern-era literary characters, an alien war-
lord who perverts the well-established modes and tropes of urban existence.
For example, Dr. Fu-Manchu violently rescripts the legacy of adventure and
conquest he inherits from Conrad's Marlow and assumes control of the
Thames, using the river for "his highway, his line of communication along
which he moved his mysterious forces" (*Mystery*, 126). The great English
river that has transported white English colonizers and their instruments
of power now becomes a conduit for Chinese villainy as Fu-Manchu smug-
gles dead bodies, scientific equipment, and foreign henchmen on the boats
and barges that cruise the Thames. Then, like Stoker's Dracula, Fu-Manchu
has the power to disappear in a crowd and reappear at will; Dr. Petrie compels us to fear "the wonderful and evil man who once walked, by the many
unsuspected, in the midst of the people of England" (155). And like
Kipling's hybrid, culturally porous hero Kim, Fu-Manchu's fluency in Eastern and Western languages facilitates his control over the international
communities that he assembles in London. Petrie marvels at how Fu-
Manchu's linguistic flexibility seduces and manipulates his followers:

> Fu-Manchu would turn slightly, and elucidate his remarks, addressing a Chi-
> naman in Chinese, a Hindu in Hindustani, or an Egyptian in Arabic. . . . It
> seemed to me that he used them as an instrument, playing upon their obvi-
> ous fanaticism, string by string, as a player upon an Eastern harp, and all the
> time weaving his harmonies to suit some giant, incredible scheme of his own
> —a scheme over and beyond any of which they had dreamed, in the fruition
> whereof they had no part—of the true nature and composition of which they
> had no comprehension. (*Si-Fan*, 602)

Faced with an alien being who can effortlessly traverse distance, time, and language, Rohmer's English heroes inevitably find the modern era's numerous promises hollow, prey to savage cultural misappropriation. As Fu-Manchu's coruscating, perverse intelligence competes against the ostensibly infallible systems of English knowledge, Rohmer transforms the discourses of science, technology, medicine, and history into the stuff of racial jeopardy. It is the specter of a futuristic Yellow Empire—a politically and technologically sovereign state ruled by Dr. Fu-Manchu—that produces a profound disjuncture between the novels' promodern rhetoric and their unwittingly antimodern turn of events.

To understand the tension between the Fu-Manchu novels' Anglocentric, imperialist bombast and the recurrent motifs of English failure, it is necessary to look beyond the prevailing conventions of popular imperial-era fiction. Although, as I have pointed out, Rohmer's novels are formally indebted to detective fiction, ideologically complicit with English adventure literature, and thematically akin to experimental modernist narratives, they nonetheless do not fit neatly into any of these genres. The continuous serialization of the original stories, combined with the racial antagonism that drove their plots, produced texts filled with rhetorical excess and embellishment. When Fu-Manchu kidnaps Dr. Petrie in *The Mystery of Dr. Fu-Manchu,* for example, Petrie's reactions fulfill a narrative obligation to hyperbolize the devil-doctor's evil:

> I have endeavoured, perhaps in extenuation of my own fears, to explain how about Dr. Fu-Manchu there rested an atmosphere of horror, peculiar, unique. He was not as other men. The dread that he inspired in all with whom he came in contact, the terrors which he controlled and hurled at whomsoever cumbered his path, rendered him an object supremely sinister. I despair of conveying to those who may read this account any but the coldest conception of the man's evil power. (*Mystery,* 125)

The constant need to remind readers of Fu-Manchu's unique brand of evil yields many similar passages, where Rohmer emphasizes the Chinese doctor's ineffably corrupt temperament. But where prose is fluid and extravagant in the Fu-Manchu novels, narrative continuity frequently suffers. When the individual, serialized Fu-Manchu stories were conflated to be published as full-length novels, Rohmer made no attempt to connect the episodes smoothly or to unify the multiple adventures. Consequently, the first three Fu-Manchu novels are awkward and lurching, punctuated by gaps in the action and inadequately explained events. I find that the racial and cultural malevolence of Sax Rohmer's novels is best understood through the tropes of melodrama, which not only compensate for the novels' narrative fissures but also sustain the continuous aura of Dr. Fu-Manchu's iniquity. Melodrama, which emerged in France during the late eighteenth century as a verse play set to music, floated free of its theatrical origins during the nineteenth century and came to stand for a more general aesthetic sensibility based on hyperbole and moral absolutism. Peter Brooks's now-classic study of the genre, *The Melodramatic Imagination,* defines melodrama's characteristics as "the indulgence of strong emotionalism; moral polarization and schematization; extreme states of being, situations, actions; overt villainy, persecution of the good, and final reward of virtue; inflated and extravagant expression; dark plottings, suspense, breathtaking peripety" (11–12). To describe the dystopian horrors of Fu-Manchu's planned Yellow Empire, Rohmer's novels merge the thematic Manichaeanisms of melodrama with the *racial* Manichaeanisms of British imperialism. Melodrama's indelible link between rhetorically elicited sensation and fixed moral codes enables Rohmer to summon the self-justifying racial paranoia that fuels his English heroes' crusade to capture Dr. Fu-Manchu. In telling "the story of Dr. Fu-Manchu and of the great secret society which sought to upset the balance of the world" (*Mystery,* 121), Rohmer avails himself of narrative devices that leave no room for racial or moral ambivalence. To sustain or renew the central textual ideology of white dominance, for example, Dr. Petrie provides overbold metaphors for character and conflict:

> A great wave of exotic perfume swept from the open window towards the curtained doorway.
> It was a breath of the East—that stretched out a yellow hand to the West. It was symbolic of the subtle, intangible power manifested in Dr. Fu-Manchu, as Nayland Smith—lean, agile, bronzed with the suns of Burma—was symbolic of the clean British efficiency which sought to combat the insidious enemy. (*Mystery,* 80)

Such melodramatic excesses grow out of an unrelenting Sinophobia that portends a racial apocalypse; the struggle to stave off this apocalypse unfolds as a series of improbable events linked together through inadequate causality. In all of these novels, Nayland Smith and Petrie survive one life-threatening adventure after another, fabricating loose connections between each incident and Fu-Manchu's master plot to rule the world. Elaborate, unrealizable strategies to capture Fu-Manchu are enacted in settings that reflect the absolute good of the white protagonists (like Petrie's brightly lit rooms) and the depraved evil of the enemy (like the darkened, filthy Chinese shops in Limehouse). Hyperbole characterizes Petrie's tales of Fu-Manchu's terrifying scientific achievements, and each new adventure provokes a variant of Petrie's claim that "I have never experienced in my life a sensation identical with that which now possessed me" (*Si-Fan*, 526). By imparting racial particulars to melodrama's explicit, unsubtle rhetoric, Rohmer pathologizes the differences between Eastern and Western races and invites his readers to share Dr. Petrie's "sensations" of horror and revulsion for "the mighty Chinaman who represented things unutterable, whose potentialities for evil were boundless as his genius, who personified a secret danger, the extent and nature of which none of us truly understood" (*Devil*, 269).

The logical demands of short-story serialization—Rohmer had to keep Fu-Manchu alive and invulnerable while partially achieving white England's goal of casting foreigners out of the metropole—posed a challenge for maintaining the ongoing sensations of racial paranoia. Since teleological narrative formulas would spell the demise of the entire series, Rohmer had to keep the *imperative* to kill Fu-Manchu at the ideological center of the novels, while the actual plots had to move forward *without* ever achieving that goal. By using Fu-Manchu's henchmen to represent the essentialized, underevolved Oriental body and the devil-doctor himself to represent an extraordinarily brilliant and perverse Oriental mind, Rohmer eliminates segments of Fu-Manchu's dark-skinned army while ensuring that Fu-Manchu's own enduring, transcendent evil is never contained or controlled. In other words, dividing Oriental evil between the body and the mind allows Rohmer to destroy specific incarnations of racial Otherness while simultaneously showing that the Orient's overarching degeneracy—embodied in Fu-Manchu—can never be fully repressed.

On one level, Rohmer's race-inflected melodrama appeals effortlessly to a middle-class readership accustomed to and complicit with the late Victorian onslaught of imperial propaganda.[61] Recruited from "the darkest places of the East" (*Devil*, 356), Fu-Manchu's pan-Asian "murder-gang" includes Negro and mulatto henchmen, Burmese thugs, Chinese martial artists, Malaysian dacoits (thieves), Indian lascars (seamen), phansigars (stranglers), hashishin (assassins), and houris (Muslim virgins). In *The Mystery of Dr. Fu-Manchu*, for example, an Indian dacoit who holds a knife to Dr. Petrie's throat evokes "pure horror" because of his "wicked, pockmarked face, with wolfish fangs bared, and jaundiced eyes squinting obliquely" (129). Similarly, in *The Si-Fan Mysteries,* Nayland Smith tries to escape from the "repellent figure" of a Chinaman who "approached, stooping, apish, with a sort of loping gait," and "perched between his shoulders —bending forward—the wicked yellow fingers at work, tightening—tightening—tightening the strangle cord!" (552). Such characters frighten because they stand for a coalesced, mingled East that challenges Western authority; the literal crowding of their foreign bodies around Nayland Smith and Petrie portends the larger encroachment of the Yellow Empire on the West.[62] When Nayland Smith and Petrie kill anonymous members of Fu-Manchu's cohort, as they do in nearly every episode, they comply with a melodramatic imperative to reassert the purity of white Englishness. But while Rohmer's protagonists kill or enact violence against these dark foreign bodies, they remain powerless to combat Dr. Fu-Manchu, the elusive mastermind who commands the henchmen. Unlike his brutish, nameless henchmen, Fu-Manchu's actual physical presence does not gain its gravitas from musculature or bulk. It is an unthreatening body that eludes the bestial corporeality of his faceless yellow hordes: "Who could mistake that long, gaunt shape, with the high, mummy-like shoulders, and the indescribable gait, which I can only liken to that of an awkward cat?" asks Petrie (*Mystery,* 204). In Nayland Smith and Petrie's confrontations with the devil-doctor, moral depravity shifts its locus from the *body* of the anonymous non-white Other to the *intellect* of Fu-Manchu.

Rohmer's novels attribute Fu-Manchu's pathological evil to his magnificent brain, whose foreignness and abnormal size suggest brilliance as well as dementia. In *The Mystery of Dr. Fu-Manchu,* one of Petrie's early confrontations with the Chinese doctor begins with a description of the latter's head:

> In his long, yellow robe, his mask-like, intellectual face bent forward amongst the riot of singular appliances before him, his great, high brow gleaming in the light of the shaded lamp above, and with the abnormal eyes, filmed and green, raised to us, he seemed a figure from the realms of delirium. (*Mystery,* 128)

Similar, oft-repeated comments on the immensity of Fu-Manchu's head, his "brow like Shakespeare" and his "face like Satan," frame every encounter between Nayland Smith and Petrie and their Chinese nemesis. The "gaunt ugliness" (*Si-Fan,* 531) of Fu-Manchu's body remains insignificant next to "the aura, the glamour" (*Devil,* 308) suggested by his gargantuan brain. If his hordes will pollute England with their bodies, Fu-Manchu threatens to claim total authority over the modern Western nation-state with his mental capacities. Thus, Petrie imagines the looming Yellow Empire as "a veritable octopus whose head was that of Dr. Fu-Manchu, whose tentacles were dacoity, thuggee, modes of death secret and swift" (*Mystery,* 179).

The exaggerated proportions of Fu-Manchu's head position him in an interstice between two late nineteenth-century scientific theories about skull size and intelligence. On one hand, the burgeoning science of craniometry—made famous by the Italian surgeon Paul Broca—theorized that a large, long skull indicated an individual's intellectual prowess, cultural refinement, and capacity for contributing to civilization. Those individuals with small, short skulls were less developed mentally, more prone to moral corruption, and incapable of substantial achievement. Typically, craniometry justified Western imperial conquest and sovereignty by "proving" that the short-skulled inhabitants of subject nations (like Fu-Manchu's henchmen) were unfit to govern themselves.[63] But Fu-Manchu transcends science's racial hierarchy: although the Chinese and other supposedly small-skulled Asian races were assumed to occupy lower orders within Western science's physiological hierarchies, Fu-Manchu's "tremendous intellectual force" (*Devil,* 311) and the "height of the great dome-like brow" (*Si-Fan,* 526–27) elevate him above his thuggish servants and make him a foe worthy of white Englishmen. Even as Petrie experiences loathing and revulsion for Fu-Manchu's cruelty, he confesses that Fu-Manchu "had the brow of a genius, the features of a born ruler," and that his face, "saving the indescribable evil of its expression, was identical with that of Seti I, the mighty Pharaoh" (*Devil,* 311).

Dr. Petrie's awe of the Chinese doctor's brilliance, however, alternates with comments on Fu-Manchu's dementia. In accordance with another branch of fin-de-siècle science, the large skull identifies Fu-Manchu as a criminal as well as a genius. Theories linking criminal identity and racial degeneration circulated widely through England in the years immediately preceding the first Fu-Manchu stories. Works like Havelock Ellis's *The Criminal* (1890), Max Nordau's *Degeneration* (1895), and Cesare Lombroso's *Crime: Its Causes and Remedies* (1911) proffered various biologically or anthropologically grounded assertions that physiology and race are intimately linked to crime in a society. The moral character of a nation, these studies argued, could be deduced from the anatomically determined character of its citizens; skull size presented the most telling signs of criminality.[64] Thus, the elongated skull that signifies Fu-Manchu's genius also identifies him as a criminal, since abnormally large cranial capacity was considered to be the trademark of deviants, maniacs, and criminals. The alienness of Fu-Manchu's head—at once Chinese, Satanic, and Pharaonic—causes *and* denotes his deviance. At the end of *The Mystery of Dr. Fu-Manchu*, for example, Fu-Manchu tortures a group of Scotland Yard detectives with giant toxic fungi. Forced to watch his colleagues suffer and die, Dr. Petrie speculates that Fu-Manchu's deadly scientific knowledge is a product of criminal insanity:

> Like powdered snow the white spores fell from the roof, frosting the writhing shapes of the already poisoned men. Before my horrified gaze, *the fungus grew;* it spread from the head to the feet of those it touched; it enveloped them as in glittering shrouds. . . .
> "They die like flies!" screamed Fu-Manchu, with a sudden febrile excitement; and I felt assured of something I had long suspected: that that magnificent, perverted brain was the brain of a homicidal maniac—though Smith would never accept the theory. (189–90)

With his "magnificent, perverted brain," Fu-Manchu occupies a complex, racially coded space between "evil" and "genius." Petrie and Nayland Smith remain unable to decide whether Fu-Manchu is "a madman bent upon self-destruction by strange means" or "a preternaturally clever scientist and the most elusive being ever born of the land of mystery—China" (220).

The incomprehensible excesses of Fu-Manchu's intelligence and criminality always lead to unresolved or incomplete adventures. Powerless against the Chinese doctor's villainy, Petrie tells us that the urgency of capturing Fu-Manchu leaves him no time to conclude his stories:

> I may not tarry, as more leisurely penmen, to round my incidents; they were not of my choosing. I may not pause to make you better acquainted with the figures of my drama; its scheme is none of mine. . . . I have been asked many times since the days with which these records deal: Who *was* Dr. Fu-Manchu? Let me confess here that my final answer must be postponed. I can only indicate, at this place, the trend of my reasoning, and leave my reader to form whatever conclusion he pleases. (*Mystery,* 176)

Such textual moments conjoin Rohmer's melodramatic treatment of race with the demands of serialized writing to produce the irresolution so aesthetically and historically characteristic of the modern era. By complying with melodrama's insistence on the inexpressible and the unspeakable, Rohmer draws his readers' attentions to the terrible frisson of Fu-Manchu's evil and, simultaneously, defers textual resolution. The cliffhanging end-points of individual episodes frequently go unexplained and Petrie confesses, "I come to the close of my chronicle, and feel that I betray a trust—the trust of my reader. . . . I am unable to complete my task as I should desire, unable, with any consciousness of finality, to write Finis to the end of my narrative" (*Mystery,* 219). Readers of the Fu-Manchu stories, like the men fated "to hear about one of Marlow's inconclusive experiences" in *Heart of Darkness* (52), repeatedly find that the pursuit of the devil-doctor has no realizable outcome. The irresolution that so often attends modernist fiction, here a function of the Fu-Manchu novels' serialization, betrays unending racial and cultural failure. And as we will see, the inability to finalize the narrative and resolve its conflicts mirrors the white protagonists' inability to rid the modern West of Fu-Manchu: the limitations of literary authority correspond to an equally limited political authority.

The racial oppositions that heighten the Fu-Manchu novels' melodramatic aesthetic also create a discursive space for Sax Rohmer's complex negotiations of English modernity. By pitting Fu-Manchu's loathsome criminal genius against Nayland Smith and Petrie's faith in England's inherent goodness, Rohmer's novels mount a dual critique of the modern West's obsession with innovation, global sovereignty, and the acquisition of knowledge. On one hand, Fu-Manchu's expert manipulations of twentieth-century England demonstrate that modernity's assets are not the exclusive privilege of Western subjects; the Chinese villain's unlimited physical and political control splinters assumptions that equate modern cultural authority with whiteness. On the other hand, the Yellow Empire that Fu-Manchu will build using modernity's resources threatens to be the very antithesis of a post-Enlightenment nation-state. Taken to its logical conclusion, a nation that promises its citizens a newer, faster, always-progressive future harbors the potential for its own downfall; the high-tech race wars in the Fu-Manchu narratives expose what Michel Foucault famously calls "the paradox of the relations of capacity and power" ("What is Enlightenment?", 47), in which a nation's systemic powers expand in inverse proportion to the power of the individual citizen. As suggested by Nayland Smith's half-horrified, half-respectful declaration that Fu-Manchu "is the greatest novelty of his age" (*Mystery,* 151), Rohmer's novels demonstrate that innovation and modernization threaten oppression to the same degree that they promise liberation.

Rohmer's unwitting representations of English failure—whether at the level of individual characters or of larger social structures—are the points where the Fu-Manchu novels intersect most provocatively with the narratives of high modernism. Indeed, these stories offer a popular, mass-market version of the avant-garde oscillation between a fierce celebration of a fragmented, ever-accelerating present and a deep desire for wholeness and continuity. Even as Dr. Petrie and Nayland Smith laud imperial Britain's scientific, technological, and bureaucratic authority, their fruitless efforts to contain Fu-Manchu with that authority betray anxieties about the modern era's dynamism and mobility. Following one of Nayland Smith's thwarted conspiracies to kill Dr. Fu-Manchu in *The Mystery of Dr. Fu-Manchu*, for example, Petrie expresses the kind of profound urban alienation that characterizes modernist writing ranging from Baudelaire and Conrad to Lawrence and Woolf:

> It was Big Ben. It struck the half-hour, leaving the stillness complete. In that room, high above the activity which yet prevailed below, high above the supping crowds in the hotel, high above the starving crowds on the Embankment, a curious chill of isolation swept about me. Again, I realized how, in the very heart of the great metropolis, a man may be as far from aid as in the heart of a desert. (112)

Big Ben, the massive symbol of England's aggressive role in standardizing time for the entire world, becomes an ironic reminder of the "chill of isolation" that accompanies such standardization.[65] According to Nayland Smith and Petrie, the proudest aspect of the West's "blazing modernity" (*Devil*, 262) should be the imperial state's technological control over a natural world. However, in this scene and several others like it, the "muted booming of London's clocks" (*Si-Fan*, 512)—like the "leaden circles" that resonate mournfully throughout Woolf's *Mrs. Dalloway*—unintentionally come to signify the imperfections and limitations of Western technocracy. Enraged that the machinery of English power has been appropriated by the foreign hands of Dr. Fu-Manchu, Petrie unknowingly identifies two ideological paradoxes that have long vexed modern sociologists and cultural critics: first, that the resources and systems in the "heart of the great metropolis" engender failure and alienation rather than success and solidarity, and second, that the individual subject's autonomy is compromised rather than expanded by these systems.

To understand the inconsistent textual treatment of Dr. Fu-Manchu's command over the social, technological, and political systems of early twentieth-century England—that is, the English characters' simultaneous revulsion and respect for Fu-Manchu's omnipotence—it is useful to turn to Anthony Giddens's theory of modern life as a "juggernaut." In *The Consequences of Modernity,* Giddens depicts modern existence as a "runaway engine of enormous power which, collectively as human beings, we can drive to some extent but which also threatens to rush out of our control and which could rend itself asunder" (139). This juggernaut, he argues,

> crushes those who resist it, and while it sometimes seems to have a steady path, there are times when it veers away erratically in directions we cannot foresee. The ride is by no means wholly unpleasant or unrewarding; it can often be exhilarating and charged with hopeful anticipation. But, so long as the institutions of modernity endure, we shall never be able to control completely either the path or the pace of the journey. In turn, we shall never be able to feel entirely secure, because the terrain across which it runs is fraught with risks of high consequence. Feelings of ontological security and existential anxiety will coexist in ambivalence. (139)

The Fu-Manchu novels identify the labile tendencies of industrialized, systematized modern existence and point to racial identity as the dominant site of modernity's uncertainties. Dr. Fu-Manchu himself becomes the "juggernaut" of modernity: his complete control over time, space, technology, languages, and social systems makes him a monstrous reflection of the very Western civilization he threatens to subsume, and his racial alterity makes literal the alienating, unknowable character of modern urban life. Despite frequent textual insistences that modern England is a white-dominated nation whose whiteness must be preserved, Fu-Manchu's access to seminal cultural discourses and technologies keeps the relationship between racial identity and modernity unstable.

Rohmer makes the contest for modern sovereignty most explicit by means of Fu-Manchu's movements through urban geographies. Nayland Smith's declaration that "'Fu-Manchu is omnipresent; his tentacles embrace everything'" (*Mystery,* 75) speaks to the distinctly modern nature of Fu-Manchu's control over the metropole. The devil-doctor not only commands the high-speed industrialized landscape built by men like Nayland Smith and Dr. Petrie, but he reterritorializes it so that it becomes impenetrably Oriental and hence unknowable to white English characters. Seeing how "Near East and Far East rubbed shoulders" in the London streets, Nayland Smith and Petrie are appalled to realize that they "might well have stood, not in a squalid London thoroughfare, but in an equally squalid market-street of the Orient" (*Devil,* 291). Fu-Manchu's ability to commingle various Eastern cultures in England bears out Giddens's premise that space and time in modern societies operate by "fostering relations between 'absent' others, locationally distant from any given situation of face-to-face interaction" (18). Like the myriad "little Englands" that mushroomed in colonial African, Asian, and Caribbean nations, where white imperialists meticulously re-created the aspect and mores of Anglo-Saxon society to distinguish themselves from the native people they subjugated, Dr. Fu-Manchu imports a complex Oriental praxis into London, making the imperial metropolis a site of dizzying instability and racial chaos.

As Nayland Smith and Petrie pursue Fu-Manchu, the colonial peripheries that are usually invisible from the metropole become suddenly visible, violent, and horrifying. When Fu-Manchu holds a political meeting in a London warehouse on the Thames, for example, Petrie espies numerous Oriental dignitaries assembled in elaborate chambers with fittings from the East, surrounded by the instruments of Chinese alchemy. Petrie struggles to make sense of what seems culturally and racially anarchic: "I could not reconcile my ideas—the ideas of a modern, ordinary middle-class practitioner—with these far Eastern devilries which were taking place in London" (*Si-Fan*, 535). Similarly, the spectacle of Fu-Manchu torturing his slave girl, Kâramanèh, and her brother, Aziz, provokes Petrie's amazement that "the wonders of *The Arabian Nights* were wonders no longer, for here, in East End London, was a true magician's palace, lacking not its beautiful slave, lacking not its enchanted prince!" (*Mystery*, 163). Realizing that the devil-doctor has interwoven the "here" of the West with the "there" of the East, Petrie cries, "'Oh, my God . . . can this be England?'" (*Mystery*, 101), incredulous at Fu-Manchu's power to render London geographically and culturally dissonant by reordering space and time.

The Chinese doctor's ubiquity within modern London foments a racial phobia that has its roots in the material and imaginative cartographies of the late nineteenth century, when journalists, social reformers, and Christian missionaries averred that London's social ills were geographically determined, a collection of cultural maladies caused by the squalid conditions of the city's poorest areas. Books like Gustave Doré and Blanche Jerrold's illustrated volume *London: A Pilgrimage* (1872), Charles Booth's *Life and Labour of the People of London* (1889), William Booth's best-selling exposé *In Darkest England* (1890), and C. F. G. Masterman's *From the Abyss* (1902) took readers on tours of London and its "abyss" of decline in much the same way that imperial travel writing described the discovery of jungles and tribes in colonized nations.[66] In the early twentieth century, reports of rapidly expanding immigrant communities in London's East End intensified the fears of a bourgeois readership already paranoid about the urban proliferation of diseased or degenerate bodies. As Fu-Manchu recolonizes the imperial metropole, usurping the seat of British authority, he overturns the imaginary geographical boundaries intended to contain nonwhite peoples and immigrants to the city's underbelly. The devil-doctor easily moves beyond the East End Chinese Limehouse district, accessing the city's major highways, occupying a beautiful mansion in Windsor, operating a laboratory on Museum Street, and holding secret meetings in a building on the banks of the Thames. Unable to find his nemesis in the labyrinths of London, Dr. Petrie is forced to admit that "it is a fact, singular but true, that few Londoners know London. . . . There are haunts in the very heart of the metropolis whose existence is unsuspected by all but the few; places unknown even to the ubiquitous copy-hunting pressman" (*Mystery*, 137). Fu-Manchu's knowledge of London and the intricate network of international power he forges from the city perfectly model Anthony Giddens's theory that "modern organisations are able to connect the local and the global in ways which would have been unthinkable in more traditional societies and in so doing routinely affect the lives of many millions of people" (20). In connecting "the local and the global," Dr. Fu-Manchu's master plan also avails itself of what Giddens calls the process of "disembedding." Giddens argues that disembedding, or the "'lifting out' of social relations from local contexts of interaction and their restructuring across indefinite spans of time-space" (21), creates the possibilities of modern social change. But Fu-Manchu's use of disembedding mechanisms shows us the alienation and violence that are the necessary offshoots of modernity's potentialities. In building his Yellow Empire, Dr. Fu-Manchu literally "lifts out" material resources from the modern West and relocates them to China. He steals the plans for an aero-torpedo from a famous U.S. aviator; he kidnaps Harley Street physicians and renowned toxicologists in order to develop sophisticated, deadly chemical and biological warfare; and he infiltrates the homes of imperial officers, explorers, and Orientalists whose instruments and documents get assimilated into the Yellow Empire's intelligence. Modern Western technology, which enables the global dissemination of information and makes portable the processes of manufacturing and production, allows Fu-Manchu to disembed these structures of Western power and to position them in the service of an evil Orient. The Chinese doctor tells Petrie and Nayland Smith that they themselves will soon be "disembedded" from England, drawn to the Yellow Empire by the allure of limitless knowledge:

"'I look to you, when you shall have overcome your prejudices—due to ignorance of my true motives—to assist me in establishing that intellectual
control which is destined to be the new World Force'" (*Devil*, 346). Although Nayland Smith and Petrie attribute Fu-Manchu's evil schemes to
his Oriental pathology, these novels unintentionally showcase the menacing obverse of early twentieth-century Western technocracy: the worship of
"intellectual control" can splinter the very racial and national communities
it works to fortify.

Rohmer's depictions of high-wire encounters between Dr. Fu-Manchu
and his white English pursuers demonstrate how national institutions and
modern technology can betray the very society they were intended to define. Such betrayals provoke a recursive self-critique that exemplifies the
modern world's double-edged relationship to its own prowess. In a telling
episode from *The Si-Fan Mysteries*, Nayland Smith and Petrie learn that Fu-
Manchu has kidnapped the world-renowned surgeon Sir Baldwin Frazer,
and promptly mobilize their forces to track down the missing Englishman.
When Petrie discovers that Fu-Manchu's henchmen have surrounded his
hotel chambers, he immediately protests against the loss of urban sanctity:
"'It seems almost absurd,' I said incredulously, 'to expect any member of
the Yellow group to attempt anything in a huge hotel like the New Louvre, here in the heart of London!'" (500). But the "heart of London"—
Petrie's metonym for what should be the virtuous, civilized core of the modern world—fails to protect its white English defenders. Fu-Manchu's dacoits not only attack Petrie and Nayland Smith in the New Louvre Hotel,
but they also escape unharmed in a taxi. A futile chase causes Nayland
Smith to rage, "'It is mortifying to think that with all the facilities of New
Scotland Yard at our disposal we cannot trace that damnable cab! We cannot find the head-quarters of the group—we cannot *move*!'" (521). Nayland Smith's acknowledgment of this paralysis calls attention to the
impotence of modern British institutions; further, it alerts us to the
uniquely modern phenomenon of maintaining a self-consciously critical
relationship to the practices or formations that enable daily life.

As Petrie and Nayland Smith agonize over the Yellow Empire's co-opta-
tion of Western knowledge, they nevertheless find themselves hungering
for the Yellow Empire's own knowledge. Profoundly envious of "the com-
plicated appliances unknown to civilized laboratories wherewith he pur-
sued his strange experiments, of the tubes wherein he isolated the bacilli
of unclassified diseases, of the yellow-bound volumes for a glimpse at which
(had they known their contents) the great men of Harley Street would have

given a fortune" (*Mystery*, 181), Petrie is forced to concede that "for all my training, I knew as little of Chemistry—of Chemistry as understood by this man's genius—as a junior student in surgery" (*Devil*, 347). Fu-Manchu's knowledge and his awesome ability to elude the efforts of England's cornerstone organizations are, to return to Anthony Giddens, proof that the "rise of expertise is a key part of modernity" (Giddens and Pierson, 110). Indeed, one of the Fu-Manchu novels' most troubling ironies is that Fu-Manchu's ascent to power is itself a consequence of modernity's democratic aspirations.

Ultimately, Rohmer does not celebrate the availability of modernity's democratic effects across racial and national boundaries; rather, he uses Fu-Manchu's unchecked encroachment on the Western nation-state to exemplify the conflictual nature of narratives of progress. Petrie's realization that "something inhuman" motivates his enemy demonstrates that knowledge deployed for antihumanistic purposes is the by-product of a national quest for enlightenment and progress. In the final episode of *The Mystery of Dr. Fu-Manchu*, which I have discussed earlier, the devil-doctor captures Nayland Smith and Petrie and shows off his latest scientific experiment. A gruesome demonstration of the giant toxic fungi that cause death by suffocation forces Petrie and Nayland Smith to watch Scotland Yard officers writhing and dying in agony. Even as Petrie acknowledges that "Dr. Fu-Manchu was the greatest fungologist the world had ever known," he shrinks in "pure horror" from the "valley of death" that Fu-Manchu has created (189). Each episode in which the Chinese doctor outwits his British pursuers lays bare the conflict that haunts canonical modernist authors and theorists of modernity alike: that state-sponsored democratic and humanistic institutions, and the culture that worships them, can breed indescribable brutality, corruption, and violence. Three decades before the Second World War and the Holocaust, Sax Rohmer's Fu-Manchu novels warned readers that the hallmark virtues of the modern era—access to information, individual agency, respect for scientific progress—might produce a killing machine, a brilliant and efficient path to mass death.

By displacing white English agency and manufacturing visions of an Oriental civilization in the West, Sax Rohmer's Fu-Manchu novels chart twentieth-century technocratic utopianism as a series of hollow promises. At a time when so much popular fiction functioned as a transparent, unmediated showcase for imperialist ideology, Rohmer's narratives, albeit unwittingly, expose the limitations of a Western imperial state and its white subjects. In these best-selling thrillers, the discontinuities of race provide a nexus for the broader discontinuities of a modern imperial nation whose global mastery is determined by the acquisition and dissemination of knowledge. When knowledge ceases to be the province and defining characteristic of the West, neither patriotic narrative bluster nor the resources of the *patria* itself can guarantee a racial victory over Fu-Manchu. And as the imperial metropole becomes a pawn of the discourses and technologies it prides itself on authoring, the very idea of progress ceases to be England's yardstick for measuring the world and forms the weapon of its own downfall.

2

RACE AND RUPTURE

The London Avant-Garde

It should by now be clear that novelistic investigations of modernity were deeply intertwined with cultural myths and pseudoscientific pathologies of racial identity. In an imperial Britain obsessed with historical continuity and discontinuity, early modernist literature offered up race as both locus and symbol of the era's disjunctiveness; as we have seen, race crucially shapes narratives of progress and decline in the fictions of Oscar Wilde, Joseph Conrad, and Sax Rohmer. We turn now to the spectacular world of the London avant-garde, whose short lifespan would leave a long-lasting mark on English letters and whose eclectic aims altered the racial dialogues begun by their fin-de-siècle and Edwardian predecessors. Early modernism had shifted ideas about race away from imperial contexts, and the provocateurs of the London avant-garde greatly accelerated and radicalized this shift. In the eight years between Roger Fry's 1910 postimpressionist exhibition and the end of the Great War in 1918, artists and authors propelled ideas about race out of their longstanding colonial hierarchies and launched them into a self-consciously modern artistic arena where questions of form outweighed sociopolitical questions. This chapter traces four interrelated moments in the development of the London avant-garde: the rise of the daring cabaret-nightclub, the Cave of the Golden Calf (1912–1914); the appearance of Wyndham Lewis's vorticist war journal, *BLAST* (1914); the publication of Ford Madox Ford's impressionist novel, *The Good Soldier* (1915); and the publication of Katherine Mansfield's experimental short story, "Je Ne Parle Pas Français" (1918). Each of these creative endeavors claims to mark an originary moment of metropolitan modernism. Taken together, they showcase a rich mutuality between the ruptures of race and the ruptures of avant-garde aesthetics. London's avant-garde artists were fiercely determined to achieve what Peter Bürger describes as "the detachment of art from the praxis of life and the accompanying crystallization of a special sphere of existence" (24). We will see that the much sought-after newness governing avant-garde artistic production expressed itself through abstract racial formations.

The Cave of the Golden Calf

I begin this chapter with a history of the Cave of the Golden Calf, the short-lived cabaret club whose cosmopolitanism and startling racial aesthetics heralded the spirit of avant-garde art in London.[1] In 1912, under the patronage of the notoriously eccentric Madame Frieda Strindberg, a dusty basement off Regent Street was transformed into a vibrant nightclub called the Cabaret Theatre Club.[2] Its central performance space, a large floor demarcated by plaster columns, was dubbed the Cave of the Golden Calf. For two years before Britain's entrance into the Great War, the Cave of the Golden Calf was home to riotous performances that ranged from Chinese puppet shows and Eastern European folk dances to Western classical music and literary readings. Its founding members, artists, and patrons included some of the most prominent figures in English arts and letters: Wyndham Lewis, Ezra Pound, Ford Madox Ford, Katherine Mansfield, and Rebecca West. One among several cabaret clubs that flourished in prewar London, the Cave brought together a group of artists whose attention to race is especially significant for understanding the evolution of avant-garde British modernism. The creators of the Cave of the Golden Calf applauded the artistic energy and unmediated life experience of primitive peoples and civilizations; and in the spirit of the continental European primitivism that had already reached its creative acme, the literature, visual arts, and performing arts of avant-garde London sought the racial authenticity of premodern civilizations. Bohemian cabaret, as Mary Gluck points out, "made legible and visible the secrets and hidden characteristics of what it meant to be modern" (119), and in Madame Strindberg's nightclub, ideas about race supplied the absolute modernity that all avant-garde artists hoped would distinguish their work.[3]

The Cave of the Golden Calf operated between 1912 and 1914, which placed it at the chronological center of avant-garde activity in London. The well-known events surrounding its opening and closing, especially the loud public rivalries between British and European artists, speak to the intertwining of artistic innovation and racial self-fashioning.[4] In 1909, the appearance of F. T. Marinetti's "Founding and Manifesto of Futurism" on the front page of the Paris newspaper *Le Figaro* astonished readers with its unprecedented glorification of industrial modernity. The manifesto's eleven tenets, which celebrate the concentrated energies of war, racing cars, factories, shipyards, and airplanes, are preceded by Marinetti's description of his dramatic, racially coded quest to rejuvenate Italian culture:

> We had stayed up all night—my friends and I—beneath mosque lamps hanging from the ceiling. Their brass domes were filigreed, starred like our souls; just as they were illuminated, again like our souls, by the imprisoned brilliance of an electric heart. On the opulent oriental rugs, we had crushed our ancestral lethargy, arguing all the way to the final frontiers of logic and blackening reams of paper with delirious writings. (Marinetti, 3)

Spurred by this animated dialogue amidst "mosque lamps" and "opulent oriental rugs," Marinetti tries to escape his "ancestral legacy" by taking a wild, violent automobile drive. The car crashes, famously, into a ditch of factory waste, and Marinetti has an epiphanic vision of futurist vitality: "Fair factory drain! I gulped down your bracing slime, which reminded me of the sacred black breast of my Sudanese nurse. . . . When I climbed out, a filthy and stinking rag, from underneath the capsized car, I felt my heart —deliciously—being slashed with the red-hot iron of joy!" (4). This narrative preface to the futurist manifesto introduces the aggressive cultural hybridity that marked avant-garde modernism's descriptions of its self-generation as well as the attending originality of its aesthetic. The charged Oriental atmosphere of Marinetti's conversation with his comrades, like the artist's immersion in a modern-primitive ditch that evokes a Sudanese woman's breast, establishes a new artistic order whose "founding" depends on mercurial conceptions of race.

The racial and cultural crossovers of Italian futurism rapidly found their way into the circles of London's emergent avant-garde, where they influenced the salons, manifestoes, literature, and visual arts that renounced the past and celebrated a modern metropolitan present. In December 1910— the famous date "on or about" which, in Virginia Woolf's words, "human character changed"—Roger Fry organized his landmark exhibition, "Manet and the Post-Impressionists," at the Grafton Galleries, shocking London art goers with the works of Manet, Matisse, Gauguin, and van Gogh.[5] In March 1912, a futurist exhibition was held at the Sackville Galleries, and Marinetti made an incendiary speech declaring that Great Britain was "a nation of sycophants and snobs, enslaved by old worm-eaten traditions, social conventions, and romanticism."[6] One month later—and in the minds of several critics, as a direct response to Marinetti's attack on British tradition—Madame Frieda Strindberg issued a prospectus for the Cabaret Theatre Club and the Cave of the Golden Calf, which opened its doors later that April.[7] The prospectus, an oversized brown paper document bearing the drawing of a three-headed calf, proclaimed that the new establishment would celebrate "the tendency of a return of art to imitation and simplicity," and that the club's "decoration will be entirely and exclusively the work of leading young British artists."[8] The twin ambitions crystallized in this prospectus—the cultivation of primitive simplicity and the promotion of new British arts—not only described plans for the Cave of the Golden Calf but also rehearsed the broader ambitions of avant-garde artists seeking to overthrow the "worm-eaten traditions" scorned by Marinetti.

As these ambitions became realities, the British art world rapidly caught up with coeval movements in Europe. In the fall of 1912, Roger Fry's Second Post-Impressionist Exhibition showcased the works of British artists including Vanessa Bell, Wyndham Lewis, and Spencer Gore alongside continental giants such as Picasso and Matisse. In 1913, Fry founded the Omega Workshops, the Bloomsbury arts collective devoted to creating anonymous, abstract, and distinctly British decorative objects. Wyndham Lewis, one of the Omega's original members, broke away from Fry and the workshops in 1914 to found the Rebel Art Centre, a rival organization that served as home for London's vorticist movement.[9] In March 1914, Madame Strindberg's Cave of the Golden Calf closed its doors in the wake of police raids and financial troubles. That July, three weeks before England declared war on Germany, Lewis launched the vorticist journal that he described as "that hugest and pinkest of all magazines, BLAST—whose portentous dimensions, and violent tint did more than would a score of exhibitions to make the public feel that something was happening" (*Rude Assignment*, 125). The outbreak of war, of course, altered the shock tactics of London's avant-garde artists, many of whom immediately took up arms for England; the second (and last) installment of *BLAST* in 1915 bore a sober brown cover and was filled with war propaganda rather than exhortations to create abstract art.[10] By 1918, England's tragic losses in the Great War had muted the bright energies of the nation's young artists, so that dwindling funds forced Roger Fry to close his Omega Workshops and the vorticist movement thudded to a halt. But in less than a decade, the makers of British arts and letters had permanently altered their world, disavowing ties with Britain's cultural past and promoting the aesthetic disjunctiveness of nonrepresentational art. And the sense that "something was happening," as Wyndham Lewis had phrased it, derived much of its foundational energy from a deep investment in the artistic possibilities inherent in racial alterity. As I will explain in this chapter (and, later, in chapter 3), the wide-ranging arts produced by Fry, Lewis, and their peers announced their revolutionary status through a bold attention to the peoples and art forms of "primitive," exotic, and Oriental civilizations. Aesthetics derived from Africa, Asia, South America, and Oceania shaped the spectrum of avant-garde art, from the Cave of the Golden Calf's cabaret performances to the Omega's domestic art objects and *BLAST*'s kinetic graphics. These deliberately modern aesthetics injected fresh energy into the entrenched racial matrix of British imperial attitudes: whereas an earlier generation of authors had pointed to race as the troubled site of cultural degeneration, race and its attendant discontinuities now lent daring shape to a new aesthetic horizon.

Wyndham Lewis's startling strategy to bring this aesthetic horizon into being was to "Kill John Bull with Art!"[11] Indeed, the collaborative enterprises and artistic collectives that nurtured modernism's development gathered their momentum through vocal, strident rejections of bourgeois or patriotic English culture. During the prewar years, a new Bohemia developed in the private homes, museums, and cafés where London artists gathered to exhibit and exchange ideas about their artwork.[12] For example, Roger Fry's Omega Workshops held "Art Circle" evenings featuring music, food, and exhibitions of Omega artworks; Violet Hunt and Ford Madox Ford presided over gatherings at Hunt's Kensington residence, South Lodge, where frequent guests included Jacob Epstein, D. H. Lawrence, Rebecca West, Richard Aldington, H. D., and Wyndham Lewis; T. E. Hulme held social events on Tuesday evenings, enabling artists to meet critics and buyers in his London home; and the flamboyant socialite Lady Ottoline Morrell played hostess to an enormous group of writers, politicians, painters, and critics in her Bloomsbury townhouse as well as at Garsington Manor near Oxford. London cafés like the Dieudonné and the Florence sponsored dinners for the vorticists, imagists, and futurists, while the staff of A. C. Orage's little magazine *New Age* (including Hulme, Katherine Mansfield, John Middleton Murry, and Ezra Pound) met at the ABC on Chancery Lane.[13] As part of this social-professional climate, Madame Strindberg's nightclub helped to "kill John Bull" by bringing together cutting-edge artists and a large circle of patrons, critics, and entrepreneurs, and by promoting the collective enjoyment and rule breaking that characterized coterie modernism.[14]

The opening of the Cabaret Theatre Club and the Cave of the Golden

Calf in 1912 coincided with the opening of other, similar nightclubs in London, most of which were modeled after their European predecessors. London was late to welcome cabaret entertainment, which had grown to immense popularity in nineteenth-century Paris, Berlin, and Vienna but only caught on in London during the second decade of the twentieth century.[15] The original cabarets in fin-de-siècle France had emphasized singing, but soon came to include dance, theatrical spectacle, monologues, and political satire. With an atmosphere that was at once casual and stylish, cabaret clubs offered their patrons a late-night place to eat, drink, and enjoy live entertainment, a decadent extension of the salons and cafés that artists haunted in the daytime. And the broadening artistic range of cabaret shared an affinity with nascent forms of modernism; as Lisa Appignanesi argues, cabaret was "modernism's youthful, light-hearted, sometimes raucous, late-night *doppelgänger,* its urban underbelly of utopian hopes twinned with laughter" (1). For artists seeking to disencumber themselves from Victorian aesthetic standards, to work outside the confines of a patronage system, and to dissolve the division between high art and popular culture, cabaret promised a venue that was socially liberating, financially profitable, and artistically provocative. Indeed, even Sax Rohmer's Fu-Manchu tales supply evidence of what Appignanesi calls the "kinship of cabaret and the early twentieth-century avant-garde" (74). In *The Si-Fan Mysteries* (1917), Nayland Smith and Dr. Petrie disguise themselves as futurists and hunt for Dr. Fu-Manchu in a fictional Soho nightclub called L'Egypte, a "Bohemian resort, where members of the French Colony, some of the Chelsea art people, professional models, and others of that sort, foregather at night. . . . It has much the same clientele as, say, the Café Royale, with a rather heavier sprinkling of Hindu students, Japanese, and so forth. It's celebrated for Turkish coffee" (559). Rohmer's description not only points to cabaret's presence in the popular imagination, but also underscores the cosmopolitanism that distinguished the modern club: multiple races and nationalities mingling over "exotic" food and drink heightened the sense of daring that cabaret entertainment introduced to England.

If Londoners regarded cabaret itself as "alien from its very inception" (xxv), as Harold Segel claims, the milieu of Madame Strindberg's cabaret would only have intensified a sense of the art form's strangeness. The Cave of the Golden Calf's antibourgeois spirit could be summed up in the foreignness that pervaded its every aspect, from the images emblazoned on its programs to the interior decor and the entertainment itself. Its very name—an allusion to Exodus and the Israelites' worship of a calf-shaped gold idol—conjured up an atmosphere of pagan revelry, hedonism, and excess.[16] Eric Gill created two sculptures of the golden calf itself, a bas-relief tablet and a free-standing statue whose unabashed eroticism epitomized the Cave's playful attitude. (Roger Fry was so taken with Gill's statue that he featured it in the Second Post-Impressionist Exhibition: it was the only British work in a room filled with canvases by Cézanne, Picasso, and Derain.) The original brochure from May 1912 bristled with drawings of savage dancers and animals and listed the "Aims and Programme of the Cabaret Theatre Club," which claimed for England the social and artistic freedoms long associated with Europe and the Mediterranean:

> We want a place given up to gaiety, to a gaiety stimulating thought, rather than crushing it.
> We want a gaiety that does not have to count with midnight.
> We want surroundings, which after the reality of daily life, reveal the reality of the unreal.
> We want light and we want song.
> With these quite modest wishes we desire to harm nobody, unless it be such "outré-mer" purveyors of entertainment as flourish, not necessarily on their merits so much as on the drastic dullness of our home-life. We do not want to Continentalise, we only want to do away, to some degree, with the distinction that the word "Continental" implies, and with the necessity of crossing the Channel to laugh freely, and to sit up after nursery hours. . . .
> During and after supper, the picturesque dances of the South, its fervid melodies, Parisian wit, English humour, will create a surrounding which, if it has no other merit, will at least endeavour to limit emigration.[17]

These aggressive directives reveal that London's avant-garde summoned its energy from racial and cultural difference; to escape "the drastic dullness of our home-life" was to embrace "Continental" practices and the "fervid" aesthetic of a hot-blooded "South." The architects of Madame Strindberg's cabaret, like the modern authors who had begun to overthrow the tyranny of realism, trained their gaze on the world outside of Britain to purchase "gaiety that does not have to count with midnight" and "the reality of the unreal." In keeping with its preliminary prospectus, the Cave's program directed British aesthetics toward racial heterogeneity and, by extension, reimagined the boundaries of national character. Dissociating itself from England's repressive, hierarchical, and convention-bound past, the Cave of the Golden Calf sought a new England whose defining trait was an invigorating and democratic internationalism. The Cave's cultural purview anticipated the incendiary pages of *BLAST* and the vorticist movement, which, as we will see, similarly laid claim to forms of Englishness rooted in the foreign and the cosmopolitan.

True to the intentions in the original prospectus, the Cave's decor was "entirely and exclusively the work of leading young British artists." A glance at paintings and carvings by these artists—Jacob Epstein, Spencer Gore, Eric Gill, Charles Ginner, and Wyndham Lewis—reveals a deep absorption in non-Western cultures. The Cave's varied representations of geographies, bodies, and art forms, while partially rooted in longstanding imperial attitudes, celebrate the mutuality between racial identity and abstraction that characterizes so much avant-garde work. This mutuality caught the eye of the London press; a reviewer for *The Observer,* for example, lauded the "artistic revolutionaries" whose startling work filled Madame Strindberg's nightclub:

> The "Troglodytes" or "Cave-dwellers", is a singularly appropriate appellation for a coterie of artists, who are not only connected with the "Cave of the Calf", but who aim—most of them—at the primitive simplicity of the days when art was in its infancy. It was, after all, on bones and walls of caves, that the artistic instinct found its first expression.[18]

The desire to depict "artistic instinct" as a function of racial identity is visible throughout the Cave's decor. Jacob Epstein, whose controversial Assyrian-inspired tomb for Oscar Wilde had recently been erected in Paris, installed a series of carved, painted columns around the floor of the Cave. These totemic pillars, deeply influenced by ancient Hindu erotic sculpture (and which would in turn influence the gifted young sculptor Henri Gaudier-Brzeska), featured the entwined, minimalist figures of humans with the heads of animals. Jewel-toned and sexually primal, the energy of Epstein's columns complemented the images of untamed nature and premodern culture on the Cave's walls. Spencer Gore, whose painterly imagination had recently been captured by the exotica of Diaghilev's Ballets Russes, contributed two murals that, as one critic put it, suggested "swirling Eastern tapestries."[19] Gore's wall paintings of tiger hunting and deer hunting reinvented nineteenth-century imperial imagery, featuring wildly colored jungle scenes with blue-striped tigers and naked orange riders atop fanciful horses that appear to be flying. Three large paintings by Eric Gill —*Chasing Monkeys, Birds and Indians,* and *Tiger Hunting*—also described striking jungle scenes, representing flora and fauna as geometric composites. In Gill's brilliantly hued *Tiger Hunting* triptych, the African exotic emerges through the simple, abstract figures of a large elephant and a gri-

Figure 4. Wyndham Lewis, sketch for *Kermesse,* 1912. The Amazon woman's whirling dance in Lewis's oversized painting embodies the unrepressed primitivism of the Cave of the Golden Calf. Gouache and watercolor with pen and black ink over graphite on two joined sheets of wove paper, left edge is unevenly trimmed. 12 × 12 1⁄16 in. (30.5 × 30.6 cm) (Yale Center for British Art, Paul Mellon Fund and Gift of Neil F. and Ivan E. Phillips in memory of their mother, Mrs. Rosalie Phillips. New Haven, Connecticut. By kind permission of the Wyndham-Lewis Memorial Trust, a registered charity.)

macing tiger surrounded by playful monkeys, riotous vines, and bright fruits. A drop curtain designed by Wyndham Lewis repeated the hunting theme, depicting primitive figures of nude African or Amazonian men and women among saffron-tinted deer or horses. Lewis's artistic work for the Cave—which he characterized as "abstract hieroglyphics" (*Rude Assignment,* 125)—included several paintings, posters, programs, and screens; but it was his enormous nine-foot painting *Kermesse* that best captured what Laura

Winkiel dubs the Cave's "transgressive identification with the primitive" ("Cabaret Modernism," 209). Unleashing the carnivalesque energy suggested by its title, *Kermesse*'s hard-edged lines depict an Amazon woman in the throes of a frenzied dance. This arresting work hung atop the stairs descending into the Cave, "an appropriately savage, hedonistic image to challenge puritan visitors and welcome them to the subversive world of cabaret" (Appignanesi, 91).

The experimental allure of Madame Strindberg's cabaret lay in the self-conscious connections between aesthetic form and racial identity, and the nightclub's eclectic decor furnished an appropriate setting for equally eclectic cabaret entertainment. Performances that might otherwise have evoked nineteenth-century music halls channeled foreignness with an ironic, distinctly modern flair: readings by English poets and music by Schoenberg and Purcell were interspersed with items like veil dances, Granville Bantock's dance drama "The Nautch Girl," Margaret Morris and "her Greek children dancers," songs by Negro minstrels, "Romany-Chals" who enacted "Gypsy folk-lore," the Spanish chanteuse La Morenita, and a Princess Red-Feather who sang American Indian songs. Ford Madox Ford wrote and acted in an *ombre chinoise,* or Chinese shadow play, about a European man who travels abroad, survives deadly attacks from cobras and assassins, and returns to Europe with a harem girl.[20] Even a performance of Mozart's opera *Bastien und Bastienne* was compered by a Chinese-costumed Katherine Mansfield.[21] Following elaborate dinners that paid tribute to Brillat-Savarin and ended with Turkish coffee, the guests themselves—who included modern notables Ezra Pound, H. D., David Bomberg, Henri Gaudier-Brzeska, and Rebecca West—danced to live music performed by a "Gipsy Orchestra." Often barefoot, bedecked in exotic jewelry, smoking Turkish cigarettes, and sporting "Egyptian" hairstyles, the Cave's patrons broke away from prim English social tradition by dancing the Bunny Hug, the Turkey Trot, and other jazz-era imports from the United States and Europe.[22] Modern writers drew a straight line between primitivism and the Cave's obsession with artistic renewal: the poet Osbert Sitwell described the entire scene as "a super-heated Vorticist garden of gesticulating figures, dancing and talking, while the rhythm of the primitive forms of ragtime throbbed through the wide room" (208); and the historian George Dangerfield declared this a moment when "there was talk of wild young people in London . . . of night clubs; of negroid dances. People gazed in horror at the paintings of Gauguin, and listened with delighted alarm to the barbaric measures of Stravinsky" (67).

Programme

▼

Amongst others:—Zette; Greville Moore; La Morenita; Margaret Morris and her Greek Children Dancers; Winifred Barnes; Eva Segunda; Nina; Nadia Sokoloff; Xantippe.

Romany-Chals

▼

Arthur Machen; Diogenes; Vernon D'Arnalle; The Three Impostors; Stacey Aumonier; Jean Rodor; Conti.

▼

Dalhousie Young

▼

Some Items; Veil Dance; Paul et Virginie; Jester Songs; Natural Selection; A Breton Wake; La Serva Padrona; Exultations; Cards; Magali; Diogenes' Tub; A Love Mask; Tarantella; Gipsy Folk-lore; Playing with Fire; Caprichos.

The Midnight Mail

Figure 5. Wyndham Lewis, entertainment program of the Cave of the Golden Calf and Cabaret Theatre Club, 1912. This program, bordered by Lewis's primitivist sketches, showcases a wide range of modern exotica. (Yale Center for British Art, Paul Mellon Fund. New Haven, Connecticut. By kind permission of the Wyndham-Lewis Memorial Trust, a registered charity.)

The constellation of modernists who contributed to the lively scene at the Cave of the Golden Calf was dispersed by rivalries and changes of fortune over the next few years. Significant events included Wyndham Lewis's bitter departure from the Omega Workshops and his subsequent quarrels with Jacob Epstein; Katherine Mansfield's and John Middleton Murry's falling-out with Henri Gaudier-Brzeska, who was killed in the war shortly thereafter; Spencer Gore's sudden death from pneumonia; and Ford Madox Ford's self-willed recession from the frontlines of English letters. However, even as these artists moved separately through modernism's garden of forking paths, they shared a common starting point: a determination to renovate and modernize British art through a shocking racial aesthetic. Multiple conceptions of racial alterity—and of the primitive in particular—supplied revolutionary artists with what Raymond Williams calls "the innately creative, the unformed and untamed realm of the pre-rational and unconscious, indeed that vitality of the naive which was so especially a leading edge of the avant-garde" ("Politics of the Avant-Garde," 58). Reflecting on this period of intense creativity, Wyndham Lewis wrote that "it was, after all, a new civilisation that I—and a few other people—was making the blueprints for. . . . A rough design for seeing men who as yet were not there. . . . It was more than just picture-making: one was manufacturing fresh eyes for people, and fresh souls to go with the eyes" (*Rude Assignment,* 125). In a hectic artistic moment that brought new subjects and objects into being, manufacturing a "new civilisation" with "fresh eyes" and "fresh souls" depended on sustained attention to much older and apparently alien civilizations. In other words —and as the short-lived Cave of the Golden Calf demonstrates—the art that declared itself "modern British" very often derived its inspiration and identity from the premodern and the not-British. The rest of this chapter will focus on the role of racial difference in British formalism (in vorticism and impressionism, in particular), illuminating the ways in which the avant-garde conjoined conceptions of modernity and conceptions of race to produce art that was relentlessly new.

The Negress and the Vortex

Wyndham Lewis's war journal *BLAST,* published shortly after the Cave of the Golden Calf closed its doors in 1914, continues to be the British avant-garde's best-known experimental work. Dubbing itself "The Review of the Great English Vortex," *BLAST* served as the mouthpiece for an abstract artistic force that Ezra Pound famously described as "a radiant node or cluster; it is what I can, and must perforce, call a VORTEX, from which, and through which, and into which, ideas are constantly rushing" (*Gaudier-Brzeska*, 92).[23] The "radiant cluster" of this Vortex galvanized Lewis and his collaborators to "BLAST years 1837 to 1900" (*BLAST*, 18) and shout down the "GLOOMY VICTORIAN CIRCUS" (19) whose historical, artistic, and racial legacies jeopardized modern England's creative potential. *BLAST*'s opening statements condemn Victorian England's very pathology, resurrecting the racially charged—if scientifically defunct—language of climate theory to condemn the nation's immediate past:

> BLAST First (from politeness) ENGLAND
> CURSE ITS CLIMATE FOR ITS SINS AND INFECTIONS
>   DISMAL SYMBOL, SET round our bodies,
>   of effeminate lout within.
>   VICTORIAN VAMPIRE, the LONDON cloud sucks
>   the TOWN'S heart.
> A 1000 MILE LONG, 2 KILOMETER Deep
> BODY OF WATER even, is pushed against us
> from the Floridas, TO MAKE US MILD. (11)

Cursing the "flabby sky" and the "lazy air" (12) that has for too long "DOMESTICATED" (11) England's artistic spirit, *BLAST*'s authors hail "the great art vortex sprung up in the centre of this town!" The jagged visuality of *BLAST*'s artwork and the joyous dissonance of its manifestoes proclaim that "The Art-instinct is permanently primitive" (33), promoting a premodern aesthetic through which the Anglo-Saxon London artist will reign as a "genius among races" (26). Thus, vorticism's chronotopia—a celebration of the English "now" through the language of a primitive, racially distant "then"—attained its power, in T. S. Eliot's words, by merging "the thought of the modern and the energy of the cave-man."[24]

This chronotopia is especially fascinating in Rebecca West's short story "Indissoluble Matrimony," which, despite its appearance in *BLAST*, has been obscured in scholarly dialogues about vorticism in London. "Indissoluble Matrimony" complicates the masculinist, Anglo-Saxonist vorticism espoused by *BLAST*'s male authors. As dynamic and concentrated as the historical moment in which *BLAST* was delivered to London readers, West's story depicts a married couple whose sexual and psychological alienation thrusts them into an apocalyptic physical battle. And although the story's narrator maintains a wry, faintly condescending distance from the couple's travails, "Indissoluble Matrimony" offers a number of remarkably prescient

Figure 6. Manifesto I. *BLAST,* 1914. *BLAST*'s opening manifesto invokes the racialized language of climate theory to curse Victorian England. (*BLAST.* 1914. Edited by Wyndham Lewis. Foreword by Bradford Morrow. Santa Rosa, CA: Black Sparrow Press, 2002.)

moments anticipating the social crises spawned by the Great War: West foretells of a world where men are afflicted with hysteria, teleological national histories have lost their meaning, and women assume prominent positions in the public sphere. "Indissoluble Matrimony" is focalized through its ineffectual protagonist, George Silverton, a solicitor's clerk who returns one evening to his suburban home and is outraged to find that his black wife Evadne has been invited to speak at a socialist meeting. George first accuses Evadne of having an affair with a prominent local socialist, and then forbids her from speaking at the meeting. Evadne, whose physical passions and intellectual acuity terrify George, bursts furiously out of the house; George follows her to a nearby reservoir and holds her under the whirling waters until he is convinced that she has drowned. But when George returns home intent on committing a martyr's suicide, he finds Evadne sleeping on their bed and realizes, anticlimactically, that she has simply escaped from him in the reservoir. The story ends with George abjectly getting into bed next to Evadne "as he had done every night for ten years, and as he would every night until he died" (West, 117).[25] Like T. S. Eliot's J. Alfred Prufrock, marginal and paralyzed in a metropolis where women "come and go" freely, George Silverton's Anglo-Saxon masculinity gives him neither autonomy nor authority in an aggressively modern world.

Despite the story's cultural foresight, "Indissoluble Matrimony" does not hold a prominent position in critical responses to *BLAST*.[26] Written while Rebecca West was trying to launch her acting career in London (the actual date of the story's composition is unknown), the piece was rejected by both *The English Review* and *The Blue Review* before Wyndham Lewis decided to include it in *BLAST* in 1914.[27] In a letter written in 1930 to the U.S. literary critic William Troy, West herself dismissed "Indissoluble Matrimony" as unimportant, disavowing her involvement with the vorticist movement:

> It was published in *Blast*—a publication of which I knew nothing—by Wyndham Lewis—whom I never met till years after—for no other reason than that Wyndham Lewis found the manuscript in the chest of drawers in the spare room of Violet Hunt & Ford Madox Hueffer's home at Selsey. . . . But I was literary editor of the *Egoist* for some months at the beginning of its career, and set its tone before I left: a fact I would rather you had mentioned than my fictional appearance in *Blast*. (*Selected Letters*, 119–20)[28]

Obviously more committed to feminism than to a movement championing abstract art, West did not go on to write any more vorticist literature. Following the outbreak of the First World War, her literary career remained separate from Wyndham Lewis's and Ezra Pound's short-lived efforts to sustain vorticism in England.[29] Indeed, in the context of a stunning eight-decade career—during which West wrote for and edited pioneering modernist-feminist magazines such as *The New Freewoman* and *The Egoist*, wrote eleven novels including *The Return of the Soldier* (1918) and *The Judge* (1922), produced her sociopolitical masterpiece on Yugoslavia, *Black Falcon and Grey Lamb* (1941), and contributed prolifically to newspapers and magazines in the United States and England—"Indissoluble Matrimony" certainly appears as a young author's relatively insignificant creation.

But read in the context of Wyndham Lewis's *BLAST,* the "puce monster" that deployed the concentrated lines and angles of the Vortex to shout for a new England, "Indissoluble Matrimony" emerges as a provocative vision of who might supply the "newness" for a war-torn nation. *BLAST*'s publication on June 29, 1914, represented a breakaway moment for artists working to establish a definitive English avant-garde, and the London vorticists who contributed to Lewis's interdisciplinary and militant journal hailed the ascension of modern Anglo-Saxonist art and thought. Vorticism's political and artistic reach in the pages of *BLAST* was self-consciously vast: with their lists of "Blasts" and "Blesses," multipage manifestoes, and programmatic attacks on the past and the future, the vorticists sought to reorder what they saw as the weakened, passive priorities of Anglo-Saxon civilization. West's "Indissoluble Matrimony," bookended by excerpts from Ford Madox Ford's *The Good Soldier* and Wassily Kandinsky's *Concerning the Spiritual in Art,* reworks English vorticism for a black woman "from the back of beyond" (109), complicating the masculinist, Anglo-Saxonist vorticism espoused by *BLAST*'s male authors. Evadne Silverton's victory over her husband feminizes the Vortex; Jane Marcus has appropriately dubbed the story "A Blast from the Female Vortex."[30] But more radically, "Indissoluble Matrimony" makes the Vortex the province of a publicly visible, politically successful Negress. Evadne Silverton dominates the industrialized modern world of "Indissoluble Matrimony," a world over which the male English authors of *BLAST* claimed total sovereignty. Her racial alterity—extreme in physical attributes as well as character traits—becomes an unsuspected weapon in the vorticist crusade to be absolutely modern.

To understand how the racial politics of Rebecca West's story simultaneously uphold and rewrite vorticism, it is useful to distill the core idea that holds *BLAST*'s wild and often inconsistent statements together. This is the idea of *energy,* the Vortex's most crucial characteristic. At the end of *BLAST,* Wyndham Lewis, Ezra Pound, and the young sculptor Henri Gaudier-Brzeska all call for unceasing energy and motion in their separate definitions of the vorticist agenda. Lewis declares that "the Vorticist is at his maximum point of energy when stillest" (148), and that "our Vortex is proud of its polished sides. Our Vortex will not hear of anything but its disastrous polished dance" (149). Similarly, Pound defines the Vortex as "the point of maximum energy" (153) and explains that "VORTICISM is art before it has spread itself out into a state of flacidity [*sic*], of elaboration, of secondary applications" (154). And Gaudier-Brzeska makes perhaps the pithiest set of claims: "VORTEX OF A VORTEX!! VORTEX IS

THE POINT ONE AND INDIVISIBLE! VORTEX IS ENERGY!" (156). Militantly opposed to impressionism and postimpressionism's cultivated softness, futurism's worship of speed, and Bloomsbury's effeminate decorative arts, *BLAST* called for a concentrated, warlike energy to revitalize England.[31] The paintings and drawings of Lewis, Jacob Epstein, Edward Wadsworth, and Frederick Etchells—geometric and angular "fields of discord" (142)—conveyed this energy throughout the pages of *BLAST*.

The climax of Rebecca West's "Indissoluble Matrimony"—the violent physical battle between George and Evadne—exemplifies vorticist principles of energy. Facing each other on the edge of the Lisbech pond, George and Evadne realize "that God is war and his creatures are meant to fight" (110) and then fall into the water:

> The feathery confusion had looked so soft, yet it seemed the solid rock they struck. The breath shot out of him and suffocation warmly stuffed his ears and nose. Then the rock cleft and he was swallowed by a brawling blackness in which whirled a vortex that flung him again and again on a sharp thing that burned his shoulder. All about him fought the waters, and they cut his flesh like knives. (111)

A "vortex" of water solid like rock and polished like knives: here are the "polished sides" that Wyndham Lewis describes and the "indivisible" energy praised by Gaudier-Brzeska. The formal aesthetics of this passage provide, on one level, a literary complement to the visual art printed in *BLAST*: the battle in the whirlpool captures the intense immediacy of consciousness that Lewis and Pound describe as the still center of the Vortex. West's delineation of the physical and psychic movements of the couple's fight follows the vorticist injunction to reject the past's messy fluidity in favor of geometrically arranged lines and a worship of the present. As George and Evadne "fought to organise their sensations," for example, they enter into a state where "the past was intangible. It trailed behind this intense event as the pale hair trails behind the burning comet. They were pre-occupied with the moment" (109). However, the racial politics of "Indissoluble Matrimony"—white English masculinity trounced by larger-than-life black femininity—offer up a complex, challenging counterdiscourse to the foundational racial politics of *BLAST* and the vorticist movement.

BLAST's racial politics are usually suppressed in dialogues about its abstraction.[32] But the war journal's call for energetic, penetrating lines and angles derives from strict racial oppositions that pit modern Western humanism and rational thought against the supposedly savage or primitive instincts of non-Western cultures. Modernist scholars and historians have persuasively traced vorticism's origins to Wilhelm Worringer's 1908 treatise, *Abstraction and Empathy*.[33] Worringer divided art into two antithetical modes: "vital" art created by empathy, and "geometric" art created by abstraction. Vital art, embodied by the humanistic traditions of the ancient Greeks and the Renaissance, reflects harmony between individuals and nature; conversely, geometric art, which Worringer associates with African, Chinese, Byzantine, and Egyptian cultures, indicates a troubled, uneasy relationship between humans and their natural surroundings.[34] The English poet-philosopher T. E. Hulme, who, in Jo Anna Isaak's words, would serve as "the chief aesthetician for the vorticists" (9), disseminated Worringer's ideas to London art circles in his famous 1914 lecture, "Modern Art and Its Philosophy."[35] Following Worringer's lead, Hulme promoted the virtues of abstraction by relying on Western primitivism's core axiom: the unquestioned assumption that nonwhite, non-Western races exist in a perpetual premodern temporality without the influences of reason and philosophy.[36]

Hulme championed Worringer's distinction between vital and geometric art, insisting that modern English artists should cast off the cultural baggage of traditional naturalistic Western art and concentrate on geometric art that is "absolutely distinct from the messiness, the confusion, and the accidental details of existing things" (*Speculations*, 87). His praise for the African or Asian "tendency to abstraction" retains a belief in Western cultures as more advanced (and more capable of advancement) than non-Western cultures existing in disharmonious relationships with nature. Primitive people, Hulme argues, "live in a world whose lack of order and seeming arbitrariness must inspire them with a certain fear. . . . In art this state of mind results in a desire to create a certain abstract geometrical shape, which, being durable and permanent shall be a refuge from the flux and impermanence of outside nature" (86). To illustrate the concept of geometric art, Hulme points to Byzantine mosaics, Egyptian paintings, Indian sculpture, and Chinese ideographs. Hulme promoted his racially determined art theories to London painters and sculptors like David Bomberg, Jacob Epstein, Edward Wadsworth, and of course Wyndham Lewis, who devised the Vortex as the ultimate abstract geometric entity.[37]

In executing Worringer's and Hulme's theories, *BLAST* carved out the space for renovating English culture by lauding a "primitive" non-Western past and simultaneously exalting the dynamic newness of the machine age. Lewis and the magazine's other contributors energized their artworks and writings through what the art critic Colin Rhodes identifies as the "discontent of the Primitivist." In *Primitivism and Modern Art*, Rhodes describes the vexed temporal stance of avant-garde artists fascinated by the aesthetics of Africa, Asia, Oceania, and South America: "The Primitivist will not judge the ideal state of the world to be in the present (for in this case there can only be cultural contentment)—it will either be located in the past, or in the future, where it takes the form of a Utopian dream of a 'return' to some previous state of grace. In other words, for the Primitivist the primitive state itself has to be valued as a regrettable loss, rather than as a mere starting-point" (20). *BLAST* urges a return to this lost primitive state, seeking unrepressed cultural strength in the cityscapes of twentieth-century London. "We are Primitive Mercenaries in the Modern World" (*BLAST*, 30), roars Lewis in Manifesto II, going on to declare that "The Art-instinct is permanently primitive" (33). In keeping with these exhortations, virtually all of *BLAST*'s visual and plastic arts rely on non-Western, premodern abstraction to generate new English aesthetic practices and philosophies. The artists' fascination with the primitive is evident, for example, in Henri Gaudier-Brzeska's sculpture *Stags*, Edward Wadsworth's drawing *Cape of Good Hope*, and Frederick Etchell's pair of *Head* drawings. It gives force to Wyndham Lewis's laudatory tracts on Chinese feng-shui and his admiration for the aesthetically potent, "unvarying, vivid, harsh black of Africa" (136). Perhaps most stridently, it drives Gaudier-Brzeska's praise for the Indian "VORTEX OF BLACKNESS AND SILENCE," the "SEMITIC VORTEX" (156), and the ancient Egyptian and Mongolian "VORTEX OF DESTRUCTION" (157). If, as Rhodes argues, "Primitivism in modern art is predominantly about making the familiar strange or about maintaining the strangeness of unfamiliar experiences" (74-75), we see that *BLAST*'s awe of premodern art forms extends the aesthetic colonialism of Worringer's and Hulme's theories. Lewis and the vorticists attain the intense, monomaniacal energy of the Anglo-Saxon Vortex by reducing primitive non-Western cultures to a series of formal qualities that have to be wrested from their "backward" birthplaces and then incorporated into the modern Western metropolis. The "puce monster's" eclectic statements about race, in other words, instrumentalize non-Western cultures in order to glorify modern Anglo-Saxondom.

Vorticism's agenda explicitly aimed to separate England and Anglo-Saxon men from continental European nations and their artistic innovations, insisting that modern England, in Queen Victoria's wake, was "the most favourable country for the appearance of a great art" (*BLAST*, 33).

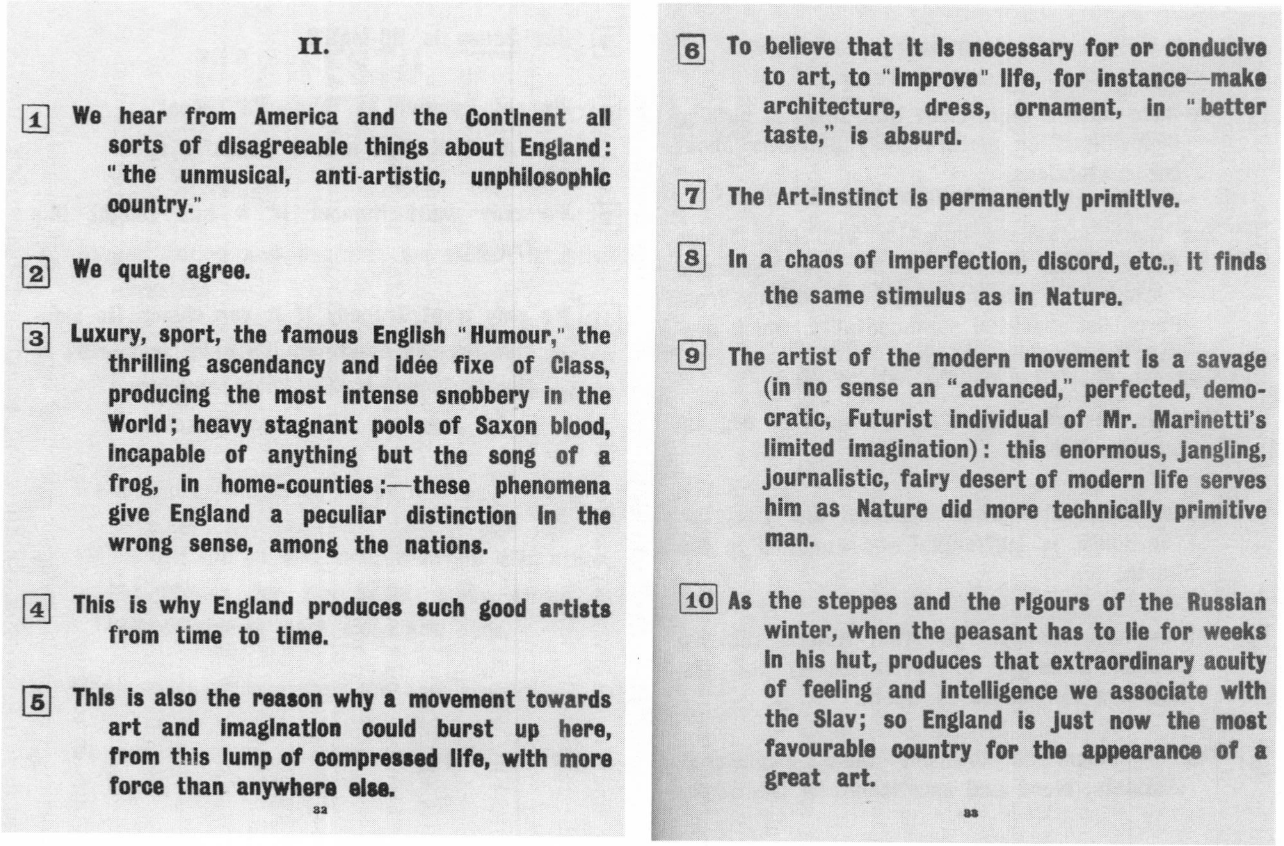

II.

1 We hear from America and the Continent all sorts of disagreeable things about England: "the unmusical, anti-artistic, unphilosophic country."

2 We quite agree.

3 Luxury, sport, the famous English "Humour," the thrilling ascendancy and idée fixe of Class, producing the most intense snobbery in the World; heavy stagnant pools of Saxon blood, incapable of anything but the song of a frog, in home-counties:—these phenomena give England a peculiar distinction in the wrong sense, among the nations.

4 This is why England produces such good artists from time to time.

5 This is also the reason why a movement towards art and imagination could burst up here, from this lump of compressed life, with more force than anywhere else.

32

6 To believe that it is necessary for or conducive to art, to "improve" life, for instance—make architecture, dress, ornament, in "better taste," is absurd.

7 The Art-instinct is permanently primitive.

8 In a chaos of imperfection, discord, etc., it finds the same stimulus as in Nature.

9 The artist of the modern movement is a savage (in no sense an "advanced," perfected, democratic, Futurist individual of Mr. Marinetti's limited imagination): this enormous, jangling, journalistic, fairy desert of modern life serves him as Nature did more technically primitive man.

10 As the steppes and the rigours of the Russian winter, when the peasant has to lie for weeks in his hut, produces that extraordinary acuity of feeling and intelligence we associate with the Slav; so England is just now the most favourable country for the appearance of a great art.

33

Figure 7. Manifesto II. *BLAST.* 1914. The vorticists laud twentieth-century England as the locus of a modern-primitive energy crucial for the birth of new art forms. (*BLAST.* 1914. Edited by Wyndham Lewis. Foreword by Bradford Morrow. Santa Rosa, CA: Black Sparrow Press, 2002.)

The English character's "unexpected universality" (35), explains *BLAST*'s first Manifesto, ensures that "a movement towards art and imagination could burst up here, from this lump of compressed life, with more force than anywhere else" (32). And because "The Modern World is due almost entirely to Anglo-Saxon genius,—its appearance and its spirit" (39), new artistic possibilities "will be more the legitimate property of Englishmen than of any other people in Europe" (41). A black conical motif printed on the opening pages of *BLAST* (in the "Great Preliminary Vortex—Manifesto I") announces the ascendance of this "Anglo-Saxon genius." The motif, Lewis's biographer Paul O'Keeffe tells us, was derived from a wood-and-canvas coastguard signal called a "storm cone": "Raised point downwards, it was known as a 'south cone,' anticipating a gale from the south. Point upwards, a 'north cone'—as in the pages of BLAST—warned of a northerly gale: a blast from the north. It was the English avant-garde's answer to the Futurist invasion of London from the Latin south" (157). The image of the north cone is repeated throughout the manifesto, whose concluding lines champion the distinctive racial status of modern England's renegade artists: "So often rebels of the North and the South are diametrically opposed species" (42). *BLAST,* therefore, presents a dizzying racial logic: the Anglo-Saxon artist proves himself a superior modern "species" through his capacity to appreciate and imitate *primitive* art forms.

Rebecca West's "Indissoluble Matrimony" reorders vorticism's cultural hegemonies, refashioning the primitive artist into the socialist-activist character of Evadne Silverton. Evadne's racial alterity is not merely a conduit to English self-fashioning but stands as a force in its own right. Her combined sensuousness, intelligence, and autonomy delegitimize the Worringer-Hulme-Lewis polarization of vital and geometric form. The following passage, which describes Evadne's entrance into the Vortex-whirlpool, illustrates the formal subversiveness of West's writing:

> She was clad in a black bathing dress, and her arms and legs and the broad streak of flesh laid bare by a rent down the back shone brilliantly white, so that she seemed like a grotesquely patterned wild animal as she ran down to the lake. Whirling her arms above her head she trampled down into the water and struck out strongly. Her movements were full of brisk delight and she swam quickly. The moonlight made her the centre of a little feathery blur of black and silver, with a comet's tail trailing in her wake. (107–8)

The controlled, penetrating energy of Evadne's dark body presents a feminized, racially marked incarnation of Pound's and Lewis's abstract Vortex.

In their elevation of the Anglo-Saxon male subject, *BLAST*'s manifestoes aver that "the artist of the modern movement is a savage" and that the "enormous, jangling, journalistic, fairy desert of modern life serves him as Nature did more technically primitive man" (33). In sharp contrast, West uses Evadne to reject the separation of nature and culture that exiles "technically primitive" dark races from industrialized modernity. No English hero strides through this text: West's reorientation of the Anglo-Saxonist Vortex transforms the "fairy desert of modern life" into the territory of a culturally potent black woman.

Insofar as West's treatment of George Silverton is both sexually and racially devastating, her narrative joins Wyndham Lewis in "blasting" the moribund English "effeminate lout" (*BLAST,* 11) who reveres the hierarchies of the past. "Indissoluble Matrimony" shatters George's understanding of himself as a Western subject determined by the master narratives of religious or imperial history, and the story upholds the vorticist claim that "the new vortex plunges to the heart of the present. . . . The Past and the Future are the prostitutes Nature has provided" (147–48). George's despair at suspecting Evadne's sexual infidelity, for example, leads to a vicious narrative mockery of traditional religious and social practices: "'Have I gone to the Unitarian chapel every Sunday morning and to the Ethical Society every evening for nothing?' his spirit asked itself in the travail. 'All those Browning lectures for nothing. . . .' He said the Lord's Prayer several times and lay for a minute quietly crying" (106). After losing his carpet slippers in a mud puddle and getting lost in his own neighborhood—"Like most people without strong primitive instincts," the narrator informs us, "he had no sense of orientation" (106)—George can only accuse Evadne of infidelity in a "horrid tenor squeak" (108). And although George likens himself to Napoleon and the Sphinx after Evadne's supposed death in the Vortex-reservoir, his horror of wet socks and a garden slug make a mockery of these imagined ties with foregone empires. Squeaky-voiced, obsessed with an imperial past, and literally lost in the ugly labyrinthine streets of his suburb, George represents the passéism that Wyndham Lewis wanted to "blast" out of a tired and tradition-bound nation. And like the *BLAST* manifestoes that surround it, West's story rejects these traditions as well as the subject who retains faith in them.

Paradoxically, West's very complicity with Wyndham Lewis's rage against a moribund Western past enables her to script the story's most pronounced *departures* from *BLAST*'s other racially determined polemics. In making

Evadne, rather than George, the text's sovereign modern character, "Indissoluble Matrimony" ironizes the primitivist tropes and discourses deployed by the avant-garde artists represented in *BLAST*'s pages. And it is significant to note that Evadne's autonomy contravenes not only against *BLAST*'s primitivism, but also against a tendency in modern primitivism more broadly, in which black or African women are stylized into voiceless corporeality. Beginning with Paul Gauguin in the late nineteenth century, avant-garde artists typically treated black femininity as a potent counterpoint to Western industrial modernity.[38] In Gauguin's Tahitian paintings, perhaps the most influential works of modern primitivism, black women's sexuality promised the European male "a redemptive union of mind and body unrealizable through contact with her European counterpart" (Antliff and Leighten, 176). Gauguin often refashioned biblical narratives or Western myths into alluring, sexual scenes from primitive societies; and although his artistic successors in the twentieth century soon abandoned the anthropological in favor of the abstract, avant-garde art continued to depict black femininity as a powerful alternative to white Western beauty, sexuality, and civility. In 1907, for example, Henri Matisse's painting *Blue Nude* —a response, possibly, to the racially charged *Olympia* paintings by Edouard Manet in 1865 and Pablo Picasso in 1901—synthesized black and white sexuality to produce an artistic revision of traditional Venus imagery.[39] Matisse's nude "Venus" lies outside on grass instead of on an elaborately decorated bed; her classical pose has been aggressively sexualized with oversized lips, breasts, and hips adapted from African sculpture. In the same year, Picasso's iconic and iconoclastic work *Les Demoiselles d'Avignon* shocked Paris audiences with its violent cubist rendering of prostitutes whose masked or mask-like faces resembled African tribal masks. Jody Blake connects the primitivist qualities of *The Blue Nude* and *Les Demoiselles d'Avignon* to the more general atmosphere of urban negrophilia in the early decades of the twentieth century:

> The "African" women that Matisse and Picasso conjured up from their study of *l'art nègre* are indeed as distinct from the marble Venuses that were among the sources for their poses as the dancers of the cakewalk and the bamboula were from the tulle-skirted ballerinas of the "white ballets." *The Blue Nude* and *Les Demoiselles d'Avignon* are endowed with the instinctual vitality, sexual energy, and demonic power that were thought to be unleashed by the beating of drums and the pounding of feet in the wilds of Dixie or in the jungles of Africa. (35)

Figure 8. Henri Matisse, *Blue Nude,* 1907. (Baltimore Museum of Art, Baltimore.)

The "instinctual vitality, sexual energy, and demonic power" of Picasso and Matisse's Africa-inspired women find literary analogues in the writings of Joseph Conrad and D. H. Lawrence. In *Heart of Darkness* and *Women in Love,* novels that explore Western alienation in the face of imperialist, capitalist modernity, the figure of the Negress suggests an unmediated connection to the uncivilized natural world. Consider Marlow's description of Kurtz's "wild and gorgeous" African mistress at the end of *Heart of Darkness:*

> She was savage and superb, wild-eyed and magnificent; there was something ominous and stately in her deliberate progress. And in the hush that had fallen suddenly upon the whole sorrowful land, the immense wilderness, the colossal body of the fecund and mysterious life seemed to look at her, pensive, as though it had been looking at the image of its own tenebrous and passionate soul. (125)

Through Marlow's eyes, the African woman suggests a totalizing metonym for the cultural condition of primitiveness itself. As Marianna Torgovnick points out, this scene (and, indeed, the novel more broadly) treats the prim-

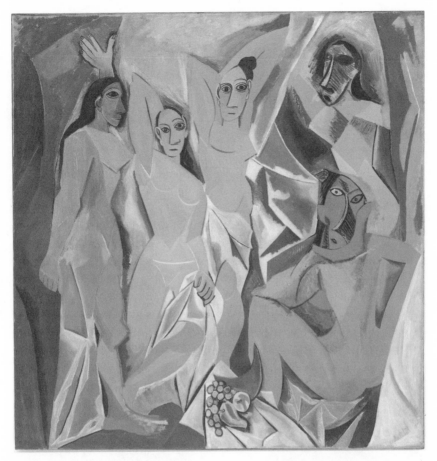

Figure 9. Pablo Picasso, *Les Demoiselles d'Avignon*, 1907. The African attributes of the women in Matisse's *Blue Nude* (figure 8) and Picasso's *Les Demoiselles d'Avignon*—the oversized features of the former and the mask-like visages of the latter—radically altered the conventions of the nineteenth-century European nude. Oil on canvas. 8 ft. × 7 ft. 8 in. (The Museum of Modern Art, New York. Acquired through the Lillie P. Bliss Bequest. Licensed by SCALA/Art Resource, New York, 2006. Estate of Pablo Picasso/Artists Rights Society, New York.)

itive as "a convenient locale for the exploration of Western dullness or degeneracy, and of ways to transcend it, and thus functions as a symbolic entity" (153).

The idea of transcendence through the primitive plays a similar role in Lawrence's *Women in Love*. Gerald Crich, the conflicted son of a successful English industrialist, encounters a collection of African statues in an urban apartment:

Figure 10. Jacob Epstein, *Female Figure in Flenite,* 1913. Three works produced by London artists in 1913 reveal the centrality of primitive femininity in the avant-garde imagination. The pregnant form of Epstein's *Female Figure in Flenite,* the tribal dance movements suggested by Gaudier-Brzeska's *Red Stone Dancer* (figure 11), and the coloring and markings in Grant's *Head of Eve* (figure 12) point to the powerful affinity between African art and modernism's quest for pure form. (© 2008 Tate, London.)

Figure 11. Henri Gaudier-Brzeska, *Red Stone Dancer,* 1913. (© 2008 Tate, London.)

Figure 12. Duncan Grant, *Head of Eve,* 1913. (Tate Gallery, London. Photo credit: Tate, London/Art Resource, New York. © 2009 Artists Rights Society, New York/DACS, London.)

It was an ordinary London sitting-room in a flat, evidently taken furnished, rather common and ugly. But there were several negro statues, wood-carvings from West Africa, strange and disturbing, the carved negroes looked almost like the foetus of a human being. One was of a woman sitting naked in a strange posture, and looking tortured, her abdomen stuck out. . . . The strange, transfixed, rudimentary face of the woman again reminded Gerald of a foetus, it was also rather wonderful, conveying the suggestion of the extreme of physical sensation, beyond the limits of mental consciousness. (74)

The totemic sculptures of African women kindle Gerald's desire to escape the "ordinary London sitting-room" as well as the boundaries of consciousness and known language. Traces of this desire appear in avant-garde co-optations of the African plastic arts, which explicitly push against received traditions of Western realism. Works such as Duncan Grant's painting *Head of Eve* (1913), Jacob Epstein's sculpture *Female Figure in Flenite* (1913), Henri Gaudier-Brzeska's sculpture *Red Stone Dancer* (1913), and the abstract works of Henry Moore, Constantin Brancusi, Henri Matisse, and Amedeo Modigliani express a shared belief in primitive femininity as a welcome source of renewal in a dreary Western world.

In sharp contrast with the fecund, barbarous, or silent black women who dominate modern primitivism, the Negress protagonist of Rebecca West's "Indissoluble Matrimony" participates wholly in—and, indeed, comes to symbolize—the modern metropolitan present. Aesthetic barriers do not limit Evadne Silverton to passive or silent spectacle; the workings of the imperial machine do not confine her within Africa or other colonized spaces; cubism and impressionism do not reduce her to fragments or blurs; and world-weary white characters do not invest her with the mythic power to rejuvenate or redeem. In sum: West overwrites the prevailing aesthetics of modern primitivism to produce the fiercely original independence of her protagonist.

In "Indissoluble Matrimony," Rebecca West makes George Silverton the voice of reductive racial assumptions and then sweeps those assumptions aside to showcase Evadne's command over urban terrain, socialist thought, and the terms of modern marriage. Through George's eyes, Evadne embodies an essential, concentrated negritude, a feminine sensuousness intent solely on physical pleasure:

Under her curious dress, designed in some pitifully cheap and worthless stuff by a successful mood of her indiscreet taste—she had black blood in her— her long body seemed pulsing with some exaltation. The blood was coursing violently under her luminous yellow skin, and her lids, dusky with fatigue, drooped contentedly over her great humid black eyes. Perpetually she raised her hand to the mass of black hair that was coiled on her thick golden neck, and stroked it with secretive enjoyment, as a cat licks its fur. And her large mouth smiled frankly, but abstractedly, at some digested pleasure. (98)

George always connects Evadne's blackness to sexual excess and indiscretion, assuming that her physicality renders impossible either serious intellectual activity or emotional depth. Initially drawn to Evadne's "smouldering contralto such as only those of black blood can possess," and inspired to rescue her from her mother's apartment, "a mean flat crowded with cheap glories of bead curtains and Oriental hangings" (101), George soon finds himself repulsed by this "depraved, over-sexed creature" (102) and her "excited candour" (101), her "uncanny, Negro" demeanor "that made him feel as though they were not properly married" (99), and the "loose-lipped hurry" of her voice (109). Her racial alterity blinds George to her political convictions and success as a socialist writer: "In the jaundiced recesses of his mind he took it for granted that her work would have the lax fibre of her character: that it would be infected with her Oriental crudities" (102). But West adopts an ironic narrative distance from George's prejudices, ridiculing his assumptions about white minds and black bodies. Indeed, the story's opening line itself—"When George Silverton opened the front door he found that the house was not empty for all its darkness" (267)—troubles, metaphorically, the hierarchical relationships of plenitude, emptiness, and racial identity. In "Indissoluble Matrimony," the negritude that has suggested a dark Vortex of premodern, prelinguistic knowledge to Pound and Lewis becomes the locus of feminine cultural autonomy.

Evadne's blackness is accompanied by a complacent, confident rationality that not only mocks George's phobic racism, but also skewers large-scale fears about women's social empowerment in England during the second decade of the twentieth century. Despite George's demeaning view of his wife's socialist activity as a crude, Oriental "caper of the sensualist" (102), Evadne has established her public credibility: "After reading enormously of economics, she had begun to write for the Socialist press and to speak successfully at meetings." George's terror of Evadne's political success expresses what Sandra Gilbert and Susan Gubar identify as "the connection between male sexual anxiety and women's entrance into the public sphere" (98). A handbill announcing Evadne's speech at Stephen Longton's socialist meeting catalyzes George's ire: "He saw her name—his name

—MRS EVADNE SILVERTON. It was at first the blaze of stout scarlet letters on the dazzling white ground that made him blink. Then he was con-
vulsed with rage" (102). Linking the Silverton name to Evadne's vocal
public socialism sparks the broader fear of women's autonomy and appropriation of male power; Eliot's J. Alfred Prufrock would express the identical fear a year later, when the war had led to the collapse of sexual codes
in both private and public spheres. Further, George's anger at the auda-
cious use of his name on the socialist handbill recalls one of vorticism's own
foundational moments. Immediately preceding *BLAST*'s publication in the
summer of 1914, Wyndham Lewis was infuriated to find his name attached
to F. T. Marinetti and C. R. W. Nevinson's futurist manifesto, "Vital English
Art." The manifesto, which was published in the *Observer* and declared that
only futurism could produce "an English art that is strong, virile and anti-
sentimental," included the unsolicited signatures of Lewis, Frederick
Etchells, Edward Wadsworth, and other artists who would contribute to
BLAST. In an aggressive letter published in *The New Weekly,* the *Observer,* and
the *Egoist,* Lewis and his vorticist supporters unambiguously disavowed any
connection to Marinetti and the futurists.[40] George Silverton's refusal to
be publicly allied with radical socialism is a tongue-in-cheek inversion of
the vorticist refusal to be publicly allied with effete or passé futurism.

"Indissoluble Matrimony" trivializes George's anxieties by casting his fear
of Evadne's intellectual and political autonomy as fear of her negritude:

> "You mustn't have anything to do with Longton," he stormed.
> A change passed over her. She became ugly. Her face was heavy with in-
> tellect, her lips coarse with power. He was at arms with a Socialist lead. Much
> he would have preferred the bland sensualist again. (102-3)

But the narrator reveals that Evadne's "coarse" and "heavy" features—characteristics stereotypically associated with black women—are merely chimeri-
cal projections of George's sexual terror. Evadne's effortless calm leads her
to victory in the argument over Stephen Longton's moral character:

> "George. I suppose you mean that he's a bad man." He nodded. "I know quite
> well that the girl who used to be his typist is his mistress." She spoke it sweetly,
> as if reasoning with an old fool. "But she's got consumption. She'll be dead
> in six months. In fact, I think it's rather nice of him. To look after her and
> all that." (103)

Evadne's sexual and social pragmatism reduces George to "a transport of
hysterical sobs" (103) and makes him wonder if the Lisbech asylum holds

any lunatic "so slavered with madness as he himself" (106). The symbolically significant equation of George's weak Anglo-Saxonism with madness and hysteria anticipates the war's shell-shock epidemic, the unprecedented psychological phenomenon that would hospitalize thousands of Englishmen just months after *BLAST*'s publication. Elaine Showalter's *The Female Malady: Women, Madness, and English Culture, 1830–1980* has persuasively demonstrated that "the Great War was a crisis of masculinity and a trial of the Victorian masculine idea. In a sense, the long-term repression of signs of fear that led to shell-shock in war was only an exaggeration of the male sex-role expectations, the self-control and emotional disguise of civilian life" (171).[41] In "Indissoluble Matrimony," feminine assertiveness, political autonomy, and sexuality are the "shells" that break down the "Victorian masculine idea." Ten years before the story's opening, we are told, the men who work in George's law firm "had been reduced to hysteria over the estates of an extraordinarily stupid old woman" (269) whose "vast income" throws the all-male legal practice into an inexplicable frenzy. And masculine paranoia suffuses George's marriage to Evadne, whose blackness and frank sexuality so threaten George that he is "determined to be a better man than her" (102). As George comes to recognize the hollowness of conventional Anglo-Saxon manliness, he falls into concentrated episodes of madness that foreshadow the agonies of shell shock caused by the Great War.

Tellingly, Rebecca West conflates George's madness with his abhorrence of sex: George shudders at "the secret obscenity of women!" (100) and wonders "why the Church did not provide a service for the absolution of men after marriage." His horror of sex and his "unnatural pride of sterility" (109-10) supply an amusing counterpoint to the suffragette leader Christabel Pankhurst's polemical 1913 text *The Great Scourge and How to End It,* which protested against the spread of venereal disease and the practice of prostitution. Pankhurst's controversial slogan, "Votes for Women and Chastity for Men," correlated female cultural empowerment with male sexual continence; and George Silverton's obsessive abstinence in "Indissoluble Matrimony" reflects an unwitting, ironic collusion with one of the suffragette movement's most radical ideas.[42] George's inability to exercise masculine authority in either the private or the public sphere crystallizes the more general psychic impotence that Englishmen confronted in the war. West's depiction of George's uncontrollable hysteria—a signifier for racial and sexual failures—provides a remarkable simulacrum of the psychic horrors that the English war poets would convey in bleak verse, that West herself would explore in *The Return of the Soldier,* and that Virginia Woolf would create for Septimus Smith in *Mrs. Dalloway.*

If the story foreshadows the sexual anarchy caused by the war, it also registers the sexual debates contemporaneous with *BLAST* 's publication. By casting Evadne as a socialist platform speaker, "Indissoluble Matrimony" yokes itself to the heated, turbulent discourses surrounding feminism and women's suffrage before the war, discourses that Rebecca West herself was instrumental in developing.[43] West does not identify Evadne as a suffragette, but her protagonist's feminism speaks directly to the dominant concerns of England's vote-seeking women. Uninterested in cultivating domestic skills, impassioned about politics, and childless, Evadne seems to conform to the vicious stereotypes linked to suffragettes who rejected late Victorian or Edwardian idealizations of passive, gentle femininity. And although Evadne makes no statements about women's votes, her violent resistance to physical confinement and political passivity evokes one of the most notorious periods in suffragette militancy. When Evadne storms out of the house to go to the reservoir, she "dashed out of the front door and banged it with such passion that a glass pane shivered to fragments behind her" (105). The glass door that shatters when Evadne refuses to acquiesce to George's demands evokes the shop windows smashed by suffragettes in London's West End in 1912, an unrepentant striking out against the strictures and structures of a patriarchal establishment. (Indeed, suffragette window smashing and the subsequent, violent phase of arson, property damage, and slashing of paintings, had a direct impact on *BLAST,* inspiring Wyndham Lewis's "Note To Suffragettes" at the end of the war journal: "WE MAKE YOU A PRESENT OF OUR VOTES. ONLY LEAVE WORKS OF ART ALONE. YOU MIGHT SOME DAY DESTROY A GOOD PICTURE BY ACCIDENT. . . . IF YOU DESTROY A GREAT WORK OF ART you are destroying a greater soul than if you annihilated a whole district of London. LEAVE ART ALONE, BRAVE COMRADES!" [151–52]).[44]

Like George Silverton's charge that Evadne's political commitments make her sound "'like a woman off the streets'" (103), prewar public discourses about suffragettes cohered around definitions of morality, femininity, and womanhood. The massive campaign for women's suffrage— its demonstrations, protests, pageants, journalism, artwork—met with an equally massive barrage of antisuffrage sentiment that pathologized women's desire for autonomy as a sign of unwomanliness, madness, or disease. Lisa Tickner's study, *The Spectacle of Women: Imagery of the Suffrage Campaign 1907–1914,* catalogs the worries stirred by feminist militancy:

It was widely asserted that "masculine" women and "feminine" men were among the indices of social degeneration, that women pursuing emancipated activities in higher education or the professions impaired their fertility and maternal capacities, that the birth rate was falling among the middle classes who would be swamped by the eugenically inferior inheritance of the lower orders, and that enfranchising women would compromise the virility of the state and promote unrest in the colonies. Woman, or rather "womanliness", was the linchpin in bourgeois ideology and a structuring category in the principal discourses of civil society (medicine, law, politics, education, the family). (170)

These anxieties about "womanliness" also expressed anxiety about racial disruption and degeneration and led to a kind of antifeminist typology. Pejorative categories such as the "Shrieking Sister," the "Modern Woman," the "Hysterical Woman," and the "Militant Woman" accrued around suffragettes and politically active women in English newspapers, editorial cartoons, and propaganda.[45] In this context, Evadne's intellectual lucidity and physical magnificence reproach widespread paranoia about the racial decline augured by women's entrance into public and political spheres.

West's painterly renderings of Evadne adapt *primitivist* iconography to subvert *misogynistic* images of ugly, hysterical, or mannish suffragettes. "Indissoluble Matrimony" ironizes prewar images associated with womanliness and motherhood, putting Evadne in classic maternal poses when she is most explicitly political or self-sufficient. For example, in what George assumes is a conciliatory gesture following the fight about Evadne's speech, Evadne "lay back with his head drawn to her bosom, rocking herself rhythmically" (104). The visual image of a black woman providing nonverbal solace to an Anglo-Saxon man troubled by the processes of modernization seems complicit with avant-garde primitive semiotics. But the rhythms of Evadne's body express neither the abstract natural harmony that *BLAST*'s authors attribute to dark races nor the abundant generosity conventionally associated with wives and mothers. Rather, Evadne rocks herself according to the phrases of the socialist speech she is rehearsing: "Then it struck [George] that each breath was a muttered phrase. He stiffened, and hatred flamed through his veins. The words came clearly through her lips. . . . 'The present system of wage-slavery . . .'" (104). Evadne's racial alterity radicalizes the iconic feminine images directed against politically active Englishwomen for the antimaternalism and antifamilialism that supposedly threaten England's racial integrity.[46]

Similarly, the formal virtues of primitive aesthetics work to feminist ad-

We Want the Vote

9026

Figure 13. "We Want the Vote," 1909. Like much antisuffrage propaganda, this image depicts a vote-seeking woman as monstrous and racially degenerate. (Anonymous picture postcard. Cynicus Publishing Company. Museum of London.)

vantage at the story's close, when George returns home and makes the anticlimactic realization that Evadne has not drowned in the Lisbech reservoir:

> Evadne lay on his deathbed. She slept there soundly, with her head flung back on the pillows so that her eyes and brow seemed small in shadow, and her mouth and jaw huge above her thick throat in the light. . . . Her breast, silvered with sweat, shone in the ray of the street lamp that had always disturbed their nights. The counterpane rose enormously over her hips in rolls of glazed linen. Out of mere innocent sleep her sensuality was distilling a most drunken pleasure. (116)

On one hand, the gigantism of Evadne's black body suggests the primitivist sculptures of Epstein and Gaudier-Brzeska, or the Africanized Venus of Matisse's *Blue Nude*. But the spectacle of Evadne's magnificent self-sufficiency forces George to admit that the whirlpool battle "had never even put her into danger" (117), collapsing his already-tenuous belief in his own racial or sexual dominance. His anti-epiphanic realization that "bodies like his do not kill bodies like hers" confesses the Anglo-Saxon male's powerlessness to control or destroy the modern-primitive-feminist Evadne, whose physical strength and intelligence trivialize masculine tradition and virulent misogyny. The story's concluding lines augur an ineluctable masculine cultural paralysis: "He was beaten. He undressed and got into bed: as he had done every night for ten years, and as he would do every night until he died. Still sleeping, Evadne caressed him with warm arms" (117). While George surrenders to the devastation of his worldview and his agency, Evadne presents a final, compelling imbrication of vorticist doctrine, primitivist imagery, and feminine independence. The single image of her unconscious caresses offers a précis of Rebecca West's feminist appropriation of Pound's and Lewis's Vortex, where maximum energy can be found at a still center.

Jo Anna Isaak argues that avant-garde primitivism "was one of the major strategies to facilitate the creation of the autonomous, autotelic work of art—a work of art relieved of its semantic or representational function, precisely because meaning with an a priori existence had been repudiated" (73). Rebecca West's Evadne Silverton redirects the modernist idea of autotelic art: the sensuous calm of her body corresponds to a self-sufficiency that is both aesthetic *and* political. In other words, the primitive form of Evadne's body gives rise to a public cultural autonomy that liberates her from the history and patriarchy represented by George. Simultaneously primitive and contemporary, sexual and intellectual, Evadne wrests modernity's private, public, and natural spaces from the Anglo-Saxon artists who claim to dominate them. Her blackness operates as a powerful instrument of critique in the story's sexual and political battles, upholding and upending Wyndham Lewis's vorticist principles.

"A race that will have no successors": *The Good Soldier* and the Discontinuities of Modernity

While the sharp wit of "Indissoluble Matrimony" lobs a good-humored blow at the racial foundations of vorticism in *BLAST*, a more sobering view of race and modernity emerges in "The Saddest Story," the first three chapters of Ford Madox Ford's 1915 novel *The Good Soldier*. This short fiction, and the full-length novel that it became less than a year later, reveals another layer of racial complexity in BLAST and its historical moment. *The Good Soldier*'s completion and publication between 1914 and 1915 mark a crucial moment in the embattled maturing of the London avant-garde, and the novel's obsession with key events falling on August 4—the date Great Britain entered the war—invites us to read it as a bridge between prewar and postwar aesthetic priorities.[47] As vague and imprecise as the aims of *BLAST* were deliberate and explicit, *The Good Soldier* poses an odd contrast to the rest of Lewis's militant war journal.[48] The philosophical differences between Ford's story of a cuckolded husband and *BLAST*'s other elements are immediately apparent: where *BLAST* celebrates the end of the Victorian era, blasting "the years 1837 to 1900," *The Good Soldier* mourns the advent of twentieth-century modernity and the end of a known civilization. In contrast with the ringing, uncompromising language and hard-edged visual arts of Lewis, Pound, and Gaudier-Brzeska, Ford offers his readers frustrating loops of recursive, tentative narrative. But in concert with the broader thematics of *BLAST*, *The Good Soldier* investigates the mutually constitutive relationships of race, Englishness, and modernity. Against the backdrop of a war journal that hails a new Anglo-Saxon vitality to repair England's national and artistic lassitude, *The Good Soldier* despairs about the displacement that has supplanted longstanding paradigms of racial and cultural continuity. It is my aim to demonstrate that *The Good Soldier*'s famed uncertainties and narrative innovations converge in its striking and surprisingly unexplored racial tropes.

BLAST, as we know, was published in London on June 29, 1914. In the weeks immediately preceding the magazine's appearance, several of its chief contributors (along with their peers and rivals in the metropolitan avant-garde) participated in a show at the Whitechapel Art Gallery titled *Twentieth Century Art: A Review of Modern Movements*. The exhibit ran from May 8 to June 20, 1914, and illustrated the explicit aesthetic change making that Wyndham Lewis and his colleagues had taken on as their mission. One hundred and thirty-three drawings and paintings by the new century's artists, including Wyndham Lewis, Walter Sickert, Augustus John, Vanessa Bell, and David Bomberg, captured the dynamic, contradictory ambitions of impressionism, postimpressionism, cubism, futurism, and vorticism. As Lisa Tickner observes, the Whitechapel exhibit "projected with particular clarity a series of underlying transitions: from a more representational to a more controversially abstract, expressive or 'primitivising' art, certainly, but also, and more structurally, from a broadly nineteenth-century set of institutions, expectations and vocabularies to something more familiar today" (*Modern Life*, 1). Like the Whitechapel Art Gallery's *Review of Modern Movements*, *The Good Soldier* bears eloquent witness to the conflicted aesthetic leanings of its historical moment. Ford's work advances the aesthetic projects of its fin-de-siècle and Edwardian predecessors, and, simultaneously, begins the work that postwar modernist experimentation would extend. This transitional novel's anxieties about the traffic between Europe and the United States, for example, look back to Henry James; and its fully realized impressionist methods evoke Joseph Conrad and his decade-long creative and critical collaboration with Ford.[49] At the same time, however, this novel's fragmented depiction of history and subjectivity reveals a thorough rejection of the Victorian realism that lingers in James and Conrad and anticipates the narrative radicalism that would soon come to be associated with Joyce and Woolf.

Ford Madox Ford's famous 1927 dedicatory letter to Stella Bowen describes the novel in precisely the terms I wish to use to guide my analysis.[50] Reflecting on the rapidly changing avant-garde scene in London during the war years, Ford remarks that *The Good Soldier* "remains my great auk's egg for me as being something of a race that will have no successors" (xxi). Describing his sense of his own aging and imminent extinction in the face of the "tapageur and riotous Jeunes of that young decade" (xx), Ford tells Stella Bowen that he intended *The Good Soldier* to be his final novel, a swan song to commemorate the end of an era. Although Ford did go on to write prolifically after *The Good Soldier*, his description of this work as a member of a "race that will have no successors" calls attention to *The Good Soldier*'s status in literary history, and, further, pinpoints the novel's central anxieties about filiation and affiliation, racial continuity and discontinuity. John Dowell's tortuous, self-conscious storytelling reveals that inherited racial authority holds no meaning in a modern world where the cultural structures that *maintain* that authority are collapsing. The militant racial self-definition that runs through *BLAST*'s manifestoes becomes the very *impossibility* of racial definition or fixity in *The Good Soldier*. Black and white, so elementally powerful in the rest of *BLAST*, become mockeries in Ford's novel, persistent, recurring reminders of the clarity and the social divisions that have been lost or are rapidly blurring.

Ford's ambivalence about twentieth-century modernity is well known, thoroughly documented over the course of a career that began in 1892 with the publication of two children's books and ended in 1938 with his compendious work *The March of Literature: From Confucius' Day to Our Own*.[51] In the decade before the Great War, Ford expressed grave anxieties about the altered state of English civilization, his somber writings paving the way for the explosive avant-garde works of "tapageur and riotous Jeunes" like Lewis and Pound.[52] Ford's essays for *Outlook* magazine and for the *English Review* —the pathbreaking literary periodical he founded in 1908—as well as works like *The Critical Attitude* (1911) and *Ancient Lights and Certain New Reflections* (1911) revealed his growing disenchantment with the post-Victorian unraveling of stratified English society, the concomitant rise of mass culture, and the ascendance of rational, objective science.[53] A Baudelairean passage from Ford's 1911 work *The Critical Attitude* records the author's dual fascination with and suspicion of twentieth-century modernity:

> We have to watch modern life sweeping away the traditions that we love, the places that we considered hallowed; we have to consider that it is blowing away us ourselves as if we were no more than a little dust. And yet, if we have consciences, we must seek to perceive order in this disorder, beauty in what shocks us, and premonitions of immortality in that which sweeps us into forgotten graves. (9)

In *The Good Soldier*, John Dowell tries to create precisely this "order" and "beauty" out of his shocking experiences. His efforts are thwarted, however, by the ambiguities of race and nation in a modern world whose borders are increasingly porous.

The Good Soldier explores modernity's discontents through a complex web of religious entanglements, international mésalliances, and transatlantic journeys that produce a deep—and ultimately impossible—desire for racial belonging. At the beginning of his tale, Dowell muses,

We were, if you will, one of those tall ships with the white sails upon a blue sea, one of those things that seem the proudest and the safest of all the beautiful and safe things that God has permitted the mind of men to frame. Where better could one take refuge? . . . For, if for me we were four people with the same tastes, with the same desires, acting—or, no, not acting—sitting here and there unanimously, isn't that the truth? If for nine years I have possessed a goodly apple that is rotten at the core and discover its rottenness only in nine years and six months less four days, isn't it true to say that for nine years I possessed a goodly apple? (8–9)

The historical and cultural smoothness suggested by the continuous forward motion of the tall ships gives way to the troubled metaphor of modernity's "goodly apple that is rotten at the core." Dowell borrows this metaphor from *The Merchant of Venice*. *The Good Soldier*'s guiding questions about the relationship between traditional past and modern present derive, significantly, from one of Antonio's anti-Semitic descriptions of Shylock:

> An evil soul producing holy witness
> Is like a villain with a smiling cheek,
> A goodly apple rotten at the heart.
> O what a goodly outside falsehood hath!
> (I.iii.94–99)

The encrypted racial violence of Dowell's opening metaphor sets the tone for the novel's attentions to the problem of race, a problem that subtly and yet unmistakably underpins each character's desire to perpetuate his or her sense of cultural belonging. Thus, Edward Ashburnham tries to shore up his role as the English good soldier who is the "model of humanity, the hero, the athlete, the father of his county, the law-giver" (124), while Leonora, his wife, strives to preserve the faultless image of an English county estate mistress with "coils of yellow hair" and "a butler and a footman and a maid or so behind her" (23). Florence, Dowell's Anglo-American wife, hopes to establish herself socially in the England of her ancestry, and Nancy Rufford, the Ashburnhams' young ward, struggles to retain her image of Edward and Leonora as the faultless patriarch and matriarch of English county tradition. But tradition is no longer available in a world where women are sexually autonomous, the empire has begun its precipitous decline, and the self-serving drive of capitalism has overwritten feudalism. The intrusions of modernity only illuminate the receding center of racial stability and inherited class status.

The racial confusion that afflicts *The Good Soldier*'s characters is powerfully captured by Ford Madox Ford's impressionist technique. In his 1914
essay "On Impressionism," Ford claimed that "Impressionism exists to render those queer effects of real life that are like so many views seen through
bright glass—through glass so bright that whilst you perceive through it a
landscape or a backyard, you are aware that, on its surface, it reflects a face
of a person behind you" (263). The imprecise multiplicity of John Dowell's
impressionist perceptions—the "many views" suggesting that surface ap-
pearances belie reality—describes the imprecise multiplicity of race and
nation. Dowell remarks that "the whole world for me is like spots of colour
in an immense canvas" (17): and just as these spots of color never coalesce
into a meaningful whole, the designations "English," "Irish Catholic," and
"American" serve only to denote disparate, inconstant states of being. Consider, for example, Dowell's introductory description of Edward and
Leonora Ashburnham:

> For I swear to you that they were the model couple. He was as devoted as it
> was possible to be without appearing fatuous. So well set up, with such hon-
> est blue eyes, such a touch of stupidity, such a warm goodheartedness! And
> she—so tall, so splendid in the saddle, so fair! Yes, Leonora was extraordi-
> narily fair and so extraordinarily the real thing that she seemed too good to
> be true. You don't, I mean, as a rule, get it all so superlatively together. To
> be the county family, to look the county family, to be so appropriately and
> perfectly wealthy; to be so perfect in manner—even just to the saving touch
> of insolence that seems to be necessary. To have all that and to be all that!
> No, it was too good to be true. (11)

Despite Edward's "honest blue eyes" and Leonora's "extraordinarily fair"
complexion, Dowell deems the couple's apparent racial authenticity "too
good to be true." His halting sentences—"You don't, I mean, as a rule, get
it all so superlatively together"—express a post-Victorian anxiety that whiteness and Englishness are fractured conditions, only rarely to be found "so
superlatively together."

The racial impressions that comprise Dowell's tale dispel the illusion that
ethnic, religious, or national identities might be linear or smoothly transmissible. As an expatriate American, Dowell traces his own genealogical and
geographical origins to the violent racial transactions of American history:

> I myself am a Dowell of Philadelphia, Pa., where, it is historically true, there
> are more old English families than you would find in any six English coun-
> ties taken together. I carry about with me, indeed—as if it were the only thing

that invisibly anchored me to any spot on the globe—the title deeds to my
farm, which once covered several blocks between Chestnut and Wampum
Streets. These title deeds are of wampum, the grant of an Indian chief to the
first Dowell, who left Farnham in Surrey in company with William Penn. (7)

Descended from English immigrants who relocated themselves by dislo-
cating others and only "invisibly anchored" to farmland originally inhabited by Native Americans, Dowell discovers a similar tenuousness in the
familial and racial ties of his companions. His dawning recognition that the
English Ashburnhams have not led the morally impeccable lives of feudal
benefactors, and that his American wife, Florence, compromised herself
sexually to attain a racially desirable "place in the ranks of English county
society" (88), gives rise to a despairing outburst that we could read as the
novel's thesis on racial consistency: "Permanence? Stability! I can't believe
it's gone" (8). And Dowell's eventual position as the owner of the Ashburnham family's ancestral estate—"I am that absurd figure, an American
millionaire, who has bought one of the ancient haunts of English peace. . . .
So life peters out" (275)—underscores the plight of modern individuals
whose organic ties to racial or national collectivity have been displaced by
financial transactions, migration, and exile.

"It is so difficult to keep all these people going" (241), Dowell confesses
to his readers, a narrator's anxiety about the continuity of literary character that evokes a deeper anxiety about sustaining *racial* character across time
and space. Indeed, Ford Madox Ford would explicitly correlate literary
form and the forms of race in his 1924 biography-memoir, *Joseph Conrad*.
Describing the genesis of literary impressionism in England, Ford recalls a
moment when he and Conrad sensed "that what was the matter with the
Novel, and the British novel in particular, was that it went straight forward,
whereas in your gradual making acquaintanceship with your fellows you
never do go straight forward" (136). The constraints of nineteenth-century
realist narration, Ford shows us, could not accommodate the unruliness
of modern racial character:

You meet an English gentleman at your golf club. He is beefy, full of health,
the moral of the boy from an English Public School of the finest type. You
discover, gradually, that he is hopelessly neurasthenic, dishonest in matters
of small change, but unexpectedly self-sacrificing, a dreadful liar, but a most
painfully careful student of lepidoptera and, finally, from the public prints,
a bigamist who was once, under another name, hammered on the Stock Exchange. . . . Still, there he is, the beefy, full-fed fellow, moral of an English
Public School product. (136–7)

To correctly capture the contradictions that make up the "finest type" of "English gentleman," Ford argues, "you could not begin at his beginning and work his life chronologically to the end. You must first get him in with a strong impression, and then work backwards and forwards over his past" (137).

Liberated from the linearity of realist method, the impressionist narrator works "backwards and forwards" to illuminate the fault lines that trouble—and often destroy—inherited myths of imperial Englishness. Consider the fate of Edward Ashburnham, who slits his throat when he loses Nancy Rufford and recognizes the futility of continuing to act "the fine soldier, the excellent landlord, the extraordinarily kind, careful, and industrious magnate, the upright, honest, fair-dealing, fair-thinking, public character" (102). The description of his suicide, an afterthought that Dowell appends to his story's apparent ending, literalizes Edward Ashburnham's fractured racial status. Following the seemingly conclusive statement, "That is the great desideratum of life, and that is the end of my story" (276), Dowell bursts out, "It suddenly occurs to me that I have forgotten to say how Edward met his death"; it is only then that he relays the sequence of events leading up to Edward's suicide. The ruptured conclusion of Dowell's tale demonstrates how modernist plots owe their forms to racial plots: the narrative of the English gentleman's death—like the English gentleman himself—cannot be smoothly integrated into a larger narrative of modern culture. In the final moments of his life, Edward certainly presents the impeccable appearance of the titular "good soldier": "His skin was clear-coloured; his hair was golden and perfectly brushed; the level brick-dust red of his complexion went clean up to the rims of his eyelids; his eyes were porcelain blue and they regarded me frankly and directly" (276–7). But archetypical Englishness has no place in a modern moment characterized by increasingly diffuse racial and sexual roles, and Dowell, realizing that "I didn't think he was wanted in the world," does nothing to halt his friend's suicide. Andrzej Gasiorek observes that "the unattainability of a totalising vision lies at the heart of Ford's account of modernity" (9); and this unattainability acquires painful vividness in the character of Edward Ashburnham, whose semblance of racial perfection is "too good to be true" and whose death merits only an awkward afterthought.

In this world of racial flux, Ford's characters, ironically, deliberately *violate* the very racial divisions and social traditions whose sanctity they appear desperate to "keep . . . going." Nancy Rufford, for example, propositions her married guardian Edward Ashburnham out of a perverse conviction that she can thereby safeguard the Anglican Protestant integrity that is his birthright. Edward, the perfect English gentleman, carries on affairs with English, Spanish, Russian, Anglo-Indian, and American women, while Leonora agonizes that he will enter into "intrigues with native women or Eurasians" (195) during their stay in India. To get closer to her goal of an English establishment, Florence marries the American John Dowell but then follows a "sallow and dark" (96) lover named Jimmy to Paris. Indeed, Florence's terror that Dowell "should murder her" if he discovers her infidelity arises from a public scene of racial violence. Dowell loses his temper with his black valet, Julius, when the latter drops Florence's valise: "I saw red, I saw purple. I flew at Julius. On the ferry, it was, I filled up one of his eyes; I threatened to strangle him. And, since an unresisting Negro can make a deplorable noise and a deplorable spectacle, and, since that was Florence's first adventure in the married state, she got a pretty idea of my character" (101). But like the disparate "spots of colour on an immense canvas," Dowell's "red" and "purple" attack on the "unresisting Negro" fails to cement his racial authority as a wealthy white American husband. Florence's continued unfaithfulness ultimately forces an admission of racial defeat from Dowell: "I am no doubt like every other man; only, probably because of my American origin, I am fainter" (257). Like Virginia Woolf's Clarissa Dalloway, who ten years later would worry that "we are a doomed race, chained to a sinking ship" (76), Ford's narrator remains unable to restore the "tall ship" to its steady course.

John Dowell confronts the wreckage of a civilization whose ontology is writ small in two disintegrating transatlantic marriages. This disintegration expresses itself across dual racial axes. On one hand, race in Dowell's narrative operates as an instrument of artistic abstraction; on the other, Dowell and the other characters constantly engage the social and material problematics of racial identity. We can map these dual racial axes in an early scene, the famously anticlimactic excursion to Marburg Castle where the Dowells and the Ashburnhams go to look at sixteenth-century Reformation documents and Florence unwittingly reveals her affair with Edward. Two seemingly insignificant incidents bracket the scene in the castle, which, read together, furnish a useful template of the novel's oscillation between the "controversially abstract" and the "familiar" leanings of the London avant-garde (Tickner, *Modern Life,* 1). On board the train for Marburg, Dowell looks out of a window and sees

a brown cow hitch its horns under the stomach of a black and white animal and the black and white one was thrown right into the middle of a narrow

stream. . . . It does look very funny, you know, to see a black and white cow
land on its back in the middle of a stream. It is so just exactly what one doesn't
expect of a cow. (45–46)

The absurd, unexpected image of the derailed black and white cow fore-
grounds the subsequent moments of unexpected "derailment" that Dowell abstracts into formally arresting black and white images. Whether the
complex particulars of the Catholic Leonora's sexuality, Edward's cross-
cultural and interracial infidelities, or Nancy's descent into madness while
journeying through the Red Sea, Dowell avails himself of self-consciously
formalist techniques to describe "just exactly what one doesn't expect." Pondering the condition of being a deceived husband, for example, Dowell
offers his reader a depersonalized vision of his wife's affair with his best
friend:

> Upon an immense plain, suspended in mid-air, I seem to see three figures,
> two of them clasped close in an intense embrace, and one intolerably solitary.
> It is in black and white, my picture of that judgment, an etching, perhaps; only
> I cannot tell an etching from a photographic reproduction. (75–76)

A similar aesthetic depersonalization characterizes a series of climactic moments that disrupt or muddle patterns of racial, national, or cultural continuity. Dowell tells us of Florence running to commit suicide "all in black"
(110) and with a face "whiter than paper" (111); of Nancy wearing a dress
that "glimmered" like a "phosphorescent fish in a cupboard" (121) on the
"black" evening when Edward Ashburnham falls in love with her; of the
grotesque death of Edward's Anglo-Indian amour, Maisie Maidan, who was
small and dark with "dark hair, like the hair of a Japanese" (81) in life, but
who assumes a bridal whiteness in death; and of Leonora, "golden-haired,
all in black" (247), at the moment she tells Nancy that Edward is dying of
love for her. Dowell stylizes each of these moments of rupture and discontinuity into dark and light, black and white, so that questions of form
and art repeatedly supplant questions of morality and sentiment. As the
creator of such images, Dowell aligns himself with the avant-gardists who,
to return to Peter Bürger, sought "the detachment of art from the praxis
of life and the accompanying crystallization of a special sphere of existence." That black and white are the primary pigments of Dowell's literary
canvas lends ironic detachment to a tale about ambiguous nationhood and
racial hybridity in a fast-changing modern world.

But Dowell also engages the racially unstable character of that world on its own terms, as we see in another seemingly unimportant occurrence once the characters arrive at Marburg Castle. Lecturing rapidly about the Protestant Reformation, Florence touches Edward's arm and says, "'It's because of that piece of paper that you're honest, sober, industrious, provident, and clean-lived. If it weren't for that piece of paper you'd be like the Irish or the Italians or the Poles, but particularly the Irish. . . .'" (48). Realizing that her English Protestant husband is having an affair with Florence, the Irish Catholic Leonora flees to a terrace with Dowell and cries, "Don't you see? . . . Don't you see what's going on?" (49). At the precise moment when the reader expects Leonora to divulge the affair to Dowell, Leonora

> appeared to look with interest at a gypsy caravan that was coming over a little bridge far below us.
> "Don't you know," she said, in her clear hard voice, "don't you know that I'm Irish Catholic?" (50)

In a scene that discloses the falseness of marriage and friendship—the rottenness of the "goodly apple"—the faraway Gypsy caravan crossing a bridge offers a racially complex semaphore of the modernity that torments Dowell. The foreign Gypsies who caravanned through western Europe refused to take their place in a capitalist economic system and did not claim either a geographical origin or point of destination. To the English imagination, as Janet Lyon has pointed out, Gypsies "seemed to reveal something about the leaky valves of modernity: living in the midst of 'progress' (in a country where the institutions of modernity had been established especially early) the "Gypsy" somehow—actively—avoided modernity's ineluctable telos" ("Gadže Modernism," 518). If Florence describes the Protestant Reformation as a source of racial and national uplift, then the sight of the Gypsy caravan underscores the racial motility that is modernity's promise as well as its curse. Indeed, Dowell panics that "it was as if we were going to run and cry out; all four of us in separate directions" (48). Like the Gypsies who move freely across borders and yet belong nowhere, characters in Ford's impressionist novel move in "separate directions," unprotected by the linear conventions of the Victorian marriage plot, the Edwardian novel of manners, or even tragedy itself:

> I call this the Saddest Story rather than "The Ashburnham Tragedy," just because it is so sad, just because there was no current to draw things along to a swift and inevitable end. There is about this story none of the elevation that accompanies tragedy; there is about it no nemesis, no destiny. Here were

two noble people—for I am convinced that both Edward and Leonora had noble natures—here then, were two noble natures, drifting down life, like fireships afloat on a lagoon and causing miseries, heartaches, agony of the mind, and death. And they themselves steadily deteriorated. And why? For what purpose? To point what lesson? It is all a darkness. (179)

Drifting, deteriorating forms of Englishness produce similarly drifting and fragmented narrative forms. Dowell's self-reflexive remarks affirm that modernist impressionism—which conveys, in Jesse Matz's words, "an inchoate sense of things" (15)—comes into being when extant literary forms are no longer adequate to express the directionlessness of race and nation.

The characters' drifting movements repeatedly centralize the problem of racial authority. As a colonial couple, Edward and Leonora vacillate between their English estate and India, Germany, and France. Florence sails from America to Europe on the *Pocahontas,* and, like the Native American woman for whom the ship is named, dies abroad, unable to successfully integrate herself into European and English society. Nancy Rufford is shipped out to Ceylon where her father owns a tea plantation and then brought back to an England in which she has no place. Dowell makes all of these journeys in one form or another and learns bitterly that geographical permanence and the racial continuity that attends it are but the illusions of a defunct historical moment. The fear that haunts this convoluted novel—and the fear that formal autonomy only intensifies—is the fear of belonging to a "race that will have no successors." Florence and Edward commit suicide without having legitimate or illegitimate children; and Dowell's future is similarly childless, as he now serves as nursemaid rather than husband to the sorrow-maddened Nancy. And although Leonora remarries and is pregnant by the novel's close, she sells the Ashburnham estate Branshaw Teleragh in order to live in a "modern mansion, replete with every convenience" (273–74). The child she will bear represents a radical break, a "separate direction," from the fading world of feudalism, imperialism, and chivalry.

Ford's social and aesthetic treatments of race converge in the character of Nancy Rufford, who is always described in terms of black and white, and whose disastrous madness perfectly embodies the racially disjointed condition of modernity. Initially Dowell associates a timelessness with Nancy, imagining her as a tall white ship and a cloistered nun, and attributes to her a feminine wholeness that lies outside modernity's detotalizing forces.[54] However, Nancy undergoes a brutal coming-of-age in the Ashburnham household, where she learns the "black and white" (238) facts of divorce, and, more troublingly, transgresses filial boundaries by falling in love with her guardian, Edward. Her descent into abstraction begins when she offers herself to Edward, "rising up at the foot of his bed, with her long hair falling, like a split cone of shadow, in the glimmer of a night-light that burned beside him" (220). Edward's memory of Nancy's appearance in his chamber distorts her into further unreality, evoking the antimimetic coloring of Cézanne and Matisse paintings: "That was the picture that never left his imagination—the girl, in the dim light, rising up at the foot of his bed. He said that it seemed to have a greenish sort of effect as if there were a greenish tinge in the shadows of the tall bedposts that framed her body" (262). This image recalls, too, one of Wyndham Lewis's descriptions of vorticism as a "dogmatically unreal" visual style in which "the colour green would not be confined, or related, to what was green in nature—such as grass, leaves, etc.; in the manner of form, a shape represented by fish remained a form independent of the animal, and could be made use of in a universe in which there were no fish."[55] Ford redirects the visual dissociations that are vorticism's triumph to describe Nancy's dissociative psychic state and the cultural failures that cause it.

From the moment she propositions Edward, Nancy ceases to represent uncorrupted continuity and serves instead as a cipher for the cultural fracturing that has undone the other characters:

> And to think that that vivid white thing, that saintly and swanlike being—to think that . . . Why, she was like the sail of a ship, so white and so definite in her movements. And to think that she will never . . . Why, she will never do anything again. I can't believe it . . . (141, ellipses in the original)

On learning of Edward's suicide en route to Ceylon, Nancy goes mad in the Red Sea, a place between East and West whose intemperate climate is associated with insanity. (Earlier, Edward had received the Royal Humane Society's medal for saving maddened soldiers from plunging into the Red Sea.) She then has to be removed from the similarly dangerous climate of Ceylon; doctors claim that "if Nancy could be brought to England, the sea air, the change of climate, the voyage, and all the usual sort of things might restore her reason. Of course, they haven't restored her reason" (256). *BLAST* may have gathered its racial and aesthetic momentum by cursing England's climate, but Dowell curses it because the collapsing plot of his story suggests only the collapsing integrity of imperial nationhood.

Nancy utters two telling phrases in her madness: "*Credo in unum Deum omnipotentem*" (254) and "Shuttlecocks!" (274). In the modern world, belief in an all-powerful deity, like belief in any unified or singular identity, sig-nals only madness. And the lone word "shuttlecocks," an evocation of Henry James's Maisie shuttling between her divorced parents, captures the oscil-lations of characters uprooted from their native geographies and conse-quently uncertain about the protocols of race, religion, and family. Dowell laments:

> Then she will say she believes in an Omnipotent Deity or she will utter the one word "shuttlecocks," perhaps. It is very extraordinary to see the perfect flush of health on her cheeks, to see the luster of her coiled black hair, the poise of the head upon the neck, the grace of the white hands—and to think that it all means nothing—that it is a picture without a meaning. (276)

A "picture without a meaning": here is the troubled denouement between autonomy and engagement, or, to return to Wilhelm Worringer, between abstraction and empathy. Dowell's stark image of Nancy does not suggest the celebration of formal purity that, as I address in greater detail in chap-ter 3, was codified by Clive Bell as "significant form"; nor does it produce any enabling engagement with the public domains of modernity itself, as do vorticist manifestoes and the feminist geometries of Rebecca West's "In-dissoluble Matrimony." *The Good Soldier* describes a psychic nightmare pre-cipitated by the twin crises of filiation and affiliation, and our final glimpse of Nancy, like the picture of Dorian Gray, offers an image of racial perfec-tion made suddenly, shockingly meaningless by the disintegrating forces of modernity.

Katherine Mansfield, Race, and the Appearance of an Aesthetic

"I do not know why I have such a fancy for this little café," muses Raoul Duquette, the bisexual French artist-gigolo who narrates Katherine Mans-field's "Je Ne Parle Pas Français" (121).[56] This stunning piece of short fic-tion, which Mansfield composed in 1918 and published in 1920 in *Bliss and Other Stories,* offers an apt endpoint for my discussion of avant-garde modernism and race. Upon completing "Je Ne Parle Pas Français" in 1918, Mansfield composed a letter to her husband, the critic John Middleton Murry, in which she declared, "I am in a way *grown up* as a writer—a sort of authority" (Hankin, *Letters,* 117); and indeed, the story maps the "grow-ing up" of metropolitan modernism, returning to the café scene where we began and illuminating anew the indelible link between race and modernism's aesthetic maturation. Mansfield parodies the frenzied artistic production of the war years, concocting a tale whose stylistic self-consciousness mocks the modernist obsession with making it new. Her amoral narrator, Raoul Duquette, who strives to make a name for himself in the glittering, decadent art world of Paris in the early 1900s, attributes his authorial talents to a series of clandestine sexual trysts with an African laundress from his childhood. But the negritude that liberates Raoul's imagination also precipitates a deep artistic crisis: his indeterminate, fragmented subjectivity, typically a site of avant-garde creative play, leads only to creative paralysis. Mansfield furnishes a retrospective view of the varied racial formations that enabled avant-garde modernism's development during the war years: "Je Ne Parle Pas Français" brings together the exotica of Madame Strindberg's Cave of the Golden Calf, *BLAST*'s racial assertiveness, the feminist primitivism of "Indissoluble Matrimony," and *The Good Soldier*'s abstract, conflicted racial impressions. Channeling these wide-ranging conceptions of race into a metacritique of modernism, Mansfield's story simultaneously exemplifies and challenges the avant-garde obsession with the permeable boundary between art and life. The story's narrative indirection—as sophisticated in its miniature perfection as lengthier fictions by Mansfield's literary peers—suggests how easily racial tropes and assumptions can pose dangers to the Western imagination that originally produced them.

To read race in Katherine Mansfield's stories is usually to discuss the politics of New Zealand colonialism. Mansfield's early writings, such as the 1907 travel diary published as *The Urewera Notebook* and the short fictions collected in *New Zealand Stories,* capture the stark divisions between the lives of the New Zealand Maori peoples and the wealthy industrialists or entrepreneurs who have colonized them. The later stories that established Mansfield's reputation—"Prelude," "At the Bay," "The Garden Party"—more subtly paint cultural contrasts between upper-class colonial families and their implicitly dirty, menacing, or unchaste indigenous neighbors.[57] But "Je Ne Parle Pas Français" reveals a very different kind of racial consciousness in Mansfield's work, one that ignores historical or political colonial conflict and instead considers the dynamic force of black sexuality in an urban European setting. Whereas colonized characters in Mansfield's New Zealand stories— most poignantly, perhaps, the little Kelvey girls in "A Doll's House"—are typically marginalized and abject, the African woman in "Je Ne Parle Pas Français" occupies a position of complex textual advantage. Her brief appearance in the story inaugurates the reordering of the narrator's cultural universe, a transgression of boundaries that informs his every subsequent social, artistic, and moral transaction.

The recursive, elliptical narrative of "Je Ne Parle Pas Français" gathers together many of the thematic strands of Mansfield's other pieces, recording the halftones and quavers of modern urban life, the callowness and solipsism of avant-garde bohemia, and the sexual damage visited upon young women who participate in delusory romantic cultural fictions. Like Bertha Young in "Bliss" (1918), Isabel in "Marriage á la Mode" (1921), and the abandoned female characters in "The Little Governess" (1915) and "Miss Brill" (1920), the characters in "Je Ne Parle Pas Français" continually interrogate what it means to *be modern* and how the architectures of their private lives can accommodate the flux and uncertainty of the outside world. Whereas several of Mansfield's women characters encounter metropolitan modernity from the confines of marriage or the private sphere of the nuclear family, the male narrator of "Je Ne Parle Pas Français" remains unbounded by the conventions of heterosexuality or domesticity. Neither a victim of patriarchy nor a passive witness to urban spectacle, Raoul Duquette experiences modern life as a series of social and aesthetic conflicts. His inability to resolve these conflicts—whether through action or art—derives from the episode of concentrated racial violence at the heart of the story. Like the other artists, authors, and narrators we have considered in this chapter, Raoul locates his creative energy in racial ambiguity. By the end of his tale, however, he finds himself paralyzed by an overabundance of artistic possibilities, unhappily alienated from the metropolitan world over which he has tried to assert the flâneur's sovereignty.

Sitting in an anonymous, unglamorous café, Raoul Duquette spins the flamboyant and self-congratulatory tale of a love triangle in bohemian Paris, continually interrupting himself with digressions on the French avant-garde, "the tendency of the modern novel" (130), and his own literary excellence. Aspiring to become a literary sensation, Raoul has cultivated the company of an English writer named Dick Harmon who is professionally successful but sexually innocent. Raoul makes Dick his confidant and escorts him through the sexual and artistic underworlds of Paris. The writers' friendship is severed abruptly, however, when Dick goes to London for several months and returns to Paris with a young woman named Mouse. Betrayed by Dick's casual disappearance and humiliated by his new love interest, Raoul decides to renew friendship with Dick solely for the sake of his art. To Raoul's delight, Dick provides ample material for literary drama: he runs away from Paris again, leaving Mouse a melodramatic letter confessing that he has returned to his mother in London. Abandoned in a new city where she does not speak the language ("'je ne parle pas français,'" ironically, is Mouse's sole French utterance), Mouse gladly turns to Raoul for the help and protection he promises. But the story ends with Raoul's disclosure that he never returns to Mouse's hotel. Despite his declaration that "regret is an appalling waste of energy, and no one who intends to be a serious writer can afford to indulge in it" (125), Raoul finds himself caught between guilt at abandoning Mouse and perverse pleasure in the various narratives he concocts from the experience. The story concludes, painfully, with Raoul's grotesque fantasies of pimping Mouse to a "dirty old gallant" (144) and of sleeping with the proprietress of the Paris café from which he has told the entire tale.[58]

"Je Ne Parle Pas Français" casts an unwavering gaze on the conflicted formation of the metropolitan avant-garde, suggesting that the creation and promotion of a self-consciously daring aesthetic exacts a harsh moral penalty from the modern artist. Despite the clarity of the story's insights, however, it remains relatively obscure in Mansfield's oeuvre, which itself did not find a place in the modernist firmament until late in the twentieth century. Katherine Mansfield's preferred métier was the short story, a genre —even within an artistic movement as defiantly diverse as modernism— never accorded the status reserved for novels and poetry. (Whereas the brevity of Pound's two-line poem "In a Station of the Metro" has never consigned it to the ranks of second-rate literature, Mansfield's stories have consistently generated critical condescension for their failure to be novels.[59]) As with a great deal of Mansfield's work, "Je Ne Parle Pas Français" has been accorded significance primarily for its biographical content. Early responses to the story praised Mansfield's pure technical mastery (*The Athenaeum* declared that "'Je Ne Parle Pas Français' is a story which possesses genius"; *The Dial* applauded Mansfield for achieving a "new and necessary form"; and the *Times Literary Supplement* called the story a "brilliant little horror"[60]); however, subsequent critical and biographical work reads the story primarily as a roman-à-clef, identifying Raoul Duquette as Mansfield's onetime French lover, the writer Francis Carco, Dick Harmon as Mansfield's husband, John Middleton Murry, and Mouse as Mansfield herself.[61] However, this story's overlooked cultural richness demands that it be read as an incisive retelling of the origins of metropolitan modernism instead of as a revenge fantasy. If Mansfield was indeed re-creating the character of Francis Carco, with whom she had a brief, unsatisfying affair in 1915, it is Carco's membership in the Parisian avant-garde—rather than his treatment of Mansfield—that gives the story its thrust.

In his memoir *De Montmartre au Quartier Latin,* Carco recounted his life
as a young poet enthralled by the Parisian aesthetic revolution taking place
in the watershed years "about 1910." Carco frequently patronized the Lapin
Agile, the Montmartre café that served as a lively experimental stage for
artists such as Picasso, Marie Laurencin, Utrillo, Apollinaire, and Max
Jacob.[62] His memoir recalls a revelatory moment when African art made its
appearance in the Lapin Agile, spurring European painters and sculptors
to depart from the conventions of realism:

> Max [Jacob]'s brother, whom we called the explorer, came back from the
> colonies and brought with him his portrait, which I believe had been done
> at Dakhar by a Negro. The likeness, very much neglected for the sake of size,
> struck all the painters at once and they noted that the gold buttons on his
> coat were not represented where they ought to have been, but as a halo
> around his face. Surprising discovery! Thus was the dissociation of objects dis-
> covered, accepted and acquired. (32)

The importance of this incident, Carco goes on to claim, cannot be over-
stated; it "must have been a stepping-stone to Picasso's first researches, for
he asserted a short time afterwards: 'If you paint a portrait, you must put
the legs beside it on the canvas.'"[63] The revolutionary "dissociation of objects" that Carco sees in the Dakhar painting plays a key role in "Je Ne Parle
Pas Français," where an African woman confers a similarly revolutionary
disjunctiveness on Raoul Duquette's perceptions and, consequently, his art.
Francis Carco's ghost haunts this story, therefore, not in the form of a callous lover, but as a witness to the crucial relationship between racial difference and experimental modernism's fragmented art forms.

Told in twenty-two chronologically disjoined episodes, "Je Ne Parle Pas
Français" exemplifies Dominic Head's claim that "dissonance is the *crux*
of the creativity" (30) in the modernist short story. Mansfield's stylized vignettes investigate the interplay of art and life, describing, performing, and
parodying literary modernism, but always stopping short of resolving the
narrator's ethical or aesthetic conflicts. Raoul's opening witticisms express
the attitude of modernist artists who privilege the fleeting present moment
over spiritual transcendence or redemption:

> I don't believe in the human soul. I never have. I believe that people are like
> portmanteaux—packed with certain things, started going, thrown about,
> tossed away, dumped down, lost and found, half emptied suddenly, or
> squeezed fatter than ever, until finally the Ultimate Porter swings them on
> to the Ultimate Train and away they rattle. . . . (122)

This godless, irreligious worldview buttresses Raoul's literary style, which interrupts itself, draws attention to its own falsities, and derides the value of mimetic or realist narration.

On one level, Raoul's elliptical asides and queries produce the story's comedy, as when he describes "a morsel of pink blotting-paper, incredibly soft and limp and almost moist, like the tongue of a little dead kitten, which I've never felt" (124), or when he undercuts an emotional moment with narcissistic attention to the "real tears" that are "glittering on my long silky lashes—so charming" (130). The very titles of his published literary volumes—*False Coins, Left Umbrellas, Wrong Doors*—point to art rooted in the partial and the inauthentic. But more darkly, the story's self-conscious artifice reveals Raoul's fear that neither artistic quality nor an authentic self lies beneath the pretty surfaces and metaphors he creates. In a brilliant narrative *mise-en-abyme*, for example, Raoul addresses his dandified reflection in a mirror and announces his intentions to make it new:

> "I am going in for serious literature. I am starting a career. The book that I shall bring out will simply stagger the critics. I am going to write about things that have never been touched before. I am going to make a name for myself as a writer about the submerged world. But not as others have done before me. Oh, no! Very naively, with a sort of tender humour and from the inside, as though it were all quite simple, quite natural. I see the way quite perfectly. Nobody has ever done it as I shall do it because none of the others have lived my experiences." (127)

Raoul makes similar pronouncements throughout "Je Ne Parle Pas Français," creating a dizzying, circular narrative that continually theorizes the very work it performs. His narrative and his literary works are, to borrow from Fredric Jameson, "allegories of their own production" (*Singular*, 159) that evoke the modernist movement itself. Jameson argues that modernism's cultural instability produces works that necessarily incorporate the shifting status of artist and art object alike:

> The point is not only that the emergent artists of modernism have no social status or institutional social role except as ill-defined positions within the *bohème*, not yet even intellectuals in any strict sense; it is also that their works are increasingly unclassifiable, and begin to resist the commercial categories of the genres in the effort to distinguish themselves from commodity forms at the same time that they invent various mythic and ideological claims for some unique formal status which has no social recognition or acknowledgement. In this void, they are obliged to recognize and acknowledge themselves; and auto-referentiality is the very dynamic of this process, in which the work

of art designates itself and supplies the criteria whereby it is supposed to be used and evaluated. (159)

Raoul Duquette, creating art from "ill-defined positions within the *bohème*," relies obsessively on the "self-designation of the modern": his "mythic and ideological claims" about his literary radicalism manifest themselves in ceaseless metareflections such as the one above. On reading Mansfield's draft of "Je Ne Parle Pas Français," John Middleton Murry noted that Raoul is "conscious of a piece out of him. . . . But what it is he hasn't got, he doesn't know" (*Letters*, 112). This absent "piece," which Jameson terms modernism's "void," produces the anxious, self-referential layers of Raoul's narrative:

> If you think what I've written is merely superficial and impudent and cheap you're wrong. I'll admit it does sound so, but then it is not all. If it were, how could I have experienced what I did when I read that stale little phrase written in green ink, in the writing-pad? That proves there's more in me and that I really am important, doesn't it? (128)

And Raoul's stylized alienation, which Mansfield offers as cause, symptom, and symbol of the avant-garde worship of form, has its roots in an originary moment of racial violence.

This moment appears in the story despite Raoul's resistance to the formal conventions of biographical narrative. Raoul mocks realist fictions of development, introducing himself by name to the reader only after several pages of self-absorbed musings about popular culture, high art, and American tourists in France. He presents himself as eternally modern, a figure who has escaped the freight of familial influences by apprehending his experiences only through their artistic potential. Here, to return to Edward Said and the opening terms of my argument, we find the modern vexations of filiation and affiliation: "My name is Raoul Duquette. I am twenty-six years old and a Parisian, a true Parisian. About my family—it really doesn't matter. I have no family; I don't want any. I never think about my childhood. I've forgotten it" (125–26). And as in all of the fiction we have considered, this story's vision of modern identity and modern artistry unfolds along an explicitly racialized axis. The single memory that Raoul describes from his otherwise opaque childhood, the racially charged incident involving his African laundress, discloses the inaugural moment of his adult literary and social personae.

The nonverbal physicality of this remembered incident initiates Raoul Duquette's journey into metropolitan modernity and artistic modernism:

In fact, there's only one memory that stands out at all. That is rather interesting because it seems to me now so very significant as regards myself from the literary point of view. It is this.

When I was about ten our laundress was an African woman, very big, very dark, with a check handkerchief over her frizzy hair. When she came to our house she always took particular notice of me, and after the clothes had been taken out of the basket she would lift me up into it and give me a rock while I held tight to the handles and screamed for joy and fright. I was tiny for my age, and pale, with a lovely little half-open mouth—I feel sure of that. (126)

On one hand, the hyperbolic racial contrast between the "very big, very dark" African laundress and the tiny, pale, open-mouthed Raoul draws on the most elementary and obvious tropes of primitivist discourse. A black woman rocks a young boy in a womblike basket, a merging of eros and terror that gives birth to Raoul's screams of "joy and fright." But at the same time, Mansfield parodies the very idea of primal, prelinguistic essence or experience. Raoul's last aside, "I feel sure of that," alerts the reader to the unreliability of memory. Avant-garde primitivism, as we have seen, depends on the evocation of transcendent meaning that cuts across the alienating institutions of twentieth-century society, but Raoul's aside challenges the possibility of such transcendence. This childhood incident embodies a characteristically modern tension between Raoul's desire to believe in himself as a unified, knowable subject and his contradictory desire to revel in contingency and artifice.

The African laundress's interest in Raoul eventually becomes sexualized and violent:

One day when I was standing at the door, watching her go, she turned round and beckoned to me, nodding and smiling in a strange secret way I never thought of not following. She took me into a little outhouse at the end of the passage, caught me up in her arms and began kissing me. Ah, those kisses! Especially those kisses inside my ears that nearly deafened me.

And then with a soft growl she tore open her bodice and put me to her. When she set me down she took from her pocket a little round fried cake covered with sugar, and I reeled along the passage back to our door. (126)

The "strange secret" language of the black woman's body derealizes an entire system of Western sexual and racial taboos. With the image of a white French child being kissed violently by a frizzy-haired African laundress in an outhouse, Mansfield renders porous the boundaries that would traditionally mandate the sexual separation of black from white, servant from employer, adult from child.[64] And by purchasing Raoul's affections (and, presumably, his silence) with a sweet fried cake, the laundress teaches him to exploit his sexuality and exchange it for other pleasures. Sex, unmoored from marital or procreative economies, becomes the coin that purchases delectations greater than itself.

This incident's flagrant disregard for racial and sexual propriety stands for modernism's broader stripping away of cultural and aesthetic traditions. The African laundress's sexual aggression creates the crucible in which Raoul Duquette's literary and social identities are forged:

> As this performance was repeated once a week it is no wonder that I remember it so vividly. Besides, from that very first afternoon, my childhood was, to put it prettily, "kissed away." I became very languid, very caressing, and greedy beyond measure. And so quickened, so sharpened, I seemed to understand everybody and to be able to do what I liked with everybody. (126)

Here are the encrypted origins of the modernist writer: shorn of his innocence and filled with insatiable desires, Raoul Duquette claims for himself a new mode of being. His artistic originality and fragmented subjectivity —avant-garde modernism's hallmark qualities—derive from repeating his "performance" with the African laundress who "tore open her bodice and put me to her." No unitary worldview dominates Raoul's narration or his movements through Paris; his art and his social persona have been liberated from all conventional expectations. The interracial encounters that end his childhood engender a matrix of power and knowledge that allows him to "understand everybody" and "do what [he] liked with everybody." Mansfield draws a straight line between the African woman's sexual desires and Raoul's artistry, employing the aggressive taboo violations of the former to catalyze the experimental freedom of the latter. Indeed, the profoundly enabling tie between the African laundress's breast and Raoul Duquette's authorial mastery harks back to the foundational avant-garde document with which I began this chapter, the 1909 "Founding and Manifesto of Futurism," in which Marinetti had identified "the sacred black breast of my Sudanese nurse" as a source of his propulsive new artistry.

The adult Raoul Duquette, a self-styled demimonde, transforms his encounters with the African laundress into coy metaphor to describe his modern urban existence:

> It's extraordinary how one can live without money. . . . I have quantities of good clothes, silk underwear, two evening suits, four pairs of patent leather boots with light uppers, all sorts of little things, like gloves and powder boxes and a manicure set, perfumes, very good soap, and nothing is paid for. If I

find myself in need of right-down cash—well, there's always an African laundress and an outhouse, and I am very frank and *bon enfant* about plenty of sugar on the little fried cake afterwards. . . . (127)

Living on credit and prostituting himself for the luxuries he adores, Raoul willingly creates his art from the economic and sexual peripheries of metropolitan Paris, the "ill-defined positions within the *bohème*," as Jameson phrases it. And by casting his partners or "clients" as African women, Raoul implies that his willingness to exploit himself sexually is always rewarded with the expanding social autonomy he has attributed to the laundress of his childhood.

Katherine Mansfield regarded the passages about the African laundress as essential to "Je Ne Parle Pas Français." In 1920, when Constable & Co. included the story in *Bliss and Other Stories,* Mansfield's editor Michael Sadleir insisted that she cut two lines describing the laundress: first, Raoul's remembrance "And with a soft growl she tore open her bodice and put me to her"; and second, Raoul's racialized metaphor for his prostitution, "If I find myself in need of right-down cash—well, there's always an African laundress and an outhouse, and I am very frank and *bon enfant* about plenty of sugar on the little fried cake afterwards."[65] John Middleton Murry agreed with Sadleir and urged Mansfield to make the changes because "I believe that it's bad policy to shock the people by whom, after all, you do desire to be read" (*Letters,* 302). But the author defended her work passionately, expressing what Angela Smith calls her "ownership of the form of her stories" (152):

> No, I certainly won't agree to those excisions if there were 500,000,000 copies in existence. They can keep their old £40 & be hanged to them. Shall I pick the eyes out of a story for £40!! I'm *furious* with Sadler [*sic*]—No, I'll never agree. I'll supply another story, but that is all. The *outline* would be blurred —It must have those sharp lines. (*Letters,* 303)[66]

Mansfield's conviction that to excise passages about the laundress would be to "pick the eyes out of a story" and blur its "sharp lines" affirms how crucially the frisson of racial difference provides experimental modernism with its very "eyes." Whether celebrating or lamenting the discontinuities of metropolitan modernity, modern artist-protagonists such as Raoul Duquette, who claims that the African laundress is "so very significant as regards myself from the literary point of view," repeatedly define themselves through their newly racialized artistic vision. "Je Ne Parle Pas Français"—like Dorian Gray's "new manner in art, the fresh mode of looking at life" (34), Marlow's despairing cry, "Do you see the story? Do you see anything?" (79),

Wyndham Lewis's commitment to "manufacturing fresh eyes" for a "new civilization" (*Rude Assignment,* 125) and John Dowell's repetitions of the phrase "you see"—crystallizes the centrality of race for what Mansfield calls the "*outline*" of modern narrative form.

Following his encounters with the laundress, Raoul Duquette's obsessive self-fashioning illustrates Katherine Mansfield's larger thesis that the inability to separate art from life renders impossible any teleological resolution for either. As Kate Fullbrook points out, Mansfield "conceived of self as multiple, shifting, non-consecutive, without essence, and perhaps unknowable. . . . The only protection for individuals, who are in constant danger of utter fragmentation, is the covering of a mask, a consciously wrought presentation of a coherent self that was of necessity artificial" (17). A passage from Mansfield's diaries provides a useful frame for understanding the "constant danger of utter fragmentation" in "Je Ne Parle Pas Français":

> True to oneself! which self? Which of my many—well really, that's what it looks like coming to—hundreds of selves? For what with complexes and repressions and reactions and vibrations and reflections, there are moments when I feel I am nothing but the small clerk of some hotel without a proprietor, who has all his work cut out to enter the names and hand the keys to the wilful guests. (*Journal* 1954, 205)

Mansfield channels the vision of herself as a hotel clerk into the character of Raoul Duquette, who likens himself to a customs official interrogating all the human "portmanteaux" he meets about the various "wines, spirits, cigars, perfumes, silks" (122) that represent the disunified elements of human subjectivity. But Raoul also defends the integrity of his identity as a "young, serious writer," which he has painstakingly assembled with the appropriate clothes, apartment, and lifestyle: "How can one look the part and not be the part? Or be the part and not look it? Isn't looking—being? Or being—looking?" (133). The self-doubt of Raoul's narrative voice reveals that celebrating the blurred boundary between art and life creates its own punishment. Despite Raoul's efforts to demonstrate his mastery over modern literature, his actual narration, like John Dowell's in *The Good Soldier,* is characterized most strongly by a *loss* of authorial control and self-confidence.

Raoul's various declarations of artistic purpose and authorial identity produce the two oppositional poles of his narrative: extreme narcissism and a theory of impersonal aesthetics. The tension between Raoul's worship of himself and his competing worship of art evokes a broader contradiction in modernist literature's development. Michael Levenson's *A Genealogy of Modernism: A Study of English Literary Doctrine, 1908–1922* points to the movement's "fitful oscillation between artist and art-work as the decisive value," arguing that

> insofar as [literary modernism] celebrates "pure form," then it appears to overturn anthropocentric values, to stake itself upon objective principles wholly distinct from human will, and to mark a break with a romantic aesthetic. But insofar as its basis remains the freedom of the artist and the absolute priority of personal vision, then it appears as only extreme romantic individualism. . . . If human values disappeared from the art, they simply reappeared in the aggressive and self-dramatizing artist. (135)

Raoul's inconsistent personal and aesthetic priorities embody precisely this conflict over the role of the modern artist. Raoul prides himself on a ruthless cultural objectivity that valorizes art and absolves him of moral obligation; at the same time, however, he is made vulnerable by a desperate need to affirm his own importance. Raoul's characteristically modernist "fitful oscillation" derives directly from the African laundress, whose wordless sexual advances produce his linguistically and ideologically slippery narrative: the racial violence that begets modernism, in other words, refuses fixed or stable meaning. Raoul's awareness of cultural artifice and contingency prevents him from achieving the authorial security he so nakedly desires. His representations of sex, race, nation, and art necessarily collapse against each other as a series of arbitrary, unstable, and eventually meaningless categories.

Although the African laundress never reappears in the story, her "very big, very dark" presence haunts Raoul's depiction of women who surround him. The antiwoman sentiments that pervade Raoul's narrative conjoin femininity and darkness; his prose abounds with light-dark metaphors and visual images that trivialize or scorn modern femininity. Thus, the contemptible "thin, dark girls" who frequent his café are escorted by workmen "powdered over with white flour" (122); a photograph of Dick Harmon's "dark, handsome, wild-looking" (131) mother terrifies Raoul; and eventually, the Englishwoman Mouse recedes into a "dark shadow" moving in the whiteness of Paris's "feathery snow" (125). The women whom Raoul represents as dark and despicable signify a larger urban cultural degeneration or decay; modern life itself is an "old hag," an "old bitch," and a "rag-picker on the American cinema, shuffling along wrapped in a filthy shawl with her old claws crooked over a stick" (123). Raoul's description of life as a corrupt(ing) woman with "old claws" resonates with misogynistic phrases in male modernist poetry, suggesting Eliot's "ragged claws" in "The Love Song of J. Alfred Prufrock" and Pound's view of civilization as an "old bitch gone in the teeth" in his 1920 poem "Hugh Selwyn Mauberley."[67]

Although Raoul regards himself as a male artist struggling to create art in a degenerate, feminine cultural moment, he nevertheless aggressively cultivates his own androgyny, a sexualized posture that promises to be artistically productive. As a dandy—an archetypically modern figure who values artifice and surface rather than authenticity and essence—Raoul insinuates himself into the unsuspected corners and vantage points of bohemian Paris, reveling in the endless possibility of reinventing himself and the culture around him.[68] But when Raoul admits Dick Harmon and Mouse into his free-floating, decadent modern existence, he becomes a victim of his own masquerade, caught in a desire for an authentic, knowable self.

Raoul's relationship with Dick intensifies both his insecurity about authorial identity and his pleasure in cultural iconoclasm. The fashionable literary party where he first meets Dick, like his overly stylized private life, exemplifies modernism's reflexive relationship to its own historical moment. Mansfield's tiny, delightful details parody the avant-garde world whose very emergence the story addresses; surrounded by poetesses in "full evening dress" who pose on "cubist sofas" drinking "thimbles of cherry brandy," Raoul tries to impress Dick by playing the role of a "young, serious writer who was making a special study of modern English literature" (129). Initially, Dick represents an ideal audience for Raoul, a willing initiate into the Parisian sexual and artistic underworlds that Raoul knows intimately, and a confessor for Raoul's "submerged life" (130). The Englishman becomes a second self who participates in Raoul's unfettered movements through the high and low spheres of Paris: "I took Dick about with me everywhere" (130), Raoul boasts, inventing himself variously as a "little perfumed fox-terrier of a Frenchman" (131), a "paid guide to the night pleasures of Paris" (132), and a "clown" (137). The allure of this friendship lies in the possibility of transforming the Englishman into a literary character; as Raoul relates the story of the friendship from his Paris café, he orders a whiskey because he is "going to write about an Englishman" (128) and remarks that he would be well served by "a pair of tweed knickerbockers, a pipe, some long teeth and a set of ginger whiskers." Nation, like sexuality, becomes a costume and a condition that Raoul tries to adopt at will, and the act of stepping into Dick Harmon's Englishness promises to affirm the cultural elasticity that Raoul imagines as his most valuable artistic asset.

However, Raoul's pleasures in this elasticity do not counteract his need to be recognized as a knowable, unified subject. Dick's sudden departure to England forces Raoul's outburst, "'I am a young writer, very serious, and extremely interested in modern English literature. And I have been insulted—insulted'" (132). On receiving a letter from Dick announcing his return to Paris, Raoul imagines himself as the Englishman's racial Other as well as his sexual subordinate:

> I read it standing in front of the (unpaid for) wardrobe mirror. It was early morning. I wore a blue kimono embroidered with white birds and my hair was still wet; it lay on my forehead, wet and gleaming.
> "Portrait of Madame Butterfly," said I, "on hearing of the arrival of *ce cher Pinkerton*." (132)

The Oriental image of Madame Butterfly provides a convergence point for Raoul's androgyny, artistry, and self-fashioning; the dandy cross-dresses culturally as well as sexually in this scene. Kimono-clad and adopting the pose of Puccini's fifteen-year-old tragic Japanese heroine, Raoul invites the reader to see him as a powerless, exotic, and feminine martyr to the infidelities of a foreign man.

When Dick returns to Paris with Mouse, Raoul self-consciously fictionalizes each moment with the couple, imagining himself as a dramaturg, auteur, Wildean aesthete, and dandy through whom modernity and urban sophistication will be conveyed in breathtaking prose. Offering his knowledge of Paris to Mouse just as he had earlier offered it to Dick, he also extends his project of capturing the English temperament, reducing Mouse to a series of gestures that express her national origins. Mouse shakes hands "in that strange boyish way Englishwomen do" (135); she inhabits silences that are "too difficult, too English" (136) for Raoul to endure; she wears a cloak that reminds Raoul of "pictures of Englishwomen abroad" (136); and she orders tea with "exactly the gesture and cry" that Raoul associates with "an Englishwoman faced with a great crisis" (138). Reading Mouse as a metonym of Englishness allows Raoul to pretend that she is opaque, devoid of interiority, and therefore unable to force him into a social rather than an artistic contract. Further, Raoul invokes the language of formalism to describe and defamiliarize the purity of Mouse's beauty. As in his descriptions of other women characters, the opposition of dark and light undergirds his aesthetic commentary, so that "white circles of lamplight" (136) show us Mouse's "lovely little face more like a drawing than a real face—every line was so full of meaning and so sharp cut against the swimming dark." And to contain Mouse as a character in an art world of his own creation, Raoul revives his Madame Butterfly metaphor and imbues Mouse with the exoticism and potential victimhood he earlier claimed for himself:

> She was exquisite, but so fragile and fine that each time I looked at her it was as if for the first time. She came upon you with the same kind of shock that you feel when you have been drinking tea out of a thin innocent cup and suddenly, at the bottom, you see a tiny creature, half butterfly, half woman, bowing to you with her hands in her sleeves. (136)

For Raoul, to look at Mouse is to see her repeatedly "as if for the first time" and to experience the "shock" of newness so prized by the avant-garde. Dehumanized in name and Orientalized in Raoul's metaphor, Mouse falls victim to an aesthetics of impersonality that literally refuses to acknowledge her personhood. And Raoul's pleasure in this image of a bowing, silent, and captive Mouse affirms Michael Levenson's theory that when "human values disappeared from the art, they simply reappeared in the aggressive and self-dramatizing artist" (135).

When Dick abandons Mouse in Paris, Raoul strikes a tragicomic narrative tone in order to distance himself from the couple. However, as in all his previous social transactions, Raoul finds himself trapped in the characteristic modernist "fitful oscillation" between participating in the events around him and sustaining the aesthete's detachment. On learning that Mouse is trapped in Paris—she cannot return to England because she has falsely led her friends to believe that she has married Dick—Raoul offers himself to Mouse in order to secure his continuing hold over her, replicating the childhood exchange of his body for the African laundress's fried cakes:

> "Do feel that I am your friend," I cried. "You will let me come tomorrow, early? You will let me look after you a little—take care of you a little? You'll use me just as you think fit?"
> I succeeded. She came out of her hole . . . timid . . . but she came out.
> "Yes, you're very kind. Yes. Do come to-morrow. I shall be glad. It makes things rather difficult because"—and again I clasped her boyish hand—"*je ne parle pas français.*" (143)

Desperate to prove his earlier claim that he can "understand everybody" and "do what [he] liked with everybody," Raoul justifies his callous treatment of Mouse in the name of securing his identity as a maker of modernism. Even though he "started out—got to the door—wrote and tore up letters—did all those things" (144), he never goes near Mouse's hotel again.

By the story's end, the cultural liberation and iconoclasm instilled by the African laundress become their own prison. The racial oppositions, sexual perversion, and textual indecision that have characterized Raoul's modernism continue to shape the story's concluding vignettes, but they yield alienation and paralysis rather than self-knowledge and agency. Trying to alleviate his guilt at abandoning Mouse, Raoul invents a series of possible erotic outcomes to their truncated relationship. He imagines a romantic beach fantasy where Mouse, clad exotically "in a frock rather like Red Indian women wear" (144), eats fresh fish and wild strawberries; and the natural innocence of this boy-girl fantasy momentarily betrays Raoul's desire for distance from the urban world that his narrative otherwise celebrates. But this childlike dream rapidly degenerates into the corruption of metropolitan sexual culture, where innocence itself is commodified and assigned an exchange value. Raoul imagines himself pimping Mouse to an old man in a café: "'But I've got the little girl for you, *mon vieux*. So little . . . so tiny. And a virgin.' I kiss the tips of my fingers—"A virgin"—and lay them upon my heart. 'I give you my word of honour as a gentleman, a writer, serious, young, and extremely interested in modern English literature'" (144). And, finally, Raoul has a two-line exchange with the owner of the café where he has been telling his story:

> Madame knows me. "You haven't dined yet?" she smiles.
> "No, not yet, Madame." (144)

Raoul's final "not yet"—a phrase that would be made famous by the close of E. M. Forster's 1924 novel *A Passage to India*—epitomizes the nomadic, peripatetic condition of the androgynous avant-garde aesthete. The ambiguous endings of several of Katherine Mansfield's stories—most notably, "Bliss," "Prelude," and "The Garden Party"—point to the author's refusal to allow fictional resolution or closure within cultural circumstances that themselves deny material or lived closure. In "Je Ne Parle Pas Français," Mansfield sharpens the edges of this narrative ambiguity, turning modernist self-referentiality into an inescapable psychic condition. Raoul Duquette gives us no hints about the direction of his art or his life. His desperate attempt to convince us that he is a "young, serious writer" must inevitably fail; his pleasure in cultural, racial, and sexual contingencies leave him as lost in the modern metropolis as Mouse. The journey that started with Raoul rocking in the African laundress's basket ends, fittingly, with a metaphorical "rocking": the aimless movements of a modern author whose art delivers him neither into self-knowledge nor cultural visibility.

3

ORIENTING VIRGINIA WOOLF

When 24-year-old Virginia Woolf[1] visited Constantinople in 1906, her daily journal became a vivid travelogue where she recorded her mixed, conflicting impressions of the city and its citizens. Although most of her Constantinople writings bear the trademark spiritedness of her diaries, occasional passages betray a marked uneasiness about the divisions between East and West. Watching the sun set over Constantinople, the young writer muses that

> you also realised that life was not lived after the European pattern, that it was not even a debased copy of Paris or Berlin or London, & that, you thought was the ambition of towns which could not actually be Paris or any of those inner capitals. As the lights came out in clusters all over the land, & the water was busy with lamps, you knew yourself to be the spectator of a vigorous drama, acting itself out with no thought or need of certain great countries yonder to the west. And in all this opulence there was something ominous, & something ignominious—for an English lady at her bedroom window. (*Passionate Apprentice*, 348)

Europe's global sovereignty recedes before the spectacle of this self-sufficient Constantinople, and Woolf despairs that "when we come to consider the question of the West & the East,—then indeed—we lay down the pen, & write no more" (352). Although her pen remained mute on this issue during the balance of her stay in Turkey, it regained its voice in the mature novels she wrote twenty years later. The "question of the West & the East" pervades many of Virginia Woolf's major works, transforming Englishness and modernity into sites defined by racial difference, imperialism, and Orientalism.

In this chapter, I argue that some of Virginia Woolf's most radical literary innovations arise from a material and a formalist politics of race. I begin with Woolf's Constantinople journals because they forge an early link between cultural identities and artistic representation, calling attention to the lines separating self from other. Years after her visit to Constantinople, Woolf's kaleidoscopic representations of selves and others formed the crowning achievement of her experiments with narrative. Her main aesthetic projects—developing a technique of free indirect discourse, rewriting patriarchal literary forms, pioneering new representations of time and space, and creating psychological realism—share a common goal: to draw (and redraw) human relationships by lifting the veils that divide people from one another. To alter the very idea of literary reality, Woolf devised what Alex Zwerdling has called "a seamless fictional language" (25), which describes the sometimes fluid, sometimes disjunctive condition of modern English selves and their numerous others. This chapter argues that Woolf's "seamless" language—its revelations and subversions—is shaped by a rhetoric of race and racial difference.

Certainly, Woolf's interests in the concept of race are nowhere as explicit or well developed as her interests in gender, war, class, or education. There are no racially focused tracts equivalent to *A Room of One's Own* (1929) or *Three Guineas* (1938), nor are there novels devoted to exploring race and its social construction. And yet, ideas about race shape Woolf's writing across many genres: her letters, journals, essays, and fiction allude frequently to racial difference, flirt with cultural crossovers, and draw on images of the racially marked exotic and primitive. Indeed, one of Woolf's foundational theories of the modern novel borrows from Turkish culture: in *A Room of One's Own*, Woolf declares that the novel should be "a structure leaving a shape on the mind's eye, built now in squares, now pagoda shaped, now throwing out wings and arcades, now solidly compact and domed like the Cathedral of Saint Sofia at Constantinople" (71). Like the church-turned-mosque that embodies Woolf's vision of the English novel, a collection of complex, hybrid racial identities enables the investigation of Englishness in her novels themselves.[2] In Woolf's fiction, race locates itself at the nexus of several key modernist discourses, and questions about racial difference accompany Woolf's celebrated challenges to patriarchy, literary tradition, and British imperialism.

My argument concentrates on *To the Lighthouse* (1927) and *Orlando* (1928), two experimental novels whose feminist commitments depend on contradictory and often overlooked racial politics. In *To the Lighthouse,* Woolf's elegiac novel about an English family and the brutal end of Victorianism, race provides a provocative source of feminist artistic inspiration. While *To the Lighthouse* critiques imperial Britain's master narratives, it also transforms Oriental perspectives—encoded in Lily Briscoe's "little Chinese eyes"—into arbiters of meaning in a barren, postwar world. To work against patriarchy's social and novelistic conventions, *To the Lighthouse* extends the English formalist doctrines that lauded autotelic art forms from East Asia, Africa, North America, and South America. The novel's narrative fluidity and abstraction reinvent the racial philosophies of Roger Fry's formalist tract *Vision and Design* (1920), as well as the racially marked *modernité* of art objects from Fry's Omega Workshops. As Woolf overwrites the Victorian marriage plot and the conventions of nineteenth-century literary realism, she attributes Lily Briscoe's triumphant modern "vision" to an aesthetic sensibility determined by race.

Written on the heels of *To the Lighthouse, Orlando* offers an exuberant resistance to narrative conventions that makes it a fitting text for the end of this study. *Orlando*'s stylistic looseness—its mix of biographical and novelistic form, its disregard for the constraints of time, its magical sexual conversion—ultimately reinforces very conventional ideologies about race and British imperialism. I read this work in dialogue with Vita Sackville-West's travelogue *Passenger to Teheran* (1926), revealing that *Orlando*'s jubilant challenges to genre and gender depend on the uncritical Anglocentrism of imperial travel writing. Where sexuality is reinvented and made wonderfully ambiguous in this text, Englishness and whiteness begin and end as fixed categories. Certainly as *Orlando* romps through four centuries of English history, the narrative registers a polyvalent understanding of culture and civilization: Orlando travels to Constantinople as a man, lives with Turkish peasants as a woman, and continually voices doubts about the value of aristocratic English heritage. But ultimately, Woolf recentralizes an imperial British worldview, and the novel's playful satires and chronological games do not destabilize the myth of an originary, unified, and all-powerful white England. Woolf resolves her buoyant remaking of history, biography, authorship, and sexuality by enshrining the very imperialist legacy whose foundations she has endeavored to shift: *Orlando* ends with the title character married to an imperial adventurer and returning to the ancestral estate where "nothing has been changed" (328).

Reading Woolf, Reading Race

Jane Marcus's 1992 essay "Britannia Rules *The Waves*," which argues that Woolf ironizes the imperial West's culture making in subject nations, opened the doors for a host of postcolonial readings of Woolf's work. Seizing on the imperialist current running through Woolf's writing, critics have since firmly established her place in literary dialogues traditionally dominated by Kipling, Conrad, and Forster. Postcolonial readings, of course, have added a crucial dimension to Woolf criticism. They historicize Woolf's portrayals of imperialist anxiety; they highlight imperialism's seminal role in *A Room of One's Own* and *Three Guineas*, texts traditionally associated with Woolf's gender battles; and they accord significance to previously neglected imperialist encounters and tropes in Woolf's fiction. Overwhelmingly, the body of criticism addressing Woolf's colonial politics casts her as an opponent of the British Empire, a dissenting voice exposing the far-flung consequences of imperialist praxis.[3] However, postcolonial readings of Woolf often assume a perfect symmetry between imperial power structures and patriarchal power structures. When Jane Marcus claims that imperialism abroad and class exploitation within England "fused in Woolf's imagination with her own revolt as a feminist" (149), she compresses issues of empire, class, and gender into the same critical paradigm. This compression, as scholars such as Laura Doyle and Mark Wollaeger have noted, oversimplifies the cultural dialogues in Woolf's fiction, implying that Woolf's representations of power remain identical across sociopolitical categories or discourses.[4] In yoking Woolf's feminism to her anti-imperialism, several critics have similarly reduced Woolf's novels to static political tracts and subordinated their aesthetic complexity to a falsely unified ideological stance.[5]

Discussions of race in Woolf's writings tend to be confined to the domain of British imperialism. But while Woolf's objections to British imperialism are widely known, I find that her critique of the empire is self-reflexive, focused on imperialism's damage to *England* rather than its effects on subject nations. It is crucial to note that Woolf's anti-imperialism rarely manifests itself through claims about racial or cultural equality, and, further, that opposition to empire forms only one of several racially based strands in her work. Woolf's wide, often contradictory depictions of nonwhite characters and non-Western cultures produce an ideological and aesthetic complexity that closed discussions of colonial politics cannot fully register. Her experimental novels often reproduce imperial-era assumptions about racial difference, but they also reinvent racial tropes in their reinvention of literary form. Virginia Woolf's invocations of the exotic, the primitive, and the Oriental are frequently disconnected from colonial practice, and I propose an interpretive axis that accommodates the full range of racial consciousness in Woolf's writings. Race frequently marks what is most explicitly "modern" in Woolf's novels, furnishing a provocative site for exploring the conditions of modernity as well as for furthering experimental literary technique. And rather than suggesting that Woolf is "racist" or that her anti-imperialism is false, I demonstrate the ways in which Woolf draws on race to bridge her political interests and her aesthetic goals.

A tour of Woolf's oeuvre reveals the breadth of her literary conceptualizations of race. For example, Woolf's motley cast of racially distinct characters includes polluted, anonymous Indians in *The Waves,* confident Turkish Gypsies in *Orlando,* and Peter Walsh's "dark, adorably pretty" (153) Anglo-Indian lover, Daisy, in *Mrs. Dalloway;* we also find minor, enigmatic characters like the "very fine Negress" (50) of *A Room of One's Own,* and Ellen, "the discreet black maid" (209) in *The Years* (1937). Lily Briscoe, although white and English, has "little Chinese eyes"—a crucial point to which I will return—and Elizabeth Dalloway, similarly, has "Chinese eyes in a pale face; an Oriental mystery" (120). Louis in *The Waves* is also white, but hails from Australia and therefore offers a marked racial contrast with the novel's five English characters; Miss LaTrobe in *Between the Acts* (1941) "worked like a nigger" (150) to produce her pageant play and seems "foreign" to the English characters who receive her dramatization of English history skeptically. Geographical spaces outside of Britain are as diverse as the characters inhabiting them: while the South America of *The Voyage Out* (1915) and the India of *The Waves* evoke timeless, eternal netherworlds, Woolf pinpoints specific historic moments with *Orlando*'s seventeenth-century Constantinople, *Mrs. Dalloway*'s colonial India in the 1920s, and the Africa of the mid-1930s in *The Years.* (Edward Pargiter in *The Years* also speculates anxiously about the future racial homogeneity of a fascist-ruled England, where "herds, groups, societies caparisoned" would resemble "one jelly, one mass, would be a rice pudding world, a white counterpane world" [410].) Finally, Woolf's novels burst with the spoils of colonialism (Afghan hounds, jewels from India, books on African game hunting, poisoned assegais) as well as the art objects of non-Western cultures (Egyptian pitchers, Turkish hookahs, Persian rugs, Chinese silks, Japanese plates).

It is helpful to examine how Woolf's engagement with specific political and artistic discourses contributed to the racial poetics and politics of her experimental fiction. Although Woolf's personal relationships have been exhaustively documented and commented on, I map a few of them here to establish that they encouraged her to interrogate cultural, national, and racial differences. Indeed, Virginia Woolf's exposure to conceptions of race was as wide ranging as the cultural shifts between her Victorian-era birth in 1882 and her death in the war-torn England of 1941. The core of the anti-imperialism that emerges so strongly in Woolf's 1938 polemic *Three Guineas* was a reaction against a family legacy of patriarchal nationalism and imperial administration. While Woolf's great-grandfather James Stephen (1758–1832) was an abolitionist in the West Indies, her grandfather Sir James Stephen (1789–1859) was a founding figure of Queen Victoria's empire. Sir James, who served as counsel to the Colonial Board of Trade, was dubbed "Mister Mother-Country" for his zealous devotion to the ideals and bureaucracy of the burgeoning British Empire at midcentury. His son, Woolf's father Leslie Stephen (1832–1904), immortalized England's nation builders in his *Dictionary of National Biography*. Allegiance to England's colonizing and civilizing mission carried over into Woolf's own generation, most notably in Dorothea Stephen (1871–1965), Woolf's first cousin. Dorothea worked as a Christian missionary in India and published a volume called *Studies in Early Indian Thought* (1918), and her commitment to conversion drove Woolf to comment that "tampering with beliefs seems to me impertinent, insolent, corrupt beyond measure" (*Letters IV*, 333). The Stephen family's long-standing complicity with colonialism compelled Woolf's private and public resistance to what she saw as the inevitably oppressive results of overseas conquest.

Leslie Stephen's death in 1904 prompted Woolf and her siblings Vanessa, Thoby, and Adrian to move to 46 Gordon Square in London's then-unfashionable Bloomsbury district, a physical relocation that corresponded to a realignment of Woolf's ideological compass. If "the Bloomsbury group" serves as shorthand for the assertive modernity of Woolf's new life, we should recognize that the group's disruption of Victorian social and sexual propriety frequently expressed itself in racial terms. In Thoby Stephen's famous Thursday-night "at homes" with his Cambridge friends, matters of racial and cultural difference began to shift away from the context of imperialism, and Woolf stood at the center of the racial crossovers and conflicts that frequently characterized Bloomsbury's political and artistic dialogues. She kept company with E. M. Forster and Maynard Keynes, influential figures in Britain's national and international colonial politics; with the noted Sinologist Arthur Waley; and with the neopagan artist Augustus John, who was known for his paintings of Romani Gypsies.[6] In the late 1920s and 1930s, she would meet the Indian writer Mulk Raj Anand, befriend the Argentine critic and publisher Victoria Ocampo, and correspond with the Chinese artist Ling Shuhua.[7] Woolf also brushed up against London's Oriental fashion craze through her friendship with the flamboyant hostess Lady Ottoline Morrell. In Lady Ottoline's company, Woolf not only attended salons where guests regularly wore East Asian garb, but she herself appeared at a fancy-dress party costumed as Cleopatra.[8] Racial alterity, freed from its dominant association with colonized subjects, became in Woolf's world—as it was becoming for the English avant-garde—a gateway into disruptive or subversive cultural possibilities. Woolf crossed geographical and intellectual boundaries alike in her new life, sojourning to Portugal, Spain, Turkey, and Greece during the same years that she began to assert her presence in London as a literary critic, social activist, and independent thinker. Her Constantinople journals, as we have already seen, bear witness to her deepening interests in the world outside of the modern West.

Woolf's engagement with conceptions of race was not confined to abstract discussion and comfortable travel. Her roles in two Bloomsbury incidents, the *Dreadnought* hoax of 1910 and the Post-Impressionist Ball of 1911, signal an active investment in racial difference and its possibilities for subverting English cultural authority. Woolf's brother Adrian Stephen initiated the *Dreadnought* hoax, eager to penetrate naval security and gain access to the enormous new ship, the H. M. S. *Dreadnought*. Dressed as the Abyssinian emperor and his entourage, Adrian, Virginia, and a group of friends approached navy officials and demanded a formal tour of the ship. Virginia wore "a false beard and moustache and a wig and a turban and flowing robes" and struggled to maintain an "Oriental stolidity of countenance" ("Interview," 168) during the caper, which was designed to insult governmental authority and institutional bureaucracy. Despite their intentions to undermine the British Empire's officialdom, however, the perpetrators of the hoax cheerfully and unselfconsciously adopted that empire's racist postures. Hermione Lee's description of the hoax captures these postures vividly:

> All the Abyssinians wore what would be described as "the most complete sets of nigger lips." On the train from Paddington to Weymouth, they practised their Swahili, which seemed the nearest thing to Abyssinian, from a grammar for the Society for the Propagation of the Gospel. . . . Admiral May and the Stephens' cousin, Commander William Fisher, showed them all round the

ship (the interpreter improvising in a mixture of broken Virgil, the Abyssinians responding with "Bunga-Bunga" and—this was Virginia—"Chuck-a-choi, chuck-a-choi"), offered refreshment which was declined on religious grounds, turned down the request for a 21-gun salute, and escorted the party back to shore. (*VW,* 279)

As Adrian Stephen had planned, juxtaposing incongruous cultural elements fooled the *Dreadnought*'s officials and revealed the navy's ignorance of the nations it dominated. But the success of the *Dreadnought* hoax also came from the participants' willingness to appear in blackface, to cobble together an Abyssinian "dialect" by mixing Latin and nonsense phrases with Swahili from a missionary guide, and to pretend allegiance to Islamic dietary practices.[9] (When the real Abyssinian emperor came to London soon after the hoax, Woolf recalled that "He complained that wherever he went in the streets boys ran after him calling out Bunga Bunga" ["*Dreadnought* Notes," 167]). The Bloomsburyites' antimilitarism reveals an ironic complicity with the very imperial violence the hoax intended to deride; and Woolf's participation in the incident anticipates the complex, racialized challenges to British hegemony that crowd her mature fiction.

In the year following the *Dreadnought* hoax, Roger Fry's exhibit "Manet and the Post-Impressionists" enabled Woolf to participate in a second, smaller act of racially charged social subversion. Traditionally, Woolf's response to Fry's exhibit is read in tandem with her dictum in her 1924 essay, "Mr. Bennett and Mrs. Brown" that "in or about December, 1910, human character changed" (194).[10] But well before Woolf invoked the exhibit for her manifesto about modern fiction, she used the racial politics of postimpressionism to achieve a minor sexual and social liberation for herself. The exhibit itself, with its works by Gaugin, Cézanne, Matisse, Picasso, Manet, and van Gogh, shocked London's museum-going public; art critics lambasted Fry for his choice of artists and subject matter. The poster advertising the exhibit—which Marianna Torgovnick hails as the "English debut of the primitive in high culture" (85)—featured a Gaugin painting of a nude "native" woman standing next to a Tahitian statue. Both the form and the content of the exhibit's works scandalized the public: the nakedness of nonwhite peoples presented through postimpressionism's nonmimetic contours shattered the English art world's assumptions about aesthetic civility.[11] Gleefully aware that the exhibit's focus on non-Western subjects appalled London audiences, Woolf and her sister Vanessa Bell attended the Post-Impressionist Ball in March 1911 dressed as savages "a la Gaugin" (Bishop, 22). Vanessa recalls that "we wore brilliant flowers and beads, we browned our legs and arms and had very little on beneath the draperies" (Lee, *VW*, 287), and Virginia writes, "Vanessa and I were practically naked" (*MOB*, 201). The spectacle of the "bare-shouldered bare-legged" sisters at the ball outraged "indignant ladies who swept out in protest" (Bell, *Vol. 1*, 170). Wearing "dresses of the printed cotton that is specially loved by negroes" (*MOB*, 200), Virginia and Vanessa rejected Victorian modesty in the same way the postimpressionist paintings rejected artistic conventions; and like the *Dreadnought* hoax, Woolf's cross-cultural masquerade at the Post-Impressionist Ball affirms an early interest in reordering the boundaries of Englishness through tropes of racial difference.

The 1910 postimpressionist exhibit marked the beginning of Woolf's engagement with the intersection of racial difference and the fine arts in London. The famously expansive circle of artists and writers in Bloomsbury connected Woolf to creative milieux where she encountered modernist aesthetic experimentation based on the forms of Asian and African arts. Between 1911 and 1918, several members of the Bloomsbury group attended performances by Sergei Diaghilev's fantastically eclectic Ballets Russes, who captivated Covent Garden audiences with performances that merged Western classicism with polyglot global traditions. Spectacles like Rimsky-Korsakov's *Schéhérazade,* Borodin's *Prince Igor,* and Stravinsky's *The Firebird* were lavish in their depictions of Persia, Egypt, and Arabia; under Diaghilev's direction, the Ballets Russes introduced English balletomanes to an exaggeratedly brilliant Oriental sensibility. Fascination with Diaghilev's elaborate aesthetics of Otherness propelled the Bloomsbury response to the Ballets Russes, whether intellectual, artistic, or personal.[12] Woolf attended Diaghilev's *Schéhérazade* in 1918, and despite her sense of the piece's foreignness ("We saw our ballet—Sche—I can't achieve either the spelling or the speaking of it" [*Diary I*, 201]), she was an attentive patron of a dance empire built on the merging of non-Western mythologies and narratives with classical Western technique.

In the same years that Diaghilev's ballets were the rage in London, Woolf began her loyal patronage of Roger Fry's numerous artistic ventures, most of which advocated cross-cultural aesthetic dialogues. As this chapter goes on to demonstrate, Roger Fry's formalist doctrines about mixing non-Western art with Western traditions would acquire a feminist dimension in the racially inflected narrative experimentation of *To the Lighthouse*. Woolf visited the exhibits Fry sponsored, attended his lectures on art history, and, of course, bought art objects from the short-lived Omega Workshops, whose pottery, textiles, furnishings, paintings, and sculptures bore traces of Asian,

African, and Native American influences. In 1920, one year after the Omega Workshops closed, Woolf attended a show of African carvings that Fry had organized at the Chelsea Book Club. The "obscene" sculptures at the "Niggers' show" (*Diary* II, 30), as Woolf called it, suggested to her that "something in their style might be written" (*Congenial Spirits*, 119). In this cultural moment, when, as we have seen, various factions of the London avant-garde were absorbed with expressing a new kind of English artistry through racial difference, Woolf similarly looked to the art objects of non-Western cultures for her varied renewals of the English novel.

Virginia Stephen made her most explicit move away from her family's Victorianism by marrying Leonard Woolf, a Jewish ex–colonial administrator, in 1912. A Jewish man living in England and an Englishman ruling the Ceylonese, Leonard Woolf returned to England after seven years of civil service in Ceylon and became a vocal socialist and opponent of the empire. His acute awareness of the complex vicissitudes of racial and ethnic identity surfaced in his early novel, *The Village in the Jungle* (1913), which, like his short fictions in *Stories from the East* (1921), illustrates a keen sensitivity to the internal conflicts of a Sri Lankan community. Leonard's better-known anti-imperialist works, like *Empire and Commerce in Africa* (1920), *Imperialism and Civilization* (1928), and *Barbarians at the Gate* (1939), present polemical arguments against England's economic, political, and religious dominance in other nations.[13] And although Virginia's marriage to Leonard gave rise to occasional expressions of anti-Semitism, the Woolfs were publicly united in their fierce opposition to the tyrannies and terrors of fascism in Europe.[14]

Founding the Hogarth Press in 1917 enabled the Woolfs to publish their own fiction and political writings and, further, to give voice to many contemporary authors writing on race, imperialism, and civil rights.[15] One of these authors was Vita Sackville-West, whose intimacy with Woolf is usually understood in a lesbian-feminist context. But Woolf's relationship with Sackville-West was also animated by lively debates about the politics of cultural identity. Vita's marriage to the English diplomat Harold Nicolson took her to central Asia and the Far East in 1926, and her correspondence with Woolf provided a forum for both writers to explore questions of race and nation, belonging and exile. The Hogarth Press published Vita Sackville-West's fiction, poetry, and travel writings; Woolf herself oversaw the publication of *Seducers in Ecuador* (1924) and *Passenger to Teheran* (1926), in which, as we will see, Sackville-West created a complex literary geography that simultaneously contests and affirms imperialist values. It becomes evident, therefore, that Virginia Woolf's personal relationships, like her active presence within early twentieth-century London's artistic and intellectual circles, generated wide-ranging dialogues about Englishness and racial difference. These varied dialogues resonate through *To the Lighthouse* and *Orlando,* where Woolf's treatment of race—literal and metaphorical, historical and ahistorical—lies at the heart of her artistic experiments and political subversions.

Lily Briscoe's Chinese Eyes

To the Lighthouse is Virginia Woolf's most private and domestic novel, set in a seaside house on the Isle of Skye. Of Woolf's major novels, *To the Lighthouse* is the least explicitly "about" race or empire. Whereas characters in *Mrs. Dalloway* travel to and from India, characters in *The Waves, The Years,* and *Between the Acts* serve as imperial administrators, and characters in *Orlando* participate in four centuries of the British Empire's burgeoning overseas conquests, the cast of *To the Lighthouse* moves within the secluded sphere of the Ramsay household. Government, empire, and war flicker on the novel's peripheries, subordinated to the details and politics of family life. But the nearly invisible racial paradigms in *To the Lighthouse* serve as the sites where Woolf remakes the English self. Woolf's deployment of racial alterity in this novel enables her to envision the "life of Monday or Tuesday" in terms other than those dictated by masculine privilege, and her feminist recuperation of narrative development overturns English patriarchy's worldview with discourses and tropes from non-English cultures. The historical, aesthetic, and imperial discourses running through *To the Lighthouse* meet at the site of racial difference, producing an extraordinary balance among three apparently contradictory ideological positions: this novel opposes imperialism, insists on racial hierarchies, *and* valorizes nonwhite otherness.

Each of the novel's three sections questions the stability of English identities rooted in the ideals of a racially exploitative empire. The first section, "The Window," troubles the Ramsay family's relationship to the British Empire through equal measure of nostalgia and critique; while the Ramsay house itself metonymically suggests the material and ideological goals of imperial enterprise, the members of the Ramsay family variously comply with and repudiate the empire's values. In the novel's second and shortest section, "Time Passes," the apocalyptic devastation that describes the Great War also suggests that British imperial identity is fundamentally hollow, prey to the same forces that supposedly protect it. And finally, in "The Lighthouse," Lily Briscoe supplies a new ending to an imperial English life-narrative, discovering an artistry that safeguards her from the fragmented remains of prewar tranquility. Paradoxically, Woolf secures a new English feminism by attributing non-Western characteristics and perspectives to Lily, whose "little Chinese eyes" exclude her socially *and* elevate her artistically. To break away from nineteenth-century literary mimesis, *To the Lighthouse* incorporates imperialist discourses about race as well as the racialized discourse of English formalism: Woolf's depiction of Lily Briscoe as a modern feminist rests on a connection between essentializing, Orientalist attitudes and the visual arts.

Despite continually shifting centers of consciousness, imperialism, like the lighthouse beam, remains a fixed, steady presence throughout the novel's first section, "The Window." The unremarkable events of a single day—taking a walk, going shopping, hosting a dinner party—allow Woolf to present competing angles on colonialist and racist exploitation. The Ramsay household, filled with artifacts of imperialist exploitation, emblematizes the transformation of peoples and cultures into commodities for English consumption. These commodities—a book about "the Savage Customs of Polynesia" (27), Mrs. Ramsay's "opal necklace, which Uncle James had brought her from India" (80–1), and the "horrid skull" (114) sent to the family as a hunting trophy—serve as mute reminders of colonized nations whose resources have been plundered. Mr. Ramsay, the patriarch who presides over these commodities, possesses a colonizing, linear intelligence that assimilates the world in terms of power and struggle, hierarchy and history: "Does the progress of civilisation depend upon great men? Is the lot of the average human being better now than in the time of the Pharaohs? . . . Possibly the greatest good requires the existence of a slave class" (42–43). The Ramsay house and the patriarch at its helm buttress Victorian imperialism, providing the economic and ideological motivation for expanding England's global control. But empire's solid material presence in the Ramsays' quotidian routine is only applauded by male characters. Woolf's female characters hint at England's fading allegiance to imperialist principles, mocking narratives of colonial life and the Victorian reverence for national institutions. Mrs. Ramsay famously reconstitutes her husband's patriarchal authority as "the fatal sterility of the male" (37); her richly conceived interior life ironizes the masculine rhetoric of familial hierarchy. The life story and opium-stained beard of the poet Augustus Carmichael invite Mrs. Ramsay's skepticism; his past appears to her an exercise in futility: "An early marriage; poverty; going to India; translating a little poetry 'very beautifully, I believe,' being willing to teach the boys Persian or Hindustanee, but what really was the use of that?" (10). And the daughters of the Ramsay family suggest a resistance to the late Victorian empire that will increase in future generations ("for there was in all their minds a mute questioning of deference and chivalry, of the Bank of England and the Indian Empire, of ringed fingers and lace" [7]). Thus, "The Window" represents imperialism through sexual polarities: the male characters embrace the imperialist saturation of English private life, while female characters struggle against a totalizing imperial worldview.

The cracks in imperialist and nationalist ideals broaden into chasms in "Time Passes." Using physical and metaphysical violence to represent the horrors of the Great War, Woolf annihilates the family network she has developed so carefully in the novel's opening. By truncating the stories of these characters, describing their deaths between indifferent parentheses, Woolf indicates that the larger life-narratives they represented—Mrs. Ramsay's all-encompassing maternalism, Prue Ramsay's marriage and implicit entry into her mother's role, Andrew Ramsay's dutifully enacted patriotic violence—can have no closure in the postwar modern world. The savage wrecking of these three lives exposes the impermanence of national identities rooted in conquest. By literally killing at-home support for imperialism abroad, Woolf uncovers a deep-rooted cultural need for new narratives of Englishness. And while the deaths of Mrs. Ramsay, Prue, and Andrew represent the end of Victorian England, the natural chaos assaulting the Ramsay house reaches back to the greater cultural instability of Englishness since the time of Queen Elizabeth. Although "Time Passes" never mentions a specific historical moment, Woolf's metaphors in this section evoke a historical chronology that begins far before World War I, intimating that English identity has for centuries been grounded in the asymmetrical and racially exploitative treatment of other cultures. Woolf does not illuminate racial inequalities by accommodating the perspectives of nonwhite characters or exploited colonial subjects; rather, she uses the recurring symbols of tea and china to render impossible any belief in unified or undifferentiated white Englishness.

Amid the storms and dust and dampness that beset the Ramsay house, Woolf's images of the family's teacups and china remind us that even the most banal signifiers of English civility stem from centuries of racial conflict. At the war's inception, the china is "already furred, tarnished, cracked" (129); then, the "repeated shocks" of the war "cracked the tea-cups" (133);

finally, the dishes silently embody postwar resignation to destruction: "Let the broken glass and the china lie out on the lawn and be tangled over with grass and wild berries" (138). Tea and china, although associated with Englishness since Elizabethan times, are nonetheless imported and appropriated from the East with the same violence as Mrs. Ramsay's jewels and the skull that hangs in the children's bedroom. Imperialist history making, to borrow from Sara Suleri, is always "an act of cultural transcription so overdetermined as to dissipate the logic of origins, or the rational framework of chronologies" (9). The transformation of tea and china into signifiers for Englishness participates in this kind of overdetermined historical process, and Woolf's multiple references to the Ramsays' tea sets and china form a palimpsest of absent colonial spaces and practices.

Porcelain making and widespread tea drinking both originally hail from the Tang dynasty in China during the sixth century AD; their migration to England was enabled by a vast network of British cultural appropriation. When Queen Elizabeth founded the British East India Company in 1600, Britain began its broad-based trade with China, importing silk, tea, and "China ware," as the British called Chinese porcelain dishes. In 1744, when "China ware" had become a commonplace feature of English homes, two porcelain factories opened in England to compete with and eventually undersell the Chinese imports. Although the fast-growing European porcelain industry influenced later designs in English porcelain, the first English manufacturers owed their methods as well as their aesthetics to East Asian traditions; English porcelain was for a long time produced according to Chinese and Japanese techniques.[16] By the turn of the twentieth century, British porcelain factories ranged from small operations in Ireland and Wales to the great houses of Spode and Wedgwood in England, and the flood of Chinese imports had slowed to an economically insignificant trickle. "China ware," initially valued for its foreign cachet, became assimilated into the English domestic sphere until only the name betrayed its Eastern origins.

Like porcelain, tea's Eastern origins were overwritten by English practices that burgeoned as the empire grew stronger.[17] The East India Company first introduced tea into England in 1684, when the company acquired a trade post in the Chinese province of Canton. Even more than porcelain, the history of tea drinking in England supplies a map of colonial brutality: the Opium Wars in 1839 and 1857, arising from Britain's enforced opium-for-tea exchange with China, are but the most extreme consequence.[18] As tea's popularity soared in England over the eighteenth and nineteenth centuries, the colonists worked to cultivate tea in their own territories and become less reliant on Chinese imports. Between 1850 and 1930, the English planted hybrid strains of Chinese tea in Assam, Malawi, and Uganda; Thomas Lipton founded his tea empire in Ceylon, and the Brooke Bond Company began cultivating tea in Nairobi; and English colonists introduced the practice of tea drinking to Iran, Morocco, and Turkey.[19] In *To the Lighthouse,* the Ramsays' tea set, found decaying in "oblivion" (139) by Mrs. McNab, portends the larger destiny of a nation built on what is borrowed or taken by force.[20] Tea —imported, transplanted, and imposed as social ritual—signifies the hybrid, culturally divided quality of Englishness.

The minutiae of "Time Passes," like the colonial artifacts that appear in "The Window," describe an imperial Englishness that has depended historically on the not-English and the not-white. And if the novel's second section begins by exposing the mutually constitutive relationship between racial and cultural violence and English selfhood, its conclusion foreshadows Woolf's final rewriting of English identity:

> The sigh of all the seas breaking in measure round the isles soothed them; the night wrapped them; nothing broke their sleep, until, the birds beginning and the dawn weaving their thin voices in to its whiteness, a cart grinding, a dog somewhere barking, the sun lifted the curtains, broke the veil on their eyes, and Lily Briscoe stirring in her sleep. She clutched at her blankets as a faller clutches at the turf on the edge of a cliff. Her eyes opened wide. Here she was again, she thought, sitting bolt upright in bed. Awake. (142–43)

Woolf described "Time Passes" as "all eyeless & featureless with nothing to cling to" (*Diary* III, 76), and the section's final emphasis on Lily Briscoe's eyes—which are repeatedly described as "little" and "Chinese" in the novel's opening section—hints that the novel's conflicts will end with a new visual order and that the fundamental act of perception holds the potential to transform English selfhood. Through Lily's "little Chinese eyes," the longstanding imperialist binaries (colonizer/colonized, white/not-white, civilized/primitive) symbolized by tea, china, and the other material evidence of British rule will lose their authority in the postwar world. However, Woolf replaces these binaries with modern racial divisions that make alternative modes of knowledge and perception available to the English artist. Although *To the Lighthouse* renders invisible the colonized subjects whose resources prop up the Ramsays' material existence, it also invents a new racial alterity that frees the English individual from an imperial ideal of national collectivity.

If we read Lily Briscoe's artistic development in the context of early twentieth-century English formalism's racially derived doctrines, we see how
To the Lighthouse transforms an essentializing vision of nonwhite racial identity into an *anti-essentialist* model of modern English selfhood. Clive Bell,
the influential London art critic and Woolf's brother-in-law, introduced his
stringent theories of English formalism in his 1914 volume, *Art*. Breaking
away from received Western ideas about the symbolic, religious, or en-
nobling potential of art, Bell's theory of "significant form" privileges abstraction over mimetic representation: "It need only be agreed that forms
arranged and combined according to certain unknown and mysterious laws
do move us in a particular way, and that it is the business of an artist so to
combine and arrange them that they shall move us" (11). Significant form
democratizes the aesthetic experience, because "we need bring with us
nothing from life, no knowledge of its ideas and affairs, no familiarity with
its emotions" (25). Bell views form as autotelic, rising above "the accidents
of time and place" (36), and *Art* moves freely through chronologies and geographies and claims formal commonalties among fifth-century Wei fig-
urines, Peruvian pottery, sixth-century Byzantine mosaics, and primitivist
drawings by Cézanne and Picasso.

Bell's formalist theories gesture toward but do not probe deeply into
the art of non-Western cultures. Roger Fry's formalism, however, central-
izes the impact of racial identity on artistic potential, exploring more fully
the cultural implications in Bell's rhetoric of formal aesthetic purity. Fry's
1920 collection of essays on formalist aesthetics, *Vision and Design*, spans
an eclectic range of artistic traditions, containing essays on paintings by
Giotto and Matisse as well as on artwork by Ottoman and Mohammedan
artists. The book's illustrations include a sculpted Negro head, a Persian
miniature, a Sassanian miniature, and drawings by Dürer, el Greco, and
Rouault. Whereas Bell's *Art* urges a method of aesthetic appreciation, Fry's
Vision and Design employs racial determinism to explain why non-Western
cultures create *form* and Western cultures create *concepts*. Setting forth a
complex dialectical relationship among the Eastern, Western, and African
arts, *Vision and Design* exalts the nonwhite artists whose marvelous creative
facilities shame the rational, post-Enlightenment Western artist.

Two essays from *Vision and Design* are particularly relevant to my reading of *To the Lighthouse:* "The Art of the Bushmen," where Fry examines
Paleolithic line drawings of animals, and "Negro Sculpture," where Fry discusses the artistic process of "nameless savages" (70) who create exquisitely true sculptures of the human form. In these two essays, Fry represents

Western (and, specifically, English) art as insufficiently expressive and inherently limited, counterposing instinctual, perceptual African art against rational, conceptual Western art. When a Bushman draws an animal, Fry claims, he strives for and captures the "general character of the silhouette" and not "a sum of the parts" (64). The Negro sculptor who carves and molds human figures has an extraordinary power "to create expressive plastic form" (70) and "conceive form in three dimensions" (71). Pitting Bushman drawings and Negro sculpture against Western drawing and sculpture, Fry continually urges Western artists to achieve the formal perfection common to African artistry. Despite his sincere admiration for Bushmen and Negro sculptors, however, Fry does not deliver unqualified praise for the African arts. He resorts to a colonialist mind/body distinction that lauds African artistry while maintaining the superiority of the European West's reason, civilization, and progress. If, historically, white Western artists did not draw forms as well as the Bushmen, Fry argues, their "sensual defects were more than compensated for by increased intellectual power" (67). Indeed, Fry attributes the white artist's deficiencies to his "habit of thinking of things in terms of concepts which deprived him for ages of the power to see what they looked like" (67). Conversely, the Negro sculptor has a "logical comprehension of plastic form" (72) but he has not created a great artistic culture because of his "want of a conscious critical sense and the intellectual powers of comparison and classification" (73).[21] Clive Bell's 1922 essay "Negro Sculpture" echoes Fry's theories, praising the "delicacy in the artist's sense of relief and modeling" (115) but qualifying his admiration with a comment on the "essential inferiority of Negro to the very greatest art": "Savages lack self-consciousness and the critical sense because they lack intelligence. And because they lack intelligence they are incapable of profound conceptions" (116).

To narrow the aesthetic divide between the Negro artist's formal mastery and the English artist's conceptual mastery, Roger Fry points to East Asia and proclaims that Chinese and Japanese line drawings "approach more nearly than those of any other civilized people to the immediacy and rapidity of transcription of Bushman and Paleolithic art" (68). Fry makes the "civilized" Japanese artist a conduit for the Western artist to move from intellectual creation to perceptual creation:

It is partly due to Japanese influence that our own Impressionists have made an attempt to get back to that ultra-primitivist directness of vision. Indeed they deliberately sought to deconceptualise art. The artist of today has therefore

Figure 14. Roger Fry, "Giraffe" marquetry cupboard, 1915. Direct African influences on the Omega Workshops are visible in the wooden geometrics of this cabinet. (Manchester Art Gallery, Manchester.)

to some extent a choice before him of whether he will *think* form like the
early artists of European races or will merely *see* it like the Bushmen. (68–69)

Commingling centuries and cultures to create new artistic avenues, Fry
promises English artists that accessing formal purity is a worthy and at-
tainable goal. The artistic vision of the Negro or Bushman, Fry urges, should
be wrested from its culturally paralyzed origins and transported to the sophisticated, civilized, modern Western world. If English artists hope to jet-
tison their own moribund artistic legacy, they will have to emulate those
nonwhite artists whose perceptual abilities remain unclouded by the trappings of modernity.

The theory that race determines one's relation to formal aesthetics manifested itself concretely in the art objects made by Fry's arts collective, the
Omega Workshops. Fry founded the Omega in 1913, hoping to vivify the
decorative arts in England by encouraging original and provocative designs
for furniture, textiles, and pottery. To this end, he invited twenty-five young
artists (including Vanessa Bell, Duncan Grant, Wyndham Lewis, Frederick
Etchells, Winifred Gill, Nina Hamnett, Ethel Sands, and Henri Doucet) to
join the Omega Workshops at 33 Fitzroy Street in Bloomsbury. The Omega
opened on July 8, 1913, and the artists displayed an astounding array of
works that included beads, parasols, carpets, stained glass, lamps, handbags,
tiles, vases, screens, clothing, menu cards, and children's toys. Ironically,
what Fry dubbed the Omega's "definitively English tradition" drew its primary inspiration from decidedly non-English cultures (quoted in Spalding,
176). From the workshop's outset, the Omega artists rejected effete ideas
about conventional representation by pledging to follow the paths of less
"civilized" cultures whose art is unspoiled by intellectualism and progress;
their efforts to imitate non-Western, premodern perceptual modes supported Fry's view that aesthetic integrity emerged out of an unthinking,
sensuous creative spirit. Fry's preface to the Omega Workshops Catalog
reinforces a racialized formulation of artistry consistent with the writings
in *Vision and Design:*

> If you look at a pot or a woven cloth made by a negro savage of the Congo
> with the crude instruments at his disposal, you may begin by despising it for
> its want of finish. . . . But if you will allow the poor savage's handiwork a longer
> contemplation you will find something in it of greater value and significance
> than in the Sévres china or Lyons velvet.
> It will become apparent that the negro enjoyed making his pot or cloth,
> that he pondered delightedly over the possibilities of his craft and that his

enjoyment finds expression in many ways; and as these become increasingly apparent to you, you share his joy in creation, and in that forget the roughness of the result. . . . [The Omega Workshops] try to keep the spontaneous freshness of primitive or peasant work while satisfying the needs and expressing the feelings of modern cultivated man. (201)

This guiding philosophy opened the doors for a more fully global view of decorative art than London had yet seen.[22] The Omega artists capitalized on the ahistorical leanings of formalism, confidently imitating and modifying artistic forms from Africa, the Middle East, and Asia.[23] Accordingly, the artwork produced by the Omega Workshops between 1913 and 1919 demonstrates a dizzying, dazzling cultural hybridity that anticipates Virginia Woolf's own deployment of competing racial discourses in her novels. Some Omega works, for example, focused on the bodies of nonwhite peoples as sites for exploring form, like Duncan Grant's *Elephant* marquetry tray and his paintings *The Queen of Sheba* and *The Tub,* Frederick Etchells's *The Chinese Student,* Wyndham Lewis's *Indian Dance,* Vanessa Bell's *Byzantine Lady,* and Roald Kristian's "African-looking Marionettes" (*Omega Workshops 1913–1919,* 60).[24] More frequently, the Omega artists borrowed patterns from non-Western art objects and incorporated them into decorative arts and interior design. Roger Fry's pottery shares stylistic affinities with the Mohammedan, North African, and Chinese ceramics that he collected on his travels; Omega rugs and bedspreads by Fry, Etchells, and Grant bear African-derived motifs like "bands of bold patterning and strong black outlines" (Collins, 107); a beaded bag by Jessie Etchells appropriates a Native American tribal design; Winifred Gill's necklaces feature beads from Japan and Bohemia; and Henri Gaudier-Brzeska's much-lauded animal sculptures imitate the work of Chinese and African sculptors.[25] Vanessa Bell's nursery toys—camels, rhinoceroses, elephants, and tigers—were exercises in exotic whimsy, designed to bring the forms of Indian and African animals to the British baby; and the bright abstract flowers of Bell's murals and painted linens evoked faraway tropical landscapes to contrast with England's climate. Indisputably, as Isabelle Anscombe points out, the Omega Workshops "freed itself totally from historical borrowings" and departed from the "'false unity'" of British aesthetic tradition; the deliberate modernity of the Omega aesthetic "relied upon attention to detail, texture, a subtle colour-sense and, most of all, a kind of inner integrity" ("Context," 29). But as even the brief catalogue above reveals, Omega art achieved this very modernity through the belief that non-Western art is

Figure 15. Duncan Grant, *Design with Red Nude Male Figure,* 1913–14. An abstract primitivism characterizes Grant's diverse creations for the Omega Workshops, whether a painting, a shutter (figure 16), or a textile (figure 17). (The Samuel Courtauld Trust, Courtauld Institute of Art Gallery, London. Estate of Duncan Grant, courtesy of Henrietta Garnett. © 2009 Artists Rights Society, New York/DACS, London.)

Figure 16. Duncan Grant, *Design for a Shutter at 38 Brunswick Square, London—Female Nude Dancing,* 1912. (Estate of Duncan Grant, courtesy of Henrietta Garnett. The Samuel Courtauld Trust, Courtauld Institute of Art Gallery, London. © 2009 Artists Rights Society, New York/DACS, London.)

Figure 17. Duncan Grant, *Textile Design Based on African Patterns,* 1913–14. (Estate of Duncan Grant, courtesy of Henrietta Garnett. The Samuel Courtauld Trust, Courtauld Institute of Art Gallery, London. © 2009 Artists Rights Society, New York/DACS, London.)

Figure 18. Roger Fry, Omega six-sided vase, 1913–19. Commercial porcelain, overpainted in three colors. 20.8 cm height. Omega Workshops art objects such as Fry's vase and Roald Kristian's lampshade with dragons (figure 19) incorporated East Asian aesthetics to create modern English style. (Victoria and Albert Museum, London.)

Figure 19. Roald Kristian, design for lampshade "Dragons," 1915–16. Gouache on off-white paper. 10.3 × 30.5 cm. (The Samuel Courtauld Trust, Courtauld Institute of Art Gallery, Fry Collection, London.)

shaped by purer, more direct vision than Western art, and that racial Otherness floats freely, infinitely interchangeable and adaptable.

Woolf's formalist literary inventions in *To the Lighthouse* reflect the ahistoric, nonmimetic aesthetic philosophy behind English formalist painting, sculpture, and decorative arts. In a letter to Roger Fry written shortly after *To the Lighthouse* was published, Woolf famously commits to a narrative formalism that eschews any alliance with symbolism:

> I meant *nothing* by The Lighthouse. One has to have a central line down the middle of the book to hold the design together. I saw that all sorts of feelings would accrue to this, but I refused to think them out, and trusted that people would make it the deposit for their own emotions—which they have done, one thinking it means one thing another another. I can't manage Symbolism except in this vague, generalised way. Whether its right or wrong I don't know, but directly I'm told what a thing means, it becomes hateful to me. (*Letters* III, 385)[26]

Significantly, Woolf also shares Roger Fry's approach to achieving aesthetic purity through racial difference: in *To the Lighthouse,* Woolf's most radical revisions to a nineteenth-century literary legacy stem from the racial alterity she inscribes onto Lily Briscoe. The novel's celebration of formalist aesthetics culminates in Woolf's Orientalist depiction of Lily Briscoe; race-based formalism in *To the Lighthouse* overturns a narrative economy traditionally structured around marriage and social stability. That Lily Briscoe uses her painting to escape the marriage plot is, of course, a widely accepted feminist reading of *To the Lighthouse*'s breakthrough modernist ending. Less obvious is the reading that the encrypted foreignness of Lily Briscoe's "little Chinese eyes" first forces Lily's sexual devaluation and subsequently enables her artistic freedom. Racial difference, in other words, provides a meeting ground for social critique and aesthetic innovation in *To the Lighthouse*.

Lily Briscoe's conflicted views of patriarchy and marriage shape her reactions to the Ramsay family in the novel's opening section, "The Window," where the narrative flits in and out of her consciousness. In the novel's concluding section, "The Lighthouse," when Lily has rejected marriage and conventional femininity, Woolf makes her the novel's final center of consciousness. Lily's heightened narrative authority is a function of her implicit *racial* alterity: Woolf uses Lily's "Chinese eyes" to effect the transition between Lily the "skimpy old maid" (181) and Lily the accomplished artist. To guarantee Lily's exclusion from marital and sexual economies, Woolf alludes to Lily's Chinese eyes whenever romantic possibilities arise. From Lily's first appearance in the novel, Woolf links her "Oriental" features to her sexual unavailability: "With her little Chinese eyes and her puckered-up face, she would never marry; one could not take her painting very seriously; she was an independent little creature, and Mrs. Ramsay liked her for it" (17). The "Chinese eyes" invite a host of reductive Orientalist associations; Woolf repeatedly characterizes Lily as inscrutable, diminutive, and unsuited for the married life that awaits the newly engaged Minta Doyle and Paul Rayley:

> [Lily] faded, under Minta's glow; became more inconspicuous than ever, in her little grey dress with her little puckered face and her little Chinese eyes. Everything about her was so small. . . . There was in Lily a thread of something; a flare of something; something of her own which Mrs. Ramsay liked very much indeed, but no man would, she feared. (104)

While suggestions of Oriental identity impose a mandatory sexual exile on Lily, they also grant acuity to her reactions against social convention. Lily resists sympathizing with Charles Tansley's "burning desire to break into the conversation" during Mrs. Ramsay's dinner party: "But, she thought, screwing up her Chinese eyes, and remembering how he sneered at women, 'can't paint, can't write,' why should I help him to relieve himself?" (91). Lily perceives marriage as a "degradation" and a "dilution" (102), willingly distancing herself from the model of English femininity that traps Mrs. Ramsay and Prue. The Chinese eyes work to critique as well as to exclude, and Orientalizing Lily's vision enables Woolf to write her out of Victorian patriarchal expectations. As a "foreign" object of the Victorian gaze *and* as a perceiver in her own right, Lily occupies a textual space bounded and stabilized by her racial difference.

The Chinese eyes that look mutinously on gendered social traditions also resist constraining artistic traditions. In concert with Roger Fry's praise for the nonwhite artist's aesthetic sensibility, Woolf designs Lily's resistance to artistic realism as a function of her "Oriental" vision. Lily's evolving artistic vision mirrors the novel's critique of a late nineteenth century worldview: her first painting is a tortured attempt to express meaning in the Ramsays' world, while the complete self-sufficiency of her final painting rejects prewar social and artistic tradition alike. As she recognizes that she has no place in conventionally ordered Victorian society, Lily's paintings become less mimetic and increasingly abstract, formalist art works whose self-referentiality protects her from patriarchy's demands. She enters the novel at work on a portrait of Mrs. Ramsay and James, executing this painting in a prewar moment when other artists paint impressionistic "lemon-coloured sailing-boats, and pink women on the beach" (13). Rejecting impressionism's injunction to "see everything pale, elegant, semitransparent" (19), Lily struggles for an art form that breaks completely free of its object. And although the "triangular purple shape" (52) she paints to represent Mrs. Ramsay and James seems detached from conventional reverence for a mother and child, Lily subordinates aesthetic achievement to her worry that the painting will "never be seen; never be hung" (48). Because Lily looks beyond the canvas boundaries to determine the painting's worth, this first effort at formal purity fails to achieve what Roger Fry calls "the conviction of a new and definite reality" (*Vision and Design*, 167). The broken and devastated material world of the war's aftermath demands the creation of such a reality; it is only then that Lily's Chinese eyes envision a painting that breaks free of the patriarchal and imperialist hierarchies of the Ramsays' world.

Lily awakens to a newly broken civilization at the end of "Time Passes," when, after a stormy night, "tenderly the light fell (it seemed to come through her eyelids)" (142). Eyelids have long been used to differentiate

"Oriental" peoples from "Caucasian" peoples; this image not only calls attention to Lily's race-based social exile, but also anticipates the fruitful connection between her racial identity and her artistic capabilities. After returning to the Ramsay household and rediscovering her old canvas, Lily hunts for an art form that bears no trace of late Victorian culture. Anguished by the bleak spectacle of Mr. Ramsay, James, and Cam, bereft of their matriarch and struggling to complete the long-deferred journey to the lighthouse, Lily turns to her easel, "screwing up her little Chinese eyes in her small puckered face" (157). She feels the "mass" of abstract imagery "pressing on her eyeballs" (159) and, as she applies brush to canvas, reflects that "one wanted fifty pairs of eyes to see with" (198). Her final, triumphant painting floats free of any signifiers of imperial Victorianism:

> There it was—her picture. Yes, with all its greens and blues, its lines running up and across, its attempt at something. It would be hung in the attics, she thought; it would be destroyed. But what did that matter? she asked herself, taking up her brush again. She looked at the steps; they were empty; she looked at her canvas; it was blurred. With a sudden intensity, as if she saw it clear for a second, she drew a line there, in the center. It was done; it was finished. Yes, she thought, laying down her brush in extreme fatigue, I have had my vision. (208–9)

Neither the painting's impermanence nor its absence of symbolic meaning hinders Lily from a sense of completion. Her "little Chinese eyes" attain the "ultra-primitive directness of vision" that Roger Fry attributes to East Asian cultures, and her arrangement of forms is liberating because it is finally autotelic. In privileging the completion of Lily's painting over Cam and James's reconciliation with their father, Woolf creates a racially differentiated model for modern Englishness that holds itself separate from longstanding patriarchal and imperial hierarchies. Lily Briscoe's "vision" signals the arrival of a modern English artist whose Oriental creativity, paradoxically, liberates her from an Englishness rooted in the colonial domination of nonwhite races.

Read in the context of Roger Fry's ideas and the creative ambitions of the Omega Workshops, *To the Lighthouse* resonates with an Orientalism that elevates and emulates the nonwhite, non-Western Other's artistry. The art that will grant fresh meaning to postwar England is as marked by cultural appropriation as the nineteenth-century life-narratives destroyed by the war: by scripting Lily's Chinese-eyed aesthetic "vision" as modernity's response to the Victorian era's sociocultural vision, *To the Lighthouse* answers one set of racialized codes with another. The novel's different modes of racial appropriation, which by turn exploit, essentialize, or redeem the resources of non-Western cultures, work together in Woolf's text to create an arc of Englishness that is always racially divided. And despite the novel's wholly private English setting, we see that Woolf carves out abundant textual space for multiple negotiations of racial difference. To read *To the Lighthouse* merely as an opposition to imperialist or nationalist violence is to ignore the rich cultural texture of Woolf's writing: the several discourses operating in the novel's exploration of feminism and aesthetics rewrite Englishness as a confluence of racially differentiated perspectives.

"Slicing at the head of a Moor"

Orlando incorporates racial discourses with an explicitness very unlike *To the Lighthouse*'s subtle interplay of colonial history, Orientalism, and modern formalism. Whereas race marks the absence of the transcendent in *To the Lighthouse*, Woolf redirects it into a powerful guarantor of transcendence and continuity in *Orlando*. In this metamodernist text, race operates as a source of liberation, anxiety, and stability for a prolix narrator who traces the evolution of literary style, maps the development of the modern artist, probes the boundary between truth and fiction, challenges the foundations of sexual identity, and lambastes the profiteering machinery of the literary marketplace. *Orlando*'s aggressively experimental racial mosaic, which at once extends and works against all of the racialized aesthetics we have seen thus far, provides a fitting end for this study of modern fiction. Like my opening text, *The Picture of Dorian Gray*, where magical time shifts reveal deep cultural anxiety about race and modernity, *Orlando*'s great chronological leaps portray the twinned histories of nation and narration as a series of racial plots. These plots provide a clear vision into Woolf's complex work with history, which, as Melba Cuddy-Keane has eloquently written, involves "locating the text in a discrete historical period known by its unlikeliness to the present, reflecting on the way the present is interrogated through this comparison, and translating both past and present (always problematically and provisionally) into the continuous now" (156). The "continuous now" that flows through *Orlando*'s multiple histories—whether the life story of the novel's protagonist, the story of English literature, or the history of England itself—announces itself through imperialist conceptions of race.

Although biographers and critics alike read *Orlando* principally as

Woolf's lesbian celebration of Vita Sackville-West, the novel has its roots in the material work of the British Empire and the cultural assumptions of English travel writing.[27] In 1926, four years after she and Woolf began their friendship, Vita Sackville-West visited Persia, where her husband, Harold Nicolson, was stationed as a diplomat with the British Foreign Legation. During her six-week stay in Persia, Vita corresponded regularly with Woolf, writing flowing letters describing landscapes, indigenous peoples, and the royal courts of Teheran. Sackville-West's representations of central Asia and the diplomatic life fascinated Woolf, and the two writers exchanged excited ideas about the limits of perception, time and space, and cultural alienation. These letters provided the skeleton for Sackville-West's travel narrative, *Passenger to Teheran,* which Woolf herself edited and then published at the Hogarth Press in November 1926. In the spring of 1927, Sackville-West made a second journey to Persia, and her letters to Woolf during these months depict a life divided between diplomatic duty and trips to the Persian countryside. Five months after Sackville-West's return to England, Woolf began writing *Orlando,* the glorious "biography" of a character based on Vita.

It is widely known that Vita Sackville-West's sexual originality inspired the narrative antics of Woolf's novel. In what follows, I hope to situate *Orlando* in a new critical arena and persuade my readers that the long-overlooked racial politics of Vita Sackville-West's writing—her private letters as well as *Passenger to Teheran*—influenced the novel as profoundly as her sexual politics. If we move past the longstanding imperative to read *Orlando* as Woolf's lesbian paean to Sackville-West, we find complex racial affinities between Woolf's novel and Vita Sackville-West's travel writing. These texts are united by what Woolf called "the question of the West & the East" in her Constantinople journals of 1906, and the racial tropes of Vita Sackville-West's work anticipate the limitations of *Orlando*'s subversiveness. The generic conventions of travel writing and modern fiction might be expected to produce divergent treatments of race: after all, the underlying principal of Vita Sackville-West's *Passenger to Teheran* is an epistemological confidence that foreign territories and peoples can *be known* by English readers, whereas *Orlando*'s narrative instability embodies a modernist reaction against objective certainties. But despite *Orlando*'s formal commitments to the modernist principles of rupture, nonlinearity, and narrative unreliability, this novel, like Vita Sackville-West's travelogue, remains ideologically wedded to the closed racial categories of British imperial discourse. Sackville-West and Woolf investigate—and revel in—the discontinuities of culture, but both writers defend the idea of race itself as fundamentally continuous. As Woolf weaves Sackville-West's travel experiences into the narrative of *Orlando,* masculinity and femininity fracture into gloriously disparate elements, but the threat of disparate *racial* identity produces anxiety rather than celebration. This novel hurtles toward twentieth-century modernity while clinging to remnants of much older racial conceptions: its all-compassing parodies and chronological games do not succeed in destabilizing the myth of an originary, unified, white English subject. Whereas *To the Lighthouse* articulates a modern English femininity through Lily Briscoe's Chinese eyes, *Orlando* insists on a racially undifferentiated Englishness with unassailable authority over people outside the modern West.

Because she was a diplomat's wife, Sackville-West's journeys to Persia were directly enabled by the British Empire, but that empire (as well as Harold Nicolson, Sackville-West's husband) remains on the periphery in her letters and *Passenger to Teheran.*[28] Although she omits specific political details in her writing, it is necessary to recognize that the British presence in Iran in 1926 was both powerful and heavily contested. Iran was never an official British colony; however, British economic, military, and political control in Iran made it a virtual possession of the empire. In the late nineteenth century, Britain's ability to control southern and eastern Iran meant a more secure hold on India. To this end, Britain imposed domestic control through the Imperial Bank of Persia, the Anglo-Persian Oil Company, and a monopoly on railroad construction and rights to Iran's natural resources. After World War I, Britain proposed the Anglo-Persian Treaty, which gave the empire almost total power over Iran's military, transportation, communication, and internal government. At the time of Vita Sackville-West's visit, the Anglo-Persian Treaty had been nullified, and Iran was moving away from Britain's control to enter a new era of national independence. The coronation of Mohammad Reza Shah in 1926 ushered in the Pahlavi dynasty that ruled Iran until the revolution of 1979; under Reza Shah's rule, Iran strengthened its central government and lessened its dependence on the West.[29] Thus, Vita Sackville-West arrived in Persia during a transformative political moment when East-West relations were being slowly redefined; and her conflicted literary authority over Persian culture reflects England's changing *material* authority over Persia.

Certainly Vita Sackville-West was by no means a "lady traveler" whose whiteness and femininity demanded constant protection or servility from "natives." Her movements through central Asia, on which Woolf patterned Orlando's Turkish sojourn, were atypical for a white Englishwoman of her class. One letter to Woolf, for example, describes a trip to Persepolis during which she "slept in ruined huts; made fires of pomegranate-wood and dried camel-dung; boiled eggs; lost all sense of civilisation; returned to the primitive state in which one thinks only of food, water, and sleep" (DeSalvo and Leaska, 189). Other letters reveal that she camped freely in the mountains, learned Parsee from a male Persian friend, and preferred wandering through the bazaars in Teheran over attending diplomats' parties. Like Woolf, Vita Sackville-West writes as much about the difficulty of accurate transcription as she does about her actual experiences: "How is it that one can *never* communicate?" she despairs in a letter from Teheran. "Only imaginary things can be communicated, like ideas, or the world of a novel; but not real experience" (DeSalvo and Leaska, 112). Versions of this characteristically modernist observation appear throughout Vita's correspondence with Woolf, frequently accompanied by the author's reflections about race, geography, and national identity.[30] Her descriptions of Eastern nations (first in her private letters to Woolf and, subsequently, for a British reading public in *Passenger to Teheran*) are scored by the tension between the desire to confess her own cultural limitations and the desire for authorial control over foreign cultures. She strives for objective accuracy as she describes what Mary Louise Pratt has termed "contact zones," the foundational sites of Western imperialism where "disparate cultures meet, clash, and grapple with each other, often in highly asymmetrical relations of domination and subordination" (4).[31] But Britain's "highly asymmetrical relations" with central Asia in 1926 beget reductive racial and cultural assumptions that inevitably find their way into literary re-creations of Egypt, India, Iraq, Iran, and Russia; Sackville-West frequently lapses into the colonizing rhetoric of a Western foreign national, unable to sustain the posture of a respectful outsider. Her different textual methods of objectification are replayed in *Orlando,* where narrative self-consciousness about the production of national culture jostles against *unselfconscious* conceptions of racial identity.

I begin reading Vita's travel writings by isolating the strand of imperialist thought that runs through her correspondence with Woolf. The Persia-England letters are undoubtedly love letters, and accordingly, they foster an intimacy that colors cultural impressions. Both writers are absorbed by the spatial and temporal coordinates of their separation; indeed, even the Latin seal on Sackville-West's missives translates as "We have left the borders and dear fields of our native land" (Desalvo and Leaska, 175).[32] Sackville-West exclaims, "My darling, I hardly know how to write to you, everything is so confused, so Einsteinian, an effect which I can never hope to communicate to you, so I won't try. Anyway, I am here. . . . And now I don't know whether England seems near or far—It is a mixture" (DeSalvo and Leaska, 171), and Woolf muses, "I believe, at this moment, more in Teheran than in Tavistock Square. I see you, somehow in long coat and trousers, like an Abyssinan Empress, stalking over those barren hills" (*Letters* III, 238). In a correspondence already crammed with ideas about reading and writing, Vita Sackville-West often makes casual literary references that both intensify and diminish the foreignness of the places she visits.[33] "Pure Conrad, this," she writes of a stop in Aden, where the "small black boys" who beg for food in "the most godforsaken spot on earth" (DeSalvo and Leaska, 98) remind her of abject natives in modern imperial fiction. (Indeed, the rhetoric of imperial adventure tales animates these letters: Virginia in London wonders whether Vita has been "eaten by brigands, wrecked, torn to pieces" [DeSalvo and Leaska, 176] or "drowned, shot, raped" [190] during her travels, while Vita writes grandly about "poor Persia," a land "divided, rotted by disease, poverty and helplessness; and the concupiscence of short sightedness, and greed of man" [181].) Upon arriving in Baghdad, Sackville-West tells Woolf, "I have reached this city of fabulous romance, which is not, believe me, as we saw it in Hassan, but just a merry muddle of donkeys, motors, Arabs, dogs, mud, cabs, and camels" (108). The reference is to James Elroy Flecker's play *Hassan: The Story of Hassan of Bagdad, and How He Came to Make the Golden Journey to Samarkand,* which Sackville-West and Woolf had seen together in 1923. Flecker's five-act double love story takes place in a Baghdad filled with two-dimensional Orientalist stereotypes: "inferior" Jewish merchants, a Chinese philosopher, veiled dancing girls, and a bloodstained Negro executioner with a taste for fair-skinned Muslim women.[34] This English-authored fiction of a romantic Baghdad falls away, however, when Sackville-West faces the city's unglamorous reality, where even "the mud is such that you would hesitate to drive an ordinary English farm-cart through it" (108). And when Sackville-West and Harold Nicolson go to see the royal jewels of Teheran, ancient and modern literature collide in a striking hybrid image:

I have been in Aladdin's cave.
Sacks of emeralds were emptied out before our eyes. Sacks of pearls. *Literally.*
We came away shaking the pearls out of our shoes. Ropes of uncut emeralds.
   Scabbards encrusted with precious stones. Great hieratic crowns.
All this in a squalid room, with grubby Persians drinking little cups of tea.

> I can't write about it now. It was simply the Arabian Nights, with décor by the
> Sitwells. Pure fantasy. (120)

The polarized literary contexts (the ancient Arabian Nights and the avant-garde poets Edith and Osbert Sitwell) elevate the jewels out of their "squalid" and "grubby" Persian surroundings.[35] Such literary allusions exemplify Edward Said's claim that Western representations of the Orient alternate between "the West's contempt for what is familiar and its shivers of delight in—or fear of—novelty" (*Orientalism*, 59). A similarly conventional mixture of racial contempt, delight, and fear, as we will see, undergirds what is intended to be most subversive in *Orlando*.

Sackville-West represents Persia's natural beauty as a partial corrective to Western civilization's flaws, pitting her distaste for diplomatic duties against her love for the Persian countryside:

> I go to call on some bloody Pole or Belgian, and we know that there is nothing to talk about except the Trebizond Road, or the Shiraz Road, and whether one has done it or not, and whether one is going away for the summer or not, and whether we may expect more snow. . . . I said to the clergyman's daughter, how was she liking Teheran? and she replied, "Well, really, the theatricals seem to be the only excitement." . . . But I looked into my ring today— an old Persian topaz, pale pink—and saw there reflected a plane tree, some blue sky, and a white mountain, all tiny and coloured, and this seemed to me worth while, so I daresay there is still something left to write about. (DeSalvo and Leaska, 174)

This and similar letters reflect, to return to Mary Louise Pratt, English travel writing's tendency to aestheticize foreign landscapes by characterizing them as "extremely rich in material and semantic substance" (204). The shallow quality of life among the Europeans compels Sackville-West to escape to the rural areas surrounding metropolitan Teheran; her favorite days, she tells Woolf, consist of "going into the mountains, and eating sandwiches beside a stream, and picking wild almond, and of coming home by incredible sunsets across the plain" (114). And in the manner of the avant-garde artists who fetishized the primitive as the truest embodiment of modernity, Sackville-West imagines an evolutionary cycle in which the acme of civilization is found in the premodern natural world:

> I have come to the conclusion that solitude is the last refuge of civilised people. . . . Social relations are just the descendants of the primitive tribal need to get together for purposes of defence; a gathering of bushmen or pygmies

is the real ancestor of a Teheran dinner party; then the wheel comes full cycle, and your truly civilised person wants to get away back to loneliness. (187)

Meditating on the contrast between the diplomatic bustle of Teheran and her idylls in the Persian countryside, she continues, "If all my life went smash, and I lost everybody, I should come and live in Persia, miles away from everywhere, and see nobody except the natives to whom I should dispense quinine. . . . I think Lady Hester Stanhope must have had a good life" (187). This escapist fantasy envisions solitude as the white woman's power over anonymous "natives"; the reference to Lady Hester Stanhope (1776–1839), more pointedly, suggests an extension of Britain's authority in the Orient.[36] Under Sackville-West's Western eyes, the Persian landscape promises an unspoiled remedy for the travails of modernity. That the countryside falls under imperial control does not enter her discussion; her freedom to avoid imperialism's most visible effects and turn instead to natural beauty is itself an exercise of colonial power.

Sackville-West's pastoral experiences furnish an escape from the stifling boundaries of the European community, and Persia, she declares to Woolf, "has become a part of me,—grafted on to me, leaving me permanently enriched" (111). But this avowed fusion, like her various literary references, harbors a complex cultural unevenness. Consider her telling description of the Persian pottery that fills her rooms in the diplomatic quarters:

> Bowls and fragments, dim greens and lustrous blues, on which patterns, figures, camels, cypresses, script disport themselves elusive and fragmentary. How I am going to get them all home God knows. For the moment they stand round my room, creating a rubbed, romantic life of forgotten centuries. It's like looking into a pool, and seeing, very far down, a dim reflection. I make all sorts of stories about them. (187)

Vita Sackville-West's pottery collection epitomizes her relationship to Persia: nature, culture, and history are here fragmented, commodified, and awaiting transport to the modern West. Dissociating the pottery from the twentieth-century artists who created it and the setting in which it was produced, Sackville-West treats it as a metonym of "forgotten centuries." In making up "all sorts of stories" about it, she participates in a version of the aesthetic colonization that Roger Fry advocates in *Vision and Design,* kindling her Western imagination with Eastern art objects. Thus, Sackville-West's Persian pastoral culminates in a vision of Persia as solace for the Western subject and sets forth a model for the Turkish interlude in *Orlando,* where Woolf details her protagonist's self-fashioning within a semantically rich Oriental landscape.

As Sackville-West revises episodes from her correspondence into the chapters of *Passenger to Teheran,* she replaces her private, healing Persia with depictions of a technologically backwards, chaotic nation of dark-skinned foreigners. As in her letters to Woolf, Sackville-West ignores the material presence of the British Empire and her connection to it; nevertheless, Englishness, rather than a condition to be escaped, stands as the implicit standard of civility and normative behavior. *Passenger to Teheran* is an armchair-traveler's book, a fast-paced travelogue whose tone seldom challenges the English reader's sense of global superiority. Filled with glossy black-and-white photographs of city scenes, the countryside, and "natives," *Passenger to Teheran* traces Sackville-West's journey through central Asia and Persia, emphasizing in each "contact zone" the hierarchical contrasts between Eastern and Western races. In each of the book's nine chapters, Sackville-West's numerous attempts at cultural open-mindedness are entangled with Orientalist or primitivist stereotypes. An early moment in the book's introduction establishes this entanglement:

> It may be that language, that distorted labyrinthine universe, was never designed to replace or even to complete the much simpler functions of the eye. We look; and there is the image in its entirety, three-dimensional, instantaneous. Language follows, a tortoise competing with the velocity of light; and after five pages of print succeeds in reproducing but a fraction of the registered vision. It reminds one of the Oriental who with engaging naivety thought that by photographing the muezzin he would record also the notes of his call to prayer. (14)

Even as Sackville-West acknowledges that a travelogue's language can never adequately capture the culture it describes, her analogy of the Oriental's "engaging naivety" reifies the East as backwards, unsophisticated, and alienated from modern technology. The book's subsequent efforts at cultural relativism fail repeatedly, as Sackville-West's cultural stereotypes enshrine the West as the modern world's source of civic organization, hygiene, and progress.

Passenger to Teheran discusses twentieth-century Persia using contradictory chronologies of development. Vita Sackville-West contributes to a longstanding imperial discourse in which non-Western peoples, to borrow from David Spurr, are "held in contempt for their lack of civility, loved for their willingness to acquire it, and ridiculed when they have acquired too much"

(86). Sackville-West praises the Persian countryside that seems to exist outside of time, but she criticizes metropolitan Teheran for its lack of Western modernization. Thus, the potters "who can do one thing, and will continue to do it all their lives, as their ancestors did it before them" (34) confirm the reductive view that "Persia had been left as it was before man's advent" (69). However, the roads "over which an English farmer might well hesitate to drive a wagon" (57) and the "objects which the average English chauffeur would scarcely recognize as motor-cars" (109) betray Teheran's failure to catch up to the civilized world. An ironic passage faults the "degenerate taste of the Persians" who prefer modern carpet designs to the old carpets which were "treasures of sixteenth-century Isfahan" (127). Sackville-West's idealized, ancient Persia cannot accommodate evolutions in native artistic traditions, but the "real" Persia is to blame for its absence of metropolitan evolution and infrastructure. Thus, Persia either stands as a shoddy imitation of the modern West, or as a beautiful spectacle that has endured, unchanging, over hundreds of years. In both versions, the technocratic Western world sets the parameters within which the East is evaluated.

The travelogue's contradictory presentations of Persian modernization are perhaps best understood in Sackville-West's chapter on the shah's coronation. Neglecting to mention that Reza Khan came to power by overthrowing the previous prime minister, Sayyed Zia, Sackville-West presents the coronation as a cultural curiosity rather than as a watershed national event. Her descriptions of local customs and oddities overshadow the particulars of the new Pahlavi regime, and she excludes any discussion of the Iranian citizens' political consciousness. Her portrait of Reza Khan debases the shah's origins and only grudgingly acknowledges his authority: "In appearance Reza was an alarming man, six foot three in height, with a sullen manner, a huge nose, grizzled hair and a brutal jowl; he looked, in fact, what he was, a Cossack trooper; but there was no denying that he had a kingly presence" (142). The shah's political power also seems dubitable to Sackville-West, because "the lax limp nation he had mastered" seems to be "easy to dominate" (142).

The shah's coronation, like the shah himself, amuses rather than impresses Sackville-West, who condescends to the Persian desire to impress the Western diplomats:

> They ordered vast quantities of glass and china from English firms; it would not arrive in time for the coronation, they had left it too late, but no matter.

> They must have red cloth for the palace servants like the red liveries worn by the servants at the English legation. They must have a copy of the proceedings at Westminster Abbey for the coronation of His Majesty George V. The copy was procured, but, stiff with ceremonial, heavy with regalia, created some consternation; one of the ministers who prided himself on his English came to ask me privately what a Rougedragon Poursuivant was, evidently under the impression that it was some kind of animal. (141)

Unimpressed by the elaborate re-creation of the rituals of British imperial monarchy, Sackville-West withholds her approval of the coronation preparations until the city fills with "wild and picturesque" tribesmen from neighboring areas: "Teheran was losing its shoddy would-be European appearance and putting on, at last, a character more reminiscent of the pen of Marco Polo" (140). Like the literary allusions that fill her letters to Woolf, Sackville-West's praise for thirteenth-century travel writings by the Christian Venetian Marco Polo betrays her need to contain Persia within romanticized Western narratives. The chapter finally undercuts the coronation's solemnity—and, by extension, Persia's entrance into modern nationhood—by demanding, "Now what can be more absurd than a coronation? It argues a veneration for kings, which no reasonable person can feel" (148). Despite *Passenger to Teheran*'s avowal that "Asia is not Europe, and all countries bestow different gifts" (100), Vita Sackville-West's depictions of Persia fall into the mythos of a modern West and an ancient East. This mythos operates as a crucial narrative stabilizer in *Orlando*, obscuring any element of the non-Western world that disrupts English assumptions about it.

The genre of travel writing conventionally features a return to native soil, and Vita Sackville-West's description of her return to England offers a final instance of the unwitting Orientalism that has run through the foregoing chapters. After a brief visit to Russia, Sackville-West goes back to London and ends her book with a series of questions that partially subverts the idea of a simple return to known life:

> Was I on the sea? Very rough, too; beautiful, green, white-crested waves; was I at Folkestone? with English voices talking round me? was that Yew Tree Cottage and the path across the fields? Were those the two pistons at Orpington, still going up and down, and still a little wrong? Was I standing on the platform at Victoria, I who had stood on so many platforms? The orange labels dangled in the glare of the electric lamps. PERSIA, they said; PERSIA. (181)

The rhetorical device of the questions suggests that England is merely one locus among many; Woolf adopts the same question strategy at the end of *Orlando* to suggest a multiselved interior for her protagonist. But Vita Sackville-West's final evocation of Persia—just a name on an official customs label—shifts Persia's ontological status, making it less real than the England to which Sackville-West has returned. David Spurr calls this kind of ontological shift "insubstantialization," a literary gesture in which "One 'finds out where one is' by putting the Orient, with its undefined categories of subjective and objective experience, over *there*" (142). Vita's final paragraph, like her opening anecdote about the naïve Oriental, enshrines England as an ideological and geographical center for understanding the rest of the world. Persia becomes a place "over *there*," a nation delineated as England's geographical Other. With the final line of *Passenger to Teheran*, Persia literally shrinks to what it has metaphorically been throughout the narrative: a label that affirms an Englishwoman's global mobility.

Virginia Woolf's response to *Passenger to Teheran* seized on Persia's remoteness; she told Sackville-West that the book "gives this sense of your being away, travelling, not in any particular geographical country: but travelling far away" (*Letters* III, 291). And Sackville-West's distant, anonymous Orient would provide a template for Woolf: anchoring *Orlando*'s aesthetic daring with the imperial tropes of *Passenger to Teheran*, Woolf plots her novel as a sequence of "contact zones" defined by asymmetric race relations. Channeling the same disjunctiveness that defines Sackville-West's relationship to England once she leaves its boundaries, Woolf prompts Orlando's self-awareness by thrusting him/her into diverse cultural spaces. To capture Sackville-West's love for the Persian countryside, Woolf's novel sets up an Oriental pastoral that stands in powerful opposition to life in the imperial metropolis.[37] Like *Passenger to Teheran*'s assessments of Persia and its lack of modern conveniences, *Orlando* situates the Orient within a chronology determined by Western narratives of progress and ultimately reduces it to an insubstantial, indeterminate, and ahistorical geographical location. Like Sackville-West contextualizing her travel experience with allusions to imperial-era British literature, *Orlando* borrows from (and, eventually, takes its place in) a Western literary tradition that stereotypes, silences, and debases the nonwhite Other. And just as questioning England's "realness" does not level the cultural playing field in *Passenger to Teheran*, articulating the contingent nature of racial and national identities does not weaken Englishness in *Orlando*. Both *Orlando* and *Passenger to Teheran* end by offering up England as an essential "home" whose absent presence pervades and dominates geographical spaces outside of itself, a *lieu de mémoire* with the power to preserve racial continuity in the face of sexual or spatiotemporal displacement.[38]

Orlando's enormous narrative arc traces its protagonist's racial identity across four hundred years, beginning and ending with an Englishness that is absolutely white and therefore entitled to the subjugation of dark races. The history of Englishness in *Orlando* reflects Woolf's lifelong interest in what Melba Cuddy-Keane terms a dialectical relation between "difference" and "continuities": "Difference implies periodization," Cuddy-Keane explains in *Virginia Woolf, the Intellectual, and the Public Sphere,* "the discrete character of each era, the distinctive characteristics in the way people lived, the way they used language, the forms to which their emotions were attached. Continuities imply an ahistorical mode, a strand of anti-periodization that focuses on the persistence of the same" (156). In *Orlando,* Woolf historicizes sexuality while leaving race in an "ahistorical mode" that cuts across the otherwise-mutable particulars of English culture. *Orlando*'s narrative, therefore, unfolds in dizzying alternations between minute, periodizing detail about sex and sweeping generalizations about race.

These alternations are visible in the novel's very first sentence. Orlando enters the novel as a boy in Elizabethan England, reenacting a racial violence that defines a tradition of imperial masculinity:

> He—for there could be no doubt of his sex, though the fashion of the time did something to disguise it—was in the act of slicing at the head of a Moor which swung from the rafters. It was the colour of an old football, and more or less the shape of one, save for the sunken cheeks and a strand or two of coarse, dry hair, like the hair on a cocoanut. Orlando's father, or perhaps his grandfather, had struck it from the shoulders of a vast Pagan who had started up under the moon in the barbarian fields of Africa; and now it swung, gently, perpetually, in the breeze which never ceased blowing through the attic rooms of the gigantic house of the lord who had slain him. (13)

The teasing gambit about Orlando's ambiguous sex cannot "disguise" his *unambiguous* claim to racial authority. This opening paragraph contains a brutally literal instance of racial discontinuity, one that recalls Mr. Kurtz's hut in the Belgian Congo: the act of separating the black head from the black body ensures the unbroken sovereignty of white Englishness. Slicing at the degraded, trivialized Moor's head establishes that to be white is to be English and participate in imperial enterprise: this fusion of race, nationality, and colonial praxis exerts its ideological power throughout the novel.[39] Sixteen-year-old Orlando embraces this fusion at the novel's inception, vowing to follow his ancestors who "had struck many heads of many colours off many shoulders, and brought them back to hang from the rafters" (13). Orlando's adventures over the next three centuries test his claim to racial continuity: as he moves away—geographically, psychologically, sexually—from ancestral tradition, he finds himself increasingly critical of the racial legacy he has assumed he will perpetuate. But Woolf gradually naturalizes imperial racial hierarchies at the same time that she denaturalizes sexual hierarchies, and Orlando overcomes his momentary lapses into racial ambivalence by renewing his commitment to the cultural protocols that distinguish white Englishnesss. Despite the claim that Orlando "belonged to the sacred race rather than to the noble—was by birth a writer, rather than an aristocrat" (83), Woolf's protagonist achieves the racial and national integration that concludes a nineteenth-century bildungsroman rather than the radical artistic autonomy that distinguishes the modernist *Künstlerroman*.

The Elizabethan chapters of *Orlando* are the novel's most lighthearted, skimming gaily through Orlando's life at court, his mediocre poetry, and his romantic escapades. Although jocular narrative distance mediates Orlando's suffering, violent racial hierarchies sharpen the thrust of Woolf's comedy. Orlando's first crisis is an unhappy love affair with Sasha, the Russian princess who betrays him with comic rapidity. A Punch-and-Judy performance of *Othello* supplies a convenient metaphor for Orlando's outrage: "A black man was waving his arms and vociferating. There was a woman in white laid upon the bed. . . . The frenzy of the Moor seemed to him his own frenzy, and when the Moor suffocated the woman in her bed it was Sasha he killed with his own hands" (56–7). Orlando's servants, regardless of race, come together to express their sympathy for Sasha's betrayal, so that "even the Blackamoor whom they called Grace Robinson by way of making a Christian woman of her, understood what they were at, and agreed that his Lordship was a handsome, pleasant, daring gentleman in the only way she could, that is to say by showing all her teeth at once in a broad grin" (70). To assuage his grief over Sasha's infidelity, Orlando writes a play (aptly titled "Xenophila a Tragedy"), which is publicly lampooned by a literary critic; the satirizing of his art leads a devastated Orlando to declare, "'I have done with men'" (96) and to retreat to his estate. His escape from the public sphere of English life takes the form of exploiting foreign resources: in the manner of Dorian Gray, Orlando finds comfort in furnishing his estate with objects from Eastern and African countries, buying a cabinet from a Moor, rugs and chests from Persia, and bears from Malaysia. The imperial enterprise that beautifies his estate also spirits him away from England:

when his lavish decor attracts the unwanted attention of the Archduchess Harriett Griselda, Orlando "did what any other young man would have done in his place, and asked King Charles to send him as Ambassador Extraordinary to Constantinople" (118). Woolf's ironizing here—like the conspicuous absence of historical detail in *Passenger to Teheran*—does not mask the ease with which Orlando can access and hold power in the East; as he has earlier occupied Othello's fictive mental space, Orlando moves away from England to occupy the geographical space of Constantinople.

If conventional racial hierarchies provided palliatives for Orlando's romantic crisis in Elizabethan England, race in seventeenth-century Constantinople no longer fits neatly into categories that Orlando can know and control. Constantinople itself, with its centuries of imperial history, challenges Orlando's ideas about unified national identity. This metropolis supplies the novel's richest metaphor for a multiply inscribed cultural identity: the city was originally founded as the Greek colony Byzantium during the seventh century BC, renamed Constantinople in 342 AD when it was appointed the capital of Christendom in the East, and sacked by the Ottomans in 1453 to become the world's most powerful empire. The fixed British hegemonies of *Orlando*'s opening seem fragile in the context of this vast seaport and its Persian, Turkish, Armenian, Jewish, Muslim, and Christian inhabitants. As long as white Englishness sits squarely atop the novel's cultural hierarchies, Woolf allows Orlando the "flexible *positional* superiority," in Edward Said's well-known formulation, of flirting with the sexual and social possibilities offered by racial difference (*Orientalism,* 7).[40] But after Orlando transforms into a woman and threatens to exchange English aristocracy for permanent residence in rural Turkey, her happy integration into the Orient ends abruptly. Her hasty return to England echoes the troubled cultural relativism of Vita Sackville-West's *Passenger to Teheran:* Orlando's desires to experience racial Otherness, while partially legitimized by the narrator, are always halted by a return to the propertied, aristocratic world of imperial England. And although the narrator-biographer devotes most of his considerable energy toward detailing Orlando's madcap antics, repatriation to England (whether literal or symbolic) becomes the drivetrain of his story.[41]

Woolf styles Orlando's experience of Constantinople after Vita Sackville-West's experience of Persia. Like the Englishwoman on diplomatic duty who dreams of blending into Persia, the English ambassador Orlando revels in racial and cultural crossovers, intent on divesting himself of the repressive particulars of imperial duty in the Oriental metropolis. Orlando gazes on the spectacle of Constantinople's "strident and multicoloured and barbaric population" (120) and questions the origins of the Englishness that appeared so unassailable in the Elizabethan era:

> That he, who was English root and fibre, should yet exult to the depths of his heart in this wild panorama, and gaze and gaze at those passes and far heights, planning journeys there alone on foot where only the goat and shepherd had gone before; should feel a passion of affection for the bright, unseasonable flowers, love the unkempt, pariah dogs beyond even his elk hounds at home, and snuff the acrid, sharp smell of the streets eagerly into his nostrils, surprised him. He wondered if, in the season of the Crusades, one of his ancestors had taken up with a Circassian peasant woman; thought it possible; fancied a certain darkness in his complexion; and, going indoors again, withdrew to his bath. (121)

Uncultivated nature, outcast animals, unmapped terrain: these "wild" aspects of Constantinople, each one a counterpoint to the civility of imperial Britain, spur Orlando to doubt the seamless racial continuum of his ancestry. His Englishness becomes less a source of self-definition and more a hindrance to be masked: he mocks the overblown English rites that herald his promotion to the Order of the Bath; he disguises himself as a Turk to "mingle with the crowd" (124) in the bazaars and the streets; and he marries a Gypsy woman named Rosina Pepita and makes real the miscegenation that he imagined in "Xenophila a Tragedy." Once Orlando becomes a woman and steps away from the public position of ambassador, however, her willful embrace of Turkishness denotes a problematic racial instability rather than the exhilarating possibilities of a multilayered self.

The change from male to female takes place during a Turkish uprising when Orlando lies in an inexplicable trance and the British in Constantinople are comically vulnerable:

> The Turks rose against the Sultan, set fire to the town, and put every foreigner they could find, either to the sword or to the bastinado. A few English managed to escape; but, as might have been expected, the gentlemen of the British Embassy preferred to die in defence of their red boxes, or, in extreme cases, to swallow bunches of keys rather than let them fall into the hands of the Infidel. The rioters broke into Orlando's room, but seeing him stretched to all appearance dead they left him untouched, and only robbed him of his coronet and the robes of the Garter. (133)

Bereft of the external markers of imperial identity, Orlando awakens the next morning and "stood upright in complete nakedness before us, and while the trumpets pealed Truth! Truth! Truth! we have no choice left but confess—he was a woman" (137). This sex change is conventionally interpreted as a soaring leap that radicalizes gender as well as literary form, a joyous modernist undoing of patriarchy and realism alike.[42] However, it is crucial to recognize that Woolf sets the transformation in Constantinople, rather than in pastoral or metropolitan England, and that Orlando's passage into femininity depends on the dual Otherness of race and place. Echoing *Passenger to Teheran*'s condescension toward natives, Woolf avails herself of the stereotype of the androgynous Oriental: the narrator remarks that "the gipsy women, except in one or two important particulars, differ very little from the gipsy men" (153), and Orlando purchases her freedom to be *biologically* female but *socially* androgynous by exchanging ambassadorial garb for "those Turkish coats and trousers which can be worn indifferently by either sex" (139).[43] Orlando's masquerade, in other words, deploys a racial trompe l'oeil to secure her daring sexual liberation.

Once the newly female Orlando abandons Constantinople and the ambassadorial post to live with the putatively androgynous Gypsies, Englishness gets focalized through Turkish eyes. The Gypsies fulfill the imaginative role so often assigned to them in English literature: their anonymous collectivity suggests, in Janet Lyon's words, "an emblem of natural liberty, unencumbered mobility, communal loyalty and harmony, admirably impervious to manipulation by the state and everywhere subverting the disciplinarity of evolving modern institutions" ("Gadže Modernism," 518). The Gypsies train Orlando to live as one of them, urging her to abandon her English instincts and desires because they "looked upon her as one of themselves (which is always the highest compliment a people can pay) and her dark hair and dark complexion bore out the belief that she was, by birth, one of them. . . . [They] taught her their arts of cheese-making and basket-weaving, their science of stealing and birdsnaring, and were even prepared to consider letting her marry among them" (141–42). As a woman performing "Gypsyness" in rural Turkey, Orlando has moved to the outermost racial and sexual margins of her imperial heritage; her absorption into the Gypsies' world both parodies and compromises the whiteness that was established in the Elizabethan section of the narrative.

Woolf designates an old Turkish man named Rustum el Sadi as the mouthpiece of the Gypsies' animosity toward Englishness. At first glance, this seemingly minor character who guides Orlando out of Constantinople offers a static racial stereotype: "He had a nose like a scimitar; his cheeks were furrowed as if from the age-long descent of iron hail; he was brown and keen-eyed, and as he sat tugging at his hookah he observed Orlando narrowly" (144). But Rustum's comments on the cultural gulf dividing East from West infiltrate Orlando's consciousness, powerfully denaturalizing her claims to race and nation. Woolf names Rustum after the warrior-hero of the tenth-century Persian epic *Shahname*, or *Book of Kings*, which delineates Iran's pre-Islamic history through the lives of the shahs. One of the *Shahname*'s most famous episodes narrates the tragic battle that Rustum fights against his son, Sohrab; both warriors fight in disguise, and Rustum unknowingly kills his son.[44] The tragedy arising from mistaken identity resonates throughout *Orlando*, as Woolf's Rustum tempts Orlando to live as a Gypsy and reject her "root and fibre" ties to England. From Rustum's perspective, each of Orlando's cherished forefathers is no more than "a vulgar upstart, an adventurer, a *nouveau riche*" (149). He demeans Orlando's four-hundred-year-old ancestral estate by reassuring her that

> she need not mind if her father were a Duke, and possessed all the bedrooms and furniture that she described. They would none of them think the worse of her for that. Then she was seized with a shame that she had never felt before. It was clear that Rustum and the other gipsies thought a descent of four or five hundred years only the meanest possible. Their own families went back at least two or three thousand years. To the gipsy whose ancestors had built the Pyramids centuries before Christ was born, the genealogy of the Howards and Plantagenets was no better and no worse than that of the Smiths and the Joneses: both were negligible. Moreover, where the shepherd boy had a lineage of such antiquity, there was nothing specially memorable or desirable in ancient birth; vagabonds and beggars alike all shared it. (147–8)

The Gypsies lay claim to a premodern genealogy that not only renders Orlando's own racial continuity insignificant but, by extension, casts aspersions on the very idea of a racially continuous England. The Gypsies' lineage quashes Orlando's conviction that "she came of an ancient and civilised race, whereas these gipsies were an ignorant people, not much better than savages" (147). National and familial pride deflated, Orlando realizes that England is merely an "imagined community" whose codes, once recontextualized, become meaningless.[45]

Orlando finds herself trapped between the pastoral, communal Turkey she now occupies and the patriarchal, imperial England she has left behind:

> "Four hundred and seventy-six bedrooms mean nothing to them," sighed Orlando.

"She prefers a sunset to a flock of goats," said the Gipsies.

What was to be done, Orlando could not think. To leave the gipsies and become once more an Ambassador seemed to her intolerable. But it was equally impossible to remain for ever where there was neither ink nor writing paper, neither reverence for the Talbots, nor respect for a multiplicity of bedrooms. (149–50)

If Lily Briscoe's racial ambiguity in *To the Lighthouse* provides the novel's richest source of perceptual originality, Orlando's racial ambiguity begets narrative panic and the attending imperative to restore English hegemony. The literal eccentricity of her love for the Gypsies can only be repaired by a return to the imperial center; and to this end, Woolf grants Orlando a mythic moment of nationalist identification. Orlando sits atop a Turkish mountain despairing over her cultural choices, when "a great park-like space opened in the flank of the hill" (150) and she has a panoramic vision of an English summer, autumn, and winter. This magical vision recalls the novel's original cultural hierarchy: England's natural beauty depletes the central Asian landscape of its semantic richness, and accordingly, Orlando "burst into a passion of tears, and striding back to the gipsies' camp, told them that she must sail for England the very next day" (151). The narrator applauds Orlando's departure by describing the formerly alluring Turkish landscape as a savage, inhospitable space that "a thousand vultures seemed to have picked bare" and by calling the Gypsies murderers who "had plotted her death" because "she did not think as they did" (151). Our final impression of Turkey is of a nation undesirable, opaque, and incomprehensible in the face of the organic Englishness that flows through Orlando.

Orlando's impassioned reaction to "seeing" England in the Turkish countryside anticipates her reaction to London's actual skyline when her ship enters the harbor. She is awed by the sight of St. Paul's Cathedral, Westminster Abbey, the Houses of Parliament, Greenwich Hospital, the Royal Pavilion, and other imperial monuments: "Her eyes had been used too long to savages and nature not to be entranced by these urban glories" (165). The imperial center's iconic architecture tempers Orlando's anxieties about racial displacement as she reenters "her native shore" (167); these first moments of Orlando's repatriation reinforce the freshly restored cultural hierarchy that subordinates Turkey to England. Like the final lines of Vita Sackville-West's travelogue, which reestablish London as the planetary center and Persia as a space "out *there*," Woolf's novel transports its protagonist to London and relegates Turkey to memory. Orlando's literal departure from the East to the West gets replicated symbolically in the rest of the novel, as Woolf weaves the pattern of racial departure-and-return into her heroine's adventures over the next three centuries.

Woolf incorporates Rustum el Sadi's presence into Orlando's London life to sustain the uneasy tension between the premodern East and the modern West. Although physically absent, Rustum continues to function as the novel's source of anti-Englishness and racial critique, and the ghost of his voice haunts Orlando when she is disenchanted with the social demands of each successive age. The defining concerns of each era—aristocratic inheritance in the eighteenth century, the "marriage plot" in the nineteenth, the absence of a fixed, unified self in the twentieth—build to pointed racial conflicts between Rustum and Orlando. However, Woolf repeatedly preserves the very Englishness she satirizes, rescuing Orlando from Rustum's cultural logic through a series of deft narrative maneuvers. And as Orlando witnesses the encroachment of twentieth-century modernity, racial continuity becomes her most powerful defense against the ruptures of history.

The chapters set during the eighteenth century, the age of "Addison, Pope, and Dryden," furnish a thorough exploration of sexual identity. Orlando "learns" her newly acquired womanhood by appearing at Queen Anne's court, attending the patriarchal literary salons where Alexander Pope presides, and passing evenings in prostitutes' quarters. Her reactions against eighteenth-century social and literary culture expose the absurdity of its elaborate sexual codes:

> And here it would seem from some ambiguity in her terms that she was censuring both sexes equally, as if she belonged to neither; and indeed, for the time being she seemed to vacillate; she was man; she was woman; she knew the secrets, shared the weaknesses of each. It was a most bewildering and whirligig state of mind to be in. (158)

This "bewildering and whirligig state of mind," while sexually freeing, unmoors Orlando's ties to her familial heritage. Wandering about the great chambers of her aristocratic estate, whose history and furnishings combine to produce a synecdochic portrait of imperial England, Orlando realizes that the house no longer fortifies her identity as it had prior to the Constantinople trip:

> But even the bones of her ancestors, Sir Miles, Sir Gervase, and the rest, had lost something of their sanctity since Rustum el Sadi had waved his hand that night in the Asian mountains. Somehow the fact that only three or four hun-

dred years ago these skeletons had been men with their way to make in the
world like any modern upstart . . . filled her with remorse. . . . The vast, empty
hills which lie above the Sea of Marmara seemed, for the moment, a finer
dwelling place than this many-roomed mansion in which no bed lacked its
quilt and no silver dish its silver cover. (174)

Troubled by having to think of an ancestor as a "modern upstart," Orlando
admits, "'I am losing my illusions,'" (175); the fissuring of her ancestral
pride forces her to acknowledge the dialectical, contingent quality of the
Englishness she had once regarded as absolute and self-contained. But Orlando's social critique has firm limits: Woolf ensures that England, no matter how foolish its particulars, remains decidedly preferable to the cultural
logic of the Orient that Orlando has just left. Orlando finds the inspiration to combat Rustum in a narrative reenactment of the magical vision
that prompted her departure from Turkey. She leans out of her estate window, hears a fox and a pheasant moving through the snowy English night,
and has a revelation spurred by her organic response to England's natural
beauty: "'By my life,' she exclaimed, 'this is a thousand times better than
Turkey. Rustum,' she cried, as if she were arguing with the gipsy . . . 'you
were wrong. This is better than Turkey'" (176). And as the century draws
to its close, Orlando stands in London admiring St. Paul's Cathedral while
Big Ben strikes midnight: like Vita Sackville-West's homecoming from Persia, both pastoral beauty and metropolitan spectacle bolster Orlando's love
for her country's "light, order, and serenity" (225). Despite the *textual* admission that nationhood and genealogy are arbitrary cultural designations,
Woolf restores the character *Orlando*'s belief in the English nation's innate virtues.

Rustum jeopardizes Orlando's adulation for her ancestors during the
eighteenth century, but his voice in the nineteenth century threatens Orlando's identity as the bearer of *future* generations. Documenting the ties
between the domestic family and the national family, Woolf supplants the
cumulative mythology of male ancestry with the nineteenth-century's ide-
alization of mothers and children: "The life of the average woman was a
succession of childbirths. She married at nineteen and had fifteen or eighteen children by the time she was thirty; for twins abounded. Thus the
British Empire came into existence" (229). Under Queen Victoria's reign,
marriage and childbirth at home provide the means for racial violence and
exploitation abroad, a merging of patriotism and patriarchy that both repulses and oppresses Orlando: "The spirit of the nineteenth century was

antipathetic to her in the extreme, and thus it took her and broke her, and she was aware of her defeat at its hands as she had never been before" (244). Determined to escape the injunction to marry and bear children, Orlando runs away from her grand estate and promptly breaks her ankle. Lying helpless on the ground, she declares, "My hands shall wear no wedding ring" (248), and, as before, the memory of Rustum's voice tempts her to part ways with an imperial English life-narrative:

> "I have sought happiness through many ages and not found it; fame and missed it; love and not known it; life—and behold, death is better. I have known many men and many women," she continued; "none have I understood. It is better that I should lie at peace here with only the sky above me —as the gipsy told me years ago. That was in Turkey." (248–49)

Once more diverting Orlando from submitting to the Gypsy's worldview, Woolf engineers her protagonist's participation in the Victorian marriage plot she loathes. In one of the novel's funniest passages, the solution to Orlando's marriage dilemma literally rides up on a horse and rescues her from her broken ankle and singlehood:

> Towering dark against the yellow-slashed sky of dawn, with the plovers rising and falling about him, she saw a man on horseback. He started. The horse stopped.
> "Madam," the man cried, leaping to the ground, "you're hurt!"
> "I'm dead, Sir!" she replied.
> A few minutes later, they became engaged. (250)

Orlando's rebellious feminism provokes a psychological return to Rustum's Turkey, but her marriage to Marmaduke Bonthrop Shelmerdine, an English sea-captain, restores imperial England's cultural authority. Certainly, narrative high jinks scale new heights over the course of this marriage, in which Orlando reveals that she is a man, Shelmerdine admits that he is a woman, and Woolf makes hay of Vita Sackville-West's and Harold Nicolson's well-known bisexuality.[46] Awed by Orlando and Shel's capacity to discourse limitlessly, the narrator declares that "it would profit little to write down what they said," and, subsequently, leaves on the page "a great blank here, which must be taken to indicate that the space is filled to repletion" (253). Woolf leaves half a page empty of text, a blank space that embodies the discontinuities of gender, history, and narrative itself. However, the actual marital discourse implied by this blank half page reminds us that *Orlando*'s racial categories remain continuous even when all other aspects of identity are disjunctive.

Orlando and Shelmerdine's sexual candor goes hand in hand with a deeply racialized epistemic violence; the whiteness of the narrator's blank page, perhaps, unintentionally literalizes the unifying element of their private language. Shel has spent his life sailing round Cape Horn and adventuring in foreign lands, and his romance with Orlando fits neatly into a master narrative of British imperial conquest and its attending domestic ideologies. The couple's engagement itself precipitates a series of symbolic racial erasures: Orlando's Turkish marriage to Rosina Pepita is annulled and the offspring declared illegitimate, and the townspeople celebrate by burning effigies of Turkish women and peasant boys in the marketplace. If Orlando earlier identified himself with Othello, she now fulfills the role of Desdemona, listening raptly to Shel's tales of geographic and sexual conquest. Shel models Cape Horn with twigs, leaves, and snail shells and describes how he

> went on shore; was trapped by a black woman; repented; reasoned it out; read Pascal; determined to write philosophy; bought a monkey; debated the true end of life; decided in favour of Cape Horn, and so on. All this and a thousand other things she understood him to say and so when she replied, Yes, negresses are seductive, aren't they? he having told her that the supply of biscuits now gave out, he was surprised and delighted to find how well she had taken his meaning. (258)

Poised on the brink of the twentieth century when "words are growing daily so scanty in comparison with ideas," the narrator notes that "'the biscuits ran out' has to stand for kissing a negress in the dark" (258). This semiotic looseness, on one hand, reflects a Woolfian obsession with language and, simultaneously, pays tribute to Vita Sackville-West's admission that travel narratives only convey "a fraction of the registered vision" because "one can *never* communicate." But Orlando and Shelmerdine's mutual understanding of "kissing a negress in the dark" signifies their complicity in colonial hierarchies under which black women function as sexual commodities for white consumption. Shel's dalliances with black women—unlike Orlando's dangerous consciousness of Rustum el Sadi—do not disrupt the logic of the British Empire's cohesiveness or sovereignty; indeed, as suggested by "how well she had taken his meaning," Orlando accepts her husband's interracial affairs as a sign of imperial masculinity. And unlike the avant-garde primitivism we considered in the previous chapter, which treats blackness as an artistically productive and therefore liberating condition, the "negress" here functions as a symbolic double for the mute, lifeless Moor's head hanging from Orlando's rafters. The interleaved sexual and imperial economies of Orlando and Shelmerdine's marriage, in other words, restore the racial matrix of the novel's first scene. And as the titled wife of an empire builder who "had been a soldier and a sailor, and had explored the East" (251), Orlando fittingly concludes the Victorian era having been "safely delivered of a son" (295).

Although Orlando meets the Victorian era's expectations of marriage and maternity, Woolf tests her allegiance to Englishness once again at the onset of the twentieth century. In the modern, postwar English metropole, the floodgates of subjectivity burst open, forcing Orlando to confront her many identities and for the last time choose whether she will remain an ideologically fragmented subject or return to a belief in wholeness and undifferentiated white English aristocracy. In the twentieth-century chapters, Woolf subsumes all of the novel's previous sources of conflict—sexual identity, miscegenation, allegiance to aristocratic codes—into a more fundamental tension about individuality and selfhood. Orlando's consciousness becomes a repository for each identity she has moved through thus far, and whenever she tries to speak in this final section, a different self comes in and interrupts her. Speech and desire become entangled in a contradictory network of past and present selves, rendering a univocal self virtually impossible. Orlando literally hails herself to make sense of the voices clashing in her consciousness, revealing her potential to be interpellated into any one of a "great variety of selves": "Orlando, at the turn by the barn, called 'Orlando?' with a note of interrogation in her voice and waited. Orlando did not come" (309).

But Woolf problematizes, rather than celebrates, Orlando's characteristically modern subjective instability, transforming it into a conflict marked by the danger of racial crossovers. The final chapters articulate Orlando's plurality of selves across racial, national, historical, and sexual categories: in the twentieth century, Orlando recognizes within herself "the boy who cut the nigger's head down; the boy who strung it up again," "the young man who fell in love with Sasha," "the Traveller," and "the Gipsy" (309). The fluctuation between continuity and discontinuity expresses itself, yet again, in the language of racial and cultural difference:

> "How strange it is! Nothing is any longer one thing. . . . When I step out of doors—as I do now," here she stepped on to the pavement of Oxford Street,

"what is it that I taste? Little herbs. I hear goat bells. I see mountains. Turkey? India? Persia?" Her eyes filled with tears.

That Orlando had gone a little too far from the present moment will, perhaps, strike the reader who sees her now preparing to get into her motor car with her eyes full of tears and visions of Persian mountains. (304–5)

The Persian mountains blind Orlando to her motor car, an unwelcome incursion of Eastern nature into Western modernity. As the psychic sway of the remembered Orient overwrites the fleeting, fast-changing spectacle of Oxford Street in 1928, the narrator chides Orlando for displacing herself from modern metropolitan flux with memories that transport her "too far from the present moment." Unlike Lily Briscoe, whose modern selfhood is defined by racial differentiation, Orlando's racial polyvalence must disappear so that "what is called, rightly or wrongly, a single self, a real self" (314) can take a stable, permanent place atop cultural hierarchies. To this end, Woolf pits Orlando against Rustum for one final clash. In a scene that reverses Orlando's magical vision of England in the Turkish hillside, Orlando has a vision of a *Turkish* landscape while looking into the English countryside:

> Here the landscape (it must have been some trick of the fading light) shook itself, heaped itself, let all this encumbrance of houses, castles, and woods slide off its tent-shaped sides. The bare mountains of Turkey were before her. It was blazing noon. She looked straight at the baked hill-side. Goats cropped the sandy tufts at her feet. An eagle soared above her. The raucous voice of old Rustum, the gipsy, croaked in her ears, "What is your antiquity and your race, and your possessions compared with this? What do you need with four hundred bedrooms and silver lids on all the dishes, and housemaids dusting?"
>
> At this moment some church clock chimed in the valley. The tent-like landscape collapsed and fell. (326)

Rustum's question—what is your antiquity and your race?—distills the concern that *Orlando,* perhaps more than any other text in my study of experimental British modernism, has proven unanswerable. But Woolf elects to answer it and thereby unify her protagonist's fragmented race-consciousness: in a final, climactic defense of Orlando's Englishness, Rustum's voice is drowned out by church bells, as though the Anglican Church were silencing Islam. As soon as Rustum falls silent, Shelmerdine returns from yet another trip to Cape Horn, "now grown a fine sea-captain" (329), and his reunion with Orlando reinstates the global dominance of white

Englishness. A long series of attempted cultural subversions ends, inevitably, by affirming Western power. Although Rustum's croaking recentralizes the enormously contingent nature of nationally and racially inscribed selfhood, *Orlando*'s narrator does not ultimately embrace this contingency.

Orlando's conclusion echoes the end of *Passenger to Teheran:* a displaced, vulnerable national identity regains its essential textual validity. When Orlando makes her final return to her estate, a queen arrives in a chariot and proclaims that an unbroken continuum of English aristocratic rule awaits her mistress: "'The house is at your service, Ma'am,' she cried, curtseying deeply. 'Nothing has been changed'" (328). This fantasy of historically enduring English monarchy works hand in glove with Orlando's very first fantasy about joining his ancestors' violent conquest of "barbarians." *Orlando* shores up a powerful collection of refutations to racial ambivalence, reifying the white imperial Englishness whose very hollowness inspires Lily Briscoe's "vision" at the conclusion of *To the Lighthouse*.

CONCLUSION

Race and the New Modernist Studies

I draw this study of race and modernism to a close by returning to the scene where we began: the multihued world of the Ballets Russes. In 1910, Sergei Diaghilev famously issued a command to the French dramatist, sculptor, and filmmaker Jean Cocteau: "Astonish me!" Cocteau obliged the Russian impresario with his libretto for *The Blue God,* a ballet about the Hindu god Krishna that debuted in Paris in 1912. The astonishments of *The Blue God*—the ancient Indian roots of its narrative, the arresting modernity of its choreography—cannot be understood apart from the *racial* astonishments that Diaghilev and his collaborators offered to their London and Paris audiences. Watching dancers strike poses inspired by Hindu statues and temple carvings, their bodies enrobed in Léon Bakst's elaborately wrought Indian costumes and their movements channeling the rhythms of music by Venezuelan-born composer Reynaldo Hahn, ballet goers recognized the arrival of an entirely new cultural moment. It was a moment that bore witness to an avalanche of such astonishments, and a moment when metropolitan modernist artists revolutionized the art world by rendering the terms of art inseparable from the terms of race.

The idea of race holds a key place in the evolution of modernism. It is an idea that should, accordingly, hold a key place in our critical engagement with the modernist movement and its varied commitments. Since the early 1990s, the rise of the "new modernist studies" has energetically rewritten the character of what had long been canonized as "the Pound era." A surge of scholarly activity has broadened the criteria for modernist aesthetics and style, realigned modernism's spatial and temporal coordinates, and uncovered modernist involvement with politics, mass culture, advertising, and fashion.[1] Consequently, the movement we once conceived of

Figure 20. Vaslav Nijinsky in the title role of *The Blue God,* costumes designed by Léon Bakst, 1912. Hindu temple statues inspired the ballet's costumes and choreography. (Bibliothèque Nationale de l'Opera, Paris. Photo Credit: Snark /Art Resource, New York.)

as austere, inward looking, and contemptuous of popular culture has emerged as a colorful mosaic of contradictory achievements, deeply invested in cultural production at every level. Our intellectual inquiries into modernist history and culture now encompass, in Douglas Mao's and Rebecca Walkowitz's words, "a pluralism or fusion of theoretical commitments, as well as a heightened attention to continuities and intersections across the boundaries of artistic media, to collaborations and influences across national and linguistic borders, and (especially) to the relationship between individual works of art and the larger cultures in which they emerged" (*Bad Modernisms,* 2). Where, then, does race fit into the new modernist studies? A look at two transformative domains in the discipline—gender and transnationalism—suggests how our understanding of modernism might be further transformed by critical approaches to race.

The new modernist studies began to shatter traditional conceptions of literary modernism through unstinting attention to discourses about gender, sexuality, and women's history. As Tamar Katz argues, these discourses powerfully determined the ways in which modernism "aspired to both anarchy and order, to stable meanings and a vertiginous, fluid refusal of reference, to both political commitments and claims for the autonomy of high culture" (3). Scholarship on gender and its relationship to authorship, cultural production, and the status of the art object gained a powerful foothold in Sandra Gilbert and Susan Gubar's massive three-volume study, *No Man's Land: The Place of the Woman Writer in the Twentieth Century* (1988, 1989, and 1994), which rewrote the history of modernist literature as a battle between the sexes. Bonnie Kime Scott's 1990 literary anthology *The Gender of Modernism,* dedicated to "the forgotten and silenced makers of modernism," recuperated the voices of modernist women authors such as Katherine Mansfield, Dorothy Richardson, Mina Loy, Djuna Barnes, and Charlotte Mew. Scott's two-volume work *Refiguring Modernism* (1995), as well as studies by Ann Ardis, Shari Benstock, Suzanne Clark, Jayne Marek, Gillian Hanscombe and Virginia Smyers, and Bridget Elliott and Jo-Ann Wallace, detailed women's vital roles in metropolitan modernism as artists, activists, publishers, editors, hostesses, critics, and entrepreneurs.[2] Perhaps most influentially, Rita Felski's *The Gender of Modernity* (1995) made visible the dominant sociological theories of masculinity and femininity that profoundly defined the modern era's sense of itself. The achievement of such scholarship has been not only to recover women's contributions to modernism but, more crucially, to establish that gender is *conceptually* essential for understanding the movement and its era. As the authoritative 2007 *Cam-*

bridge Introduction to Modernism declares, "Three major categories of human experience were reimagined in modernist literature and art: gender, space, and time" (Lewis, 26).

Race merits similar visibility as a structural category in early twentieth-century literature and art, but it has yet to be formalized as one of modernism's keywords. Prior to the reinvention of modernist studies, as I argued in my introduction, race was either largely absent from British modernist scholarship or else subsumed into conversations about British imperialism. More recently, however, race has played a complex and variable role in the new modernist studies' second major intellectual project: the "transnational turn."[3] As a consequence of the shift toward transnationalism, the once-stable narrative of Anglo-American modernism has splintered into a collection of crisscrossing *modernisms,* so that a new planetary consciousness imbues our study of art and culture in the early decades of the twentieth century. Race provides a charged locus for what Laura Doyle and Laura Winkiel call "geomodernisms," a term that denotes "modernisms' engagement with cultural and political discourses of global modernity" (3); it also operates as a powerful force in the "cultural globalization," as Melba Cuddy-Keane puts it, that shaped modernism ("Modernism," 540).[4] Scholarship on geo-, transnational, and global modernisms debates the aesthetic, material, and sexual exchanges between modernism and colonialism; it documents modernism's transatlantic currents; and, most recently, it illuminates the modernist tendencies of artists far removed from Western metropolitan capitals.[5] We are now familiar with Caribbean, Chinese, Indian, Filipino, Latin American, and Jewish modernisms, as well the "ethnic modernism," in Werner Sollors's phrase, of Anglo-American literature and arts.[6] And race serves as a core concern in other, seemingly disparate spheres of transnational modernism: consider Janet Lyon's study of decadence and disability, Christopher GoGwilt's delineation of modern geopolitics, Peter Childs's work on eugenics and modern literature, Ryan Jerving's inquiries into jazz modernism, readings of cosmopolitanism by Rebecca Walkowitz, Jessica Berman, and Kobena Mercer, and the ongoing debates about T. S. Eliot's anti-Semitism.[7] Indeed, even Bonnie Kime Scott's follow-up to *The Gender of Modernism,* an anthology titled *Gender in Modernism: New Geographies, Complex Intersections,* declares that "in the first decade of the twenty-first century, gender is most interesting as a system connected with and negotiated among various cultural identifiers" (2). As this wealth of new research suggests, transnationalism has become modernism's new racial byword, evoking an egalitarian boundary crossing that occasionally diffuses the particulars of race into broader discussions about nation and culture. But it is important to acknowledge that all of these new visions of modernism and modernity turn on the elemental concept of race and its attendant questions about continuity, discontinuity, and difference. Whether the fluidity of ethnic and national identities or the literal transmission of corporeal traits, the idea of race lies at the heart of modern culture as it is being discovered and rewritten in current scholarship. In other words, race has come to provide a rubric as well as a method for our evolving study of modernism.

At a moment when we have begun to regard modernism as a complex global phenomenon, this book returns to London—the metropolitan seat of canonical modernism—and invites readers to recognize the conceptual centrality of race in experimental British fiction and related arts. Although critical race theory has moved well beyond reductive binaries that pit white against black, center against periphery, or the West against the rest, the subject of race remains—for obvious reasons—overwhelmingly sociopolitical.[8] By subordinating the social to the aesthetic, I have endeavored to add a fresh dimension to a body of scholarship in which race tends to be circumscribed by questions about cultural asymmetry, social injustice, or colonial praxis. While such questions lead to necessary insights about collective and individual racial experiences and about the formation and dissolution of social and scientific bias, they cannot entirely explain experimental modernism's racial contours. To understand what Simon Gikandi has brilliantly called modernism's "schemata of difference" ("Picasso," 455), we need to approach race as an organizing aesthetic category, a form-giving resource that played an influential but often-overlooked role in the modernist reinvention of art and literature.[9]

I have focused on three aspects of modernism that remain constant despite our increasingly diverse study of the movement: its metropolitan origins, the cultural consciousness of a historical break, and the artistic urge to make it new. My goal has not been to articulate an "alternative" modernism, but rather to illustrate the very complex racial character of British modernism. This goal would have been unattainable without the excellent work that has preceded and informed mine. I am indebted to Edward Said's *Culture and Imperialism* and Simon Gikandi's *Maps of Englishness: Writing Identity in the Culture of Colonialism,* two pathbreaking studies that, in very different ways, made visible the connections between British literature and conceptions of race. These works created a rich point of departure for subsequent studies by Laura Doyle, Jed Esty, Pericles Lewis, Paul Peppis, and Laura Winkiel, scholars who have variously explored how the forms of modernist fiction engaged or redirected the British Empire's dominant conceptions of race.[10] I hope that my own narrative of metropolitan modernism, which brings together several of London's racial conversations between 1890 and 1930, will take its place in this growing body of scholarship, contributing to dialogues about race as a signal element in modernist interdisciplinarity and in British cultural history more generally. We are deeply familiar with the historical ruptures of the early twentieth century but less familiar with how modern artists and authors captured the discontinuities of their cultural moment through newly imagined conceptions of race. This book's mapping of modernism, from the Congolese heads outside Mr. Kurtz's hut to Lily Briscoe's Chinese eyes, demonstrates that the modernist movement's historical and aesthetic self-consciousness —its attention to the now and the new—found radical expression in the forms of race.

NOTES

Introduction

1. See Lynn Garafola, *Diaghilev's Ballets Russes*, and Garafola and Nancy Van Norman Baer, eds., *The Ballets Russes and Its World*, for excellent cultural histories of the dance company. Mary E. Davis's *Classic Chic: Music, Fashion, and Modernism* offers a detailed discussion of the Ballets Russes as a modernist institution.

2. See Peter Wollen, *Raiding the Icebox: Reflections on Twentieth-Century Culture*, Harold Acton, *Memoirs of an Actor*, and Elisabeth Ingles, *Léon Bakst: The Art of Theatre and Dance*.

3. The historical and aesthetic workings of race in the contexts of American, African American, and transatlantic modernism are superbly articulated by Michael North, *The Dialect of Modernism: Race, Language, and Twentieth-Century Literature*, Houston A. Baker, Jr., *Modernism and the Harlem Renaissance*, Laura Doyle, *Freedom's Empire: Race and the Rise of the Novel in Atlantic Modernity, 1640–1940*, and Paul Gilroy, *The Black Atlantic: Modernity and Double Consciousness*.

4. Wide-ranging treatments of this postcolonial literary canon can be found, for example, in Abdul JanMohamed, "The Economy of Manichean Allegory: The Function of Racial Difference in Colonial Literature," Howard Booth and Nigel Rigby, *Modernism and Empire: Writing and British Coloniality, 1890–1940*, Robert Young, *Colonial Desire: Hybridity in Theory, Culture and Race*, and Elleke Boehmer, *Colonial and Postcolonial Literature*.

5. I note here that all of the authors in my study were white and British, but it should be obvious that this does not denote a uniform racial identity; Polish-born Joseph Conrad, New Zealand-born Katherine Mansfield, and English-born Virginia Woolf, for example, inhabited their whiteness and Britishness in very different ways. I also note here that this book considers race principally in the contexts of Africa, Asia, and the imaginative domain called the "Orient"; I do not devote detailed attention to the question of race as it pertains, for instance, to Ireland, the Americas, or the Caribbean.

6. See Jonathan Schneer, *London 1900* and Karl Beckson, *London in the 1890s: A Cultural History*.

7. Said, *Culture and Imperialism*, and Boehmer, *Colonial and Postcolonial Literature*. Similar studies in this vein include Homi Bhabha, *The Location of Culture*, Sara Suleri, *The Rhetoric of English India*, and John Marx, *The Modernist Novel and the Decline of Empire*.

8. Henry Louis Gates Jr. offers a broadly descriptive definition of race as a cultural and biological concept in his introduction to *"Race," Writing, and Difference*. The concept of race "has both described and *inscribed* differences of language, belief system, artistic tradition, and gene pool, as well as all sorts of supposedly natural attributes such as rhythm, athletic abil-

ity, cerebration, usury, fidelity, and so forth. The relation between 'racial character' and these sorts of characteristics has been inscribed through tropes of race, lending the sanction of God, biology, or the natural order to even presumably unbiased descriptions of cultural tendencies and differences" (5). I will elaborate on the history of race thought in chapter 1.

9. Pound's phrase is especially appropriate as an implicit epigraph for my study of race and modernism. In 1934, Pound published a collection of essays about modern art and literature called *Make It New;* in 1940, Canto LIII of *The China Cantos* would attribute these words to the Emperor Tching Tang: "Tching prayed on the mountain and / wrote MAKE IT NEW / on his bath tub / Day by day make it new / cut underbrush, / pile the logs / keep it growing" (*The Cantos of Ezra Pound,* 264–65). Thus, a phrase that conjures up the vast Anglo-American modernist project owes its origins to the art and philosophy of ancient China.

10. Marx's enduring phrase dramatizes the moment of history's "radical break," as does Charles Baudelaire's *The Painter of Modern Life* (1863), which famously celebrates modernity as "the ephemeral, the fugitive, the contingent, the half of art whose other half is the eternal and the immutable" (13). Marx's and Baudelaire's theories of modernity echo through the subsequent intellectual work of twentieth-century authors such as Georg Simmel, Theodor Adorno, Walter Benjamin, Michel Foucault, and Jürgen Habermas.

11. It is significant to note that attention to the break continues to command a nearly unassailable place in contemporary *critical* discourses about modernism. An earlier generation of scholars depicted modernism primarily through the movement's insistence on its own difference from the past: in 1967, Irving Howe's introduction to *The Idea of the Modern in Literature and the Arts,* described modernism's "unyielding rage against the official order" (13) at a moment when "there is a frightening discontinuity between the traditional past and the shaken present" (15); in 1976, Malcolm Bradbury and James McFarlane emphasized modernism's "desecration of established conventions" (30); and Raymond Williams, writing in 1989, pointed to the movement's characteristic "directly competitive sequence of innovations" that were "immediately recognized by what they are breaking from" ("Metropolitan Perceptions," 43). But even as we have reconceived modernism through increasingly diverse channels—the ideological entanglements, generic variety, and fluid international boundaries of numerous "modernisms"—the movement's self-avowed distance and difference from the past continues to determine our sense of its evolution. The titles of two twenty-first century studies, Peter Gay's *Modernism: The Lure of Heresy* (2007) and Douglas Mao's and Rebecca Walkowitz's *Bad Modernisms* (2006), affirm an ongoing intellectual investment in the modernist fracturing of a cultural past. The "consciousness of a radical break" thus shapes not only our temporal understanding of modernity, but also our criteria for what constitutes modernism.

12. Several excellent literary histories (for example, Michael Levenson's *A Genealogy of Modernism* [1984], Astradur Eysteinsson's *The Concept of Modernism* [1990], Bonnie Kime Scott's *Refiguring Modernism* [1995], and Peter Nicholls's *Modernisms* [1995]) discuss British modernism's originary impulses without recognizing the movement's foundational investments in racial difference. Even as thorough a reference work as Levenson's *The Cambridge Companion to Modernism* (1999) relegates race to a two-page section titled "The Colonial Other"; and Chris Baldick's 2006 Oxford English Literary History series volume *The Modern Movement (1910–1940)* as well as Michael Whitworth's *Modernism* (2007), a Blackwell Guide to the movement's dominant characteristics and concerns, omit the subjects of race and imperialism altogether.

1. Race and the Emergence of Metropolitan Modernism

1. See Nicolás Wey Gómez's magnificent study, *Tropics of Empire: Why Columbus Sailed South to the Indies,* which explains the ancient and classical roots of western European race thought.

2. I am indebted here to Michael Banton, *Racial Theories,* Peter Fryer, *Staying Power: Black*

People in Britain since 1504, Stephen Jay Gould, *The Mismeasure of Man,* Ivan Hannaford, *Race: The History of an Idea in the West,* Nancy Stepan, *The Idea of Race in Science: Great Britain 1800– 1960,* and George Stocking, *Race, Culture, and Evolution: Essays in the History of Anthropology* and *Victorian Anthropology.*

3. See Colin Kidd, *The Forging of Races: Race and Scripture in the Protestant Atlantic World, 1600–2000.*

4. This is not to deny or erase the multiple discourses of European racism during the Enlightenment; see Emmanuel Chukwudi Eze's *Race and the Enlightenment: A Reader* and Robert Bernasconi, "Who Invented the Concept of Race? Kant's Role in the Enlightenment Construction of Race."

5. The tension between Christian belief and European xenophobia manifests itself most clearly in the large collection of stereotypes of blacks in the late eighteenth and early nineteenth centuries. Douglas Lorimer's *Colour, Class and the Victorians* describes the varied and contradictory rhetoric of European explorers, slaveholders, missionaries, and abolitionists: "The physical characteristics of the black man remained constant, but his attributes altered according to changes of social and cultural context. The Negro was at once the obedient, humble servant, and the lazy, profligate, worthless worker; the natural Christian and the unredeemable sinner; the patient, suffering slave, and the cruel, vengeful savage" (203). See also Felicity Nussbaum, *The Limits of the Human: Fictions of Anomaly, Race, and Gender in the Long Eighteenth Century.*

6. Consider, for instance, one of the most influential Enlightenment-era treatises on race and climate, Charles de Montesquieu's 1748 *On the Spirit of Laws,* which declared that "If it be true that the temper of the mind and the passions of the heart are extremely different in different climates, the laws ought to be in relation both to the variety of those passions and to the variety of those tempers" (Book XIV, "Of Laws in Relation to the Nature of Climate," 102). We should also note here that climatic theories did not always equate white skin and Northern climates with intelligence, strength, or beauty. The privileged status of whiteness in British racial discourses, as well as the accompanying tendency to understand whiteness as the stable starting-point for measuring racial identities, was the result of aggressive ideological work by England's sociopolitical institutions in the sixteenth and seventeenth centuries. See Mary Floyd-Wilson, "'Clime, Complexion, and Degree': Racialism in Early Modern England."

·7. See Urmila Seshagiri, "Modernist Ashes, Postcolonial Phoenix: Jean Rhys and the Evolution of the English Novel in the Twentieth Century."

8. See Arthur O. Lovejoy's definitive study, *The Great Chain of Being,* which demonstrates how the concept of the Chain derived from Plato and Aristotle and was deployed variously to explain relationships among life forms on earth.

9. Blumenbach's work paved the way for George Cuvier, the influential French anatomist who declared that there were only three races: Caucasian, Mongolian, and Ethiopian. Cuvier became a leading figure of nineteenth-century typology, a broadly defined system of race thought that usually did not distinguish between genus, species, and variety.

10. Note that the phalanx of new race theories countered the emergent discourses of slave narratives, which were very popular and sold well in Britain during the abolitionist movement. In the same years that blacks wrote stirring accounts of their self-actualization after escaping or being freed from slavery (e.g., the Nigerian abolitionist Olaudah Equiano's *The Interesting Narrative of the Life of Olaudah Equiano* [1789], the Bermudian fugitive slave Mary Prince's *The History of Mary Prince, A West Indian Slave* [1831], and the Jamaican slave-turned-nurse Mary Seacole's *The Wonderful Adventures of Mary Seacole in Many Lands* [1857]), science insisted on a biological determinism that made intelligence, agency, and self-governance in the dark races almost impossible.

11. See Gould, *The Mismeasure of Man.*

12. Craniometry was also applied to the white inhabitants of Great Britain. In 1885, the English doctor John Beddoe published his study *The Races of Britain*, which meticulously analyzed the heads of the peoples of the British Isles to determine their ethnic differences. Beddoe's work paved the way for Havelock Ellis's *A Study of British Genius* (1904), which linked intelligence and psychological character to an individual's race (Young, 76). As Douglas Lorimer writes, "If it could be conclusively proven that blacks were inferior by reason of their biological endowment, then there might be grounds for limiting the rights of others having white skins but inappropriately-shaped skulls. . . . This division of the British population into competing races had its most concrete application to the Irish question, and involved not simply the Home Rule issue but also the immigration of the Irish into industrial centres in England" (204–5). See Vincent Cheng's *Joyce, Race, and Empire*, which provides a detailed analysis of how craniometry (and an attending rhetoric of bestiality, savagery, and buffoonery) linked the Irish to Africans in British science and popular culture.

13. Stephen Jay Gould furnishes the anecdote that Sir Francis Galton charged money for head measuring at the International Exposition in 1884 and later operated a lab in London to amass data on the dimensions of heads and bodies (76).

14. Nietzsche's theory of the *Übermensch* and Hitler's belief in Aryan supremacy have their roots in Gobineau's work. See Banton, 62–68.

15. See Jenny Sharpe's *Allegories of Empire: The Figure of Woman in the Colonial Text* for a discussion of the Sepoy Mutiny and its political, symbolic, and sexual ramifications for the British Raj.

16. For detailed overviews of the Morant Bay Uprising, see Catherine Hall, *Civilising Subjects: Metropole and Colony in the English Imagination, 1830–1867*, 243–64 and 406–24, and Michael Craton, *Testing the Chains: Resistance to Slavery in the British West Indies*.

17. Note that Governor Eyre also received the unequivocal support of the polygenist, racialist Anthropological Society of London, which had been founded by James Hunt in 1863 as a rival organization to the monogenist Ethnological Society. Hunt's first presidential address to the Anthropological Society was a speech titled "On the Negro's Place in Nature" that insisted aggressively on the Negro's status as a species separate from the European. See Stocking's *Victorian Anthropology* for an extensive discussion of the intertwined racial politics of science and empire.

18. Darwin was not the sole author of mid-Victorian evolutionary theory. Notable contemporaries included Alfred Russel Wallace, E. B. Tylor, Herbert Spencer, Charles Lyell, Francis Galton, and T. H. Huxley.

19. Galton's ideas about strengthening races through selection methods were further developed by Karl Pearson, who founded the Galton Eugenics Laboratory at University College in London in 1907. Other important figures in social Darwinist and eugenicist thought included Herbert Spencer, author of the phrase "survival of the fittest," Edwin Lankester, who wrote *Degeneration: A Chapter in Darwinism* (1880), H. G. Wells, and George Bernard Shaw. Aldous Huxley's *Brave New World* (1932) is perhaps the best-known literary vision of a eugenicist society, adumbrating the rise of the Nazi regime and the Holocaust.

20. See John MacKenzie's *Propaganda and Empire: The Manipulation of British Public Opinion 1880–1960* for a detailed history of the methods and motives of the British Empire's various ideology-manufacturing institutions.

21. Kipling, "The White Man's Burden," 321.

22. See Gretchen Gerzina, ed., *Black Victorians, Black Victoriana* and Mica Nava and Alan O'Shea, eds., *Modern Times: Reflections on a Century of English Modernity*.

23. See Vincent Cheng, *Joyce, Race, and Empire* and Pericles Lewis, *Modernism, Nationalism, and the Novel* for detailed discussions of race in *A Portrait of the Artist as a Young Man*.

24. See Michael Patrick Gillespie, "A Note on the Texts," in the 2nd Norton Critical Edition of *The Picture of Dorian Gray;* see also Gillespie's annotations to Wilde's original 1890 text

in this same edition. For the textual backgrounds of *Heart of Darkness*, see Robert Kimbrough's introduction to the 3rd Norton Critical Edition.

25. Rebecca Walkowitz calls Conrad—born in Poland, fluent in French, famed for his English—"at once the most British and the most cosmopolitan of novelists" (*Cosmopolitan Style: Modernism beyond the Nation*, 35). Mark Wollaeger's *Joseph Conrad and the Fictions of Skepticism* and Christopher GoGwilt's *The Invention of the West: Joseph Conrad and the Double-Mapping of Europe and Empire* offer thorough accounts of Conrad's career in relation to his varied international affiliations; see also Benita Parry, "Conrad and England." On the intersection of Oscar Wilde's Irishness and his Englishness, I quote Eve Sedgwick: "Wilde, as an ambitious Irish man, and the son, intimate, and protégé of a celebrated Irish nationalist poet, can only have had as a fundamental element of his own sense of self an exquisitely exacerbated sensitivity to how by turns porous, brittle, elastic, chafing, were the membranes of 'domestic' national definition signified by the ductile and elusive terms England, Britain, Ireland" (*Epistemology of the Closet*, 175). See Coakley Davis, *Oscar Wilde: the Importance of Being Irish* and Maureen O'Connor, "*The Picture of Dorian Gray* as Irish National Tale."

26. Jed Esty's *A Shrinking Island: Modernism and National Culture in England* amplifies Jameson's argument and its significance for the creation of a national literature in twentieth-century England.

27. From the outraged London newspaper reviews in 1890 to late twentieth-century scholarship on Wilde, attention to sexuality and morality has dominated the treatment of this novel. On June 24, 1890, the *St. James's Gazette* published an anonymous, vicious review of *The Picture of Dorian Gray* titled "A Study in Puppydom," whose accusations of immorality and perversion Wilde immediately refuted in a letter to the editor. A spirited debate ensued between the author and the critics in the *St. James's Gazette*; Wilde had similar exchanges with the editors of *The Daily Chronicle* and the *Scots Observer*. See *The Artist as Critic: Critical Writings of Oscar Wilde*, ed. Richard Ellmann. Contemporary critical work attends extensively to the relationship between homosexuality and art in *Dorian Gray* and points to Wilde as a key figure for understanding gender and sexuality in Britain at the fin de siècle. See Alan Sinfield, *The Wilde Century: Effeminacy, Oscar Wilde, and the Queer Moment*, Jeff Nunokawa, *Tame Passions of Wilde: The Styles of Manageable Desire*, Joseph Bristow, "'A complex multiform creature'—Wilde's Sexual Identities," Ed Cohen, *Talk on the Wilde Side: Toward a Genealogy of a Discourse on Male Sexualities*, Jonathan Dollimore, *Sexual Dissidence: Augustine to Wilde, Freud to Foucault*, and Patricia Behrendt, *Oscar Wilde: Eros and Aesthetics*.

28. Note that, like Dorian's dalliance with Sibyl Vane, several of the novel's romance plots blur the boundaries of race, nation, and class. Dorian's own parentage, for example, is riven by racial and national conflicts: the "strange, almost modern romance" (33) between his mother, Margaret Devereaux, and "a subaltern in a foot regiment" (31) ends in tragedy when Dorian's wealthy, titled grandfather hires a "Belgian brute" to kill his "mere nobody" of a son-in-law. Similarly, when James Vane learns that his sister Sibyl is in love with a "gentleman" (54), he immediately "hated him through some curious race-instinct" (55), not only out of fraternal protectiveness, but also out of rage against the unknown "father, and a gentleman" (59) who callously abandoned his mother. Sibyl herself encourages James to seek his fortune in colonial Australia, speculating about "the wonderful heiress whose life he was to save from the wicked, red-shirted bushrangers" (55). And at the novel's end, Dorian Gray falls in love with a village girl, "not one of our own class," named Hetty Merton (160), but preserves her pastoral innocence to atone for his life of sin. In each case, a troubled racial plot determines the shape of a sexual or romantic plot.

29. *The Picture of Dorian Gray* expresses tremendous narrative animosity toward Mr. Isaacs, the Jewish manager of a "vulgar" and "tawdry" (43) theater, and, by implication, toward London's East End Jewish population. Mr. Isaacs—a "most offensive brute" alternately described as a "fat Jew," an "old Jew," and simply "the Jew"—repulses the narrator and Dorian alike

with his "oily, tremulous" smile (43), his "fat jeweled hands" (66) and his "Caliban"-like aspect. For a concise overview of London's Jewish population at the turn of the century, see David Feldman, "Jews in London, 1880–1914." For discussions of modernism and anti-Semitism, see Jonathan Freedman, *The Temple of Culture* and Ronald Schuchard, "Burbank with a Baedeker, Eliot with a Cigar: American Intellectuals, Anti-Semitism, and the Idea of Culture."

30. On Wilde and the culture of decadence, see Philip Hoare, *Oscar Wilde's Last Stand: Decadence, Conspiracy, and the Most Outrageous Trial of the Century.* See also *Perennial Decay: On the Aesthetics and Politics of Decadence,* eds. Liz Constable, Dennis Denisoff, and Matthew Potolsky, and Barbara Charlesworth's pioneering study, *Dark Passages: The Decadent Consciousness in Victorian Literature.*

31. See Regenia Gagnier, *Idylls of the Marketplace: Oscar Wilde and the Victorian Public,* 51–99. Ellen Moers's *The Dandy: Brummel to Beerbohm* offers a detailed history of dandyism; see Rita Felski, *The Gender of Modernity* for an illuminating analysis of the dandy's sexual politics. See also Richard Dellamora, *Masculine Desire: The Sexual Politics of Victorian Aestheticism* and Stephen Calloway, "Wilde and the Dandyism of the Senses."

32. See John Paul Riquelme, "Oscar Wilde's Aesthetic Gothic: Walter Pater, Dark Enlightenment, and *The Picture of Dorian Gray*" and Sinfield.

33. Matthew Potolsky's "Decadence, Nationalism, and the Logic of Canon Formation" supplies an illuminating analysis of Dorian's collecting in relation to national subjects and national literatures.

34. On criminality in this novel, see Simon Joyce, "Sexual Politics and the Aesthetics of Crime: Oscar Wilde in the Nineties."

35. For a detailed history of gender, prostitution, and metropolitan geography at the fin de siècle, see Judith Walkowitz, *City of Dreadful Delight: Narratives of Sexual Danger in Late-Victorian London;* see also Lynda Nead, *Victorian Babylon: People, Streets and Images in Nineteenth-Century London.*

36. A telling comparison between two Norton Critical Editions of *Heart of Darkness* reveals that attention to Conrad's literary methods has been subsumed into sociopolitical questions about race. Robert Kimbrough's 1988 edition is devoted to explicating textual variances between Conrad's manuscript of *Heart of Darkness,* the version serialized in *Blackwood's Magazine* in 1899, and subsequent book editions; Kimbrough's supplementary materials include background on the Belgian Congo, biographical writings by and about Conrad, and literary criticism concerned principally with narrative form. In contrast, Paul B. Armstrong's 2006 edition of *Heart of Darkness* is dominated by information about the social and historical underpinnings of race thought: Armstrong adds a lengthy background section titled "Nineteenth-Century Attitudes towards Race," includes several photographs of Congolese people abused under King Leopold's rule, and selects critical essays that offer anthropological, ethnographic, postcolonial, and primitivist approaches to the novel. It is also telling to consider the defensive or reactionary postures of scholarly introductions to editions of *Heart of Darkness* published late in the twentieth century and early in the twenty-first: John Lyon's introduction to the 1995 Penguin edition, for example, declares, "Current criticism, mixing arrogance and timidity in equal measure, seems embarrassed by great literature and incapable of conceiving or conceding the disagreeableness of such art, and its distance from us, and our priorities and prejudices" (xxxv–xxxvi); Caryl Phillips's 1999 introduction to the Modern Library Classics edition points out that "the novel should not be confused with an equal opportunity pamphlet" (xv); and Cedric Watts's introduction to the 2002 Oxford World Classics edition insists, "Critics who allege that Conrad is imperialistic may themselves be practising ideological and temporal imperialism" (xxvi). See also Benita Parry, "The Moment and Afterlife of *Heart of Darkness.*"

37. See Albert Guerard, *Conrad the Novelist* and Ian Watt, *Conrad in the Nineteenth Century* for symbolist readings of *Heart of Darkness.* See Jesse Matz, *Literary Impressionism and Modernist*

Aesthetics and Tamar Katz, *Impressionist Subjects: Gender, Interiority, and Modernist Fiction in England* for discussions of Conrad's impressionism. On the role and representation of Africa in *Heart of Darkness,* see Simon Gikandi, *Maps of Englishness: Writing Identity in the Culture of Colonialism,* Peter Firchow, *Envisioning Africa: Racism and Imperialism in Conrad's "Heart of Darkness,"* and Patrick Brantlinger's *Rule of Darkness: British Literature and Imperialism.*

38. For a detailed discussion of nineteenth-century typology and the politics of representation, see Mary Cowling, *The Artist as Anthropologist: The Representation of Type and Character in Victorian Art.*

39. On the racial and sexual identities of the Intended and the unnamed Congolese woman, see Gabrielle McIntire, "The Women Do Not Travel: Gender, Difference, and Incommensurability in Conrad's *Heart of Darkness.*"

40. See Annie E. Coombes, *Reinventing Africa: Museums, Material Culture and Popular Imagination* for a thorough discussion of the ideological motives and strategies behind imperial exhibitions. See also Elazar Barkan and Ronald Bush, eds., *Prehistories of the Future: The Primitivist Project and the Cultures of Modernism.* For anthropological readings of Kurtz's display of African heads, see James Clifford, *The Predicament of Culture* and Marianna Torgovnick, *Gone Primitive: Savage Intellects, Modern Lives.*

41. Simon Gikandi's *Maps of Englishness* is especially illuminating here: "Africa sustains the epistemology of modernism by creating circumstances in which fetishism challenges traditional modes of self-cognition and even realistic representation: if you cannot sustain clear distinctions between European subjects and African surroundings, between rational systems and evil spirits, then representation must be reduced to an impressionistic flirting with figures and images, unexpected reversals and transformation" (70).

42. W. B. Yeats, "The Second Coming"; James Joyce, *A Portrait of the Artist as a Young Man,* 213; Joyce, *Ulysses,* 28; Forster, *A Passage to India,* 149.

43. On Conrad's treatment of discourses of national character, see Pericles Lewis, *Modernism, Nationalism, and the Novel.*

44. See, for example, Edward Said, *Culture and Imperialism,* Peter Brook, *Reading for the Plot: Design and Intention in Narrative,* and Stephen Ross, *Conrad and Empire.*

45. Homi Bhabha's essay "How Newness Enters the World: Postmodern Space, Postcolonial Times and the Trials of Cultural Translation" argues that the repetition of Kurtz's and Marlow's last words embodies the "global link between colony and metropolis" (212) and thus predicts the key problematic of postcolonial literature in an age of globalization.

46. In this chapter, and throughout the book, I use the word "Oriental" as a self-conscious and historically specific term to communicate late nineteenth- and early twentieth-century Western perceptions of Asia, the Near East, and the Far East. To borrow Edward Said's classic formulation from *Orientalism,* the historical and imaginative distinction between the "Orient" and the "Occident" calls to critical attention an enormous cultural project that includes "the spice trade, colonial armies and a long tradition of colonial administrators, a formidable scholarly corpus, innumerable Oriental 'experts' and 'hands,' an Oriental professorate, a complex array of 'Oriental' ideas (Oriental despotism, Oriental splendor, cruelty, sensuality), many Eastern sects, philosophies, and wisdoms domesticated for local European use" (4). In Sax Rohmer's Fu-Manchu novels, "Orient" and "Oriental" refer predominantly to China, but Rohmer also uses these words to include the cultures and peoples of East Asia, South Asia, Southeast Asia, the Far East, or the Middle East.

47. Although Sax Rohmer was best known as the creator of Dr. Fu-Manchu, his many other novels and short story collections also enjoyed considerable market success. Like the Fu-Manchu thrillers, the rest of Rohmer's oeuvre played to the racial prejudices and desires of white bourgeois audiences: some of his well-known (and oft-reprinted) works include *The Yellow Claw* (1915), *Tales of Secret Egypt* (1918), *Tales of Chinatown* (1922), *Dreams of East and West* (1932), and *Bim-Bashi Baruk of Egypt* (1944). In the 1950s, Rohmer created a new char-

acter called Sumuru, a Eurasian heroine with a cohort of Amazon women who starred in five instantly popular novels: *The Sins of Sumuru* (1950), *Slaves of Sumuru* (1952), *Virgin in Flames* (1953), *Sand and Satin* (1955), and *Sinister Madonna* (1956). The Sumuru novels were reprinted multiple times in the United States and England, adapted for an eight-part BBC radio series, and used as the basis for a film.

48. See Ann Cvetkovich, *Mixed Feelings: Feminism, Mass Culture, and Victorian Sensationalism,* Clive Bloom, *Cult Fiction: Popular Reading and Pulp Theory,* and Brian Stableford, *Scientific Romance in Britain 1890–1950.*

49. "Specialists in Crime," *Vanity Fair* (September 1930), 56.

50. Sax Rohmer was enormously popular in the United States, and he traveled between the U.S. and England for most of his professional life. He was frequently published in the *Boston Sunday Globe,* the *Cleveland Plain Dealer,* and the *Chicago Sunday Tribune;* his most prosperous relationship was with the national weekly magazine *Collier's,* which featured Rohmer's work in 208 issues between 1913 and 1949. *Collier's* was largely responsible for Rohmer's success in America, publishing special collections of his books, offering "Orient" editions and reprints of the Fu-Manchu titles, and setting up a radio broadcast of Fu-Manchu stories. For discussions of Fu-Manchu's popularity in the context of U.S. Sinophobia, see Tina Chen, "Dissecting the 'Devil-Doctor': Stereotype and Sensationalism in Sax Rohmer's Fu-Manchu," William Wu, *The Yellow Peril: Chinese Americans in American Fiction, 1850–1940,* and Robert G. Lee, *Orientals.*

51. The films based on Rohmer's Fu-Manchu fictions enjoyed five decades of transatlantic popularity. In England in 1924, the Stoll Production Company released the very successful eight-episode film *The Further Mysteries of Fu-Manchu,* based on Rohmer's second novel *The Devil-Doctor.* Subsequently, the U.S. company Paramount Pictures took over the enterprise of adapting Rohmer's stories. Paramount made three films (*The Mysterious Dr. Fu-Manchu* [1929], *The Return of Dr. Fu-Manchu* [1930], and *Daughter of the Dragon* [1931]), casting Warner Oland (who would later achieve fame playing Charlie Chan) as Fu-Manchu. In 1932, MGM-UA Studios released *The Mask of Fu-Manchu* starring Boris Karloff as the Chinese doctor and Myrna Loy as his evil daughter Fah Lo Suee. A number of very low-budget Fu-Manchu films were produced during the 1940s and 1950s, starring the relatively unknown U.S. actors Henry Brandon and Manuel Requena. The role regained its notoriety in the 1960s when Christopher Lee played Fu-Manchu for five feature films. As late as 1980, Peter Sellers appeared as Rohmer's devil-doctor in the Warner Brothers farce *The Fiendish Plot of Dr. Fu-Manchu.* For cultural histories of the Fu-Manchu and other Yellow Peril films, see Gina Marchetti, *Romance and the "Yellow Peril": Race, Sex, and Discursive Strategies in Hollywood Fiction,* and Jun Xing, *Asian America through the Lens: History, Representations, and Identity.*

52. Dr. Fu-Manchu appears in contemporary popular culture as the arch-villain of Alan Moore and Kevin O'Neill's 2001 graphic novel, *The League of Extraordinary Gentlemen: Volume I.* This comic book is set in London in 1898 and features a group of Victorian literary heroes (e.g., H. Rider Haggard's Allan Quatermain, Bram Stoker's Mina Murray, Jules Verne's Captain Nemo, Robert Louis Stevenson's Dr. Jekyll) who band together to defeat a Chinese "devil-doctor" who plans to take over the world. Moore and O'Neill's self-conscious allusions to fin-de-siècle London satirize imperial-era propaganda in general as well as the Fu-Manchu tales in particular; one narrative aside, for example, describes the unfolding adventure as an "arresting yarn, in which the Empire's finest are brought into conflict with the sly Chinee, accompanied by a variety of coloured illustrations from our artist that are sure to prove exciting to the manly, outwardgoing youngster of today."

53. Although Rohmer would set the later Fu-Manchu tales in locations like Venice, Haiti, France, North America, and the Mediterranean, these first three novels take place entirely in England.

54. See Henry Keown-Boyd, *The Fists of Righteous Harmony: A History of the Boxer Uprising in*

China in the Year 1900 and Paul Cohen, *History in Three Keys: The Boxers as Event, Experience, and Myth.*

55. For specific details about China and the English press in the early years of the twentieth century, see Keown-Boyd, 143–7 and Cohen, 15 and 256.

56. Rohmer's prediction about "market conditions" in the years following the Boxer Uprising proved accurate: Sinophobia's appeal for a vast middle-class readership is evident in the variety of publications that serialized Rohmer's stories. The Fu-Manchu stories appeared in literary magazines such as *The Story-Teller* and *The Premier Magazine;* they were regular features in the patriotic boys' magazine *Chums;* they ran in the imperialist newspapers *Empire News* and *The Illustrated London News;* and they appeared in the largely apolitical magazine *Pearson's Weekly.* For further reading on the ideological work of popular crime fiction and adventure fiction in the early twentieth century, see Colin Watson, *Snobbery with Violence: English Crime Stories and Their Audience* and Joseph Bristow, *Empire Boys: Adventures in a Man's World.*

57. Merle Goldman and Leo Ou-Fan Lee's *An Intellectual History of Modern China* supplies detailed historical accounts of the tumultuous development of Chinese nationalism in the twentieth century; see also Wen-Hsin Yeh, "Introduction: Interpreting Chinese Modernity" in *Becoming Chinese: Passages to Modernity and Beyond.*

58. See Panikos Panayi, "Anti-Immigration Riots," 11, and Rozina Visram, *Asians in Britain: 400 Years of History*, 43–59; see also Ng Kwee Choo, *The Chinese in London.* Despite muckraking Victorian journalism, overwhelming political and sociological evidence indicates that the Chinese in London were a peaceable community and that opium smoking was not the social problem that middle-class citizens were led to believe. See Victoria Berridge and Griffith Edwards, *Opium and the People: Opiate Use in Nineteenth-Century England,* 202, Colin Holmes, *John Bull's Island: Immigration & British Society, 1871–1971,* 81, Kenneth Lunn, *Hosts, Immigrants, and Minorities: Historical Responses to Newcomers in British Society,* 5, J. P. May, "The Chinese in Britain, 1860–1914," 118–20, James Walvin, *Passage to Britain: Immigration in British History and Politics,* 69–70; see also Julian North, "The Opium-Eater as Criminal in Victorian Writing."

59. Although Limehouse, London's diminutive East End Chinatown, does not feature prominently in canonical Victorian or modernist writing, it did make its way into a small body of early twentieth-century popular literature and film. M. P. Shiel, the Edwardian writer credited with inventing the phrase "Yellow Peril," put Limehouse on the literary map in 1899 with his novel *The Yellow Danger,* a gruesome thriller about a Chinese gang that invades London. In 1919, following the opium-induced death of a British actress, Sax Rohmer wrote a novel called *Dope* to "expose" the truth behind Limehouse's drug industry; like the Fu-Manchu novels, *Dope* offered a morally heavy-handed depiction of Limehouse as a cesspool luring white bourgeois citizens into foreign vices. Thomas Burke, a contemporary of Rohmer's, wrote three short-story collections—*Limehouse Nights* (1917), *More Nights in Limehouse* (1921), and *A Tea-Shop in Limehouse* (1931)—that reinforced the image of the East End Chinese district as dirty and mysterious; and the dark geography of Limehouse lent itself to the dystopian, angular vision of the avant-garde painter C. R. W. Nevinson, who depicted the district's shadowy buildings in his 1919 vorticist painting *Limehouse.* Most famously, Limehouse was captured on film in D. W. Griffith's 1919 picture *Broken Blossoms,* the tragic story of forbidden love between a noble-hearted Chinese man and a destitute English girl.

60. See Jameson, "Modernism and Imperialism."

61. See MacKenzie, *Propaganda and Empire.*

62. V. G. Kiernan's description of the Western fear of the Yellow Peril is appropriate here: "In the minds of many ordinary people to whom the Yellow Peril brought vague alarms, it meant the thought of China's enormous population, already spilling over by millions into other lands. Europeans cradled in small cities and nation-states might well be sensitive to the vertigo of numbers. To them Asia had always stood for an overwhelming multitude of be-

ings, only to be counteracted by superior skill; the word 'horde' that had come into the European languages from the steppes of central Asia signified a mass of creatures on the move, less human than animal, a blind menace" (172).

63. John S. Haller, *Outcasts from Evolution: Scientific Attitudes of Racial Inferiority*, 1859–1900, 3–39, Stepan, 97–100, Gould 98–102.

64. It is helpful here to consider Bram Stoker's *Dracula* (1897), which illustrates the late Victorian and early modern English attentiveness to criminology and skull size. Endeavoring to explain Dracula's habits and desires, Dr. Van Helsing declares that "'This criminal has not full man-brain,'" which Mina Harker affirms by saying, "'The Count is a criminal and of criminal type. Nordau and Lombroso would so classify him, and *qua* criminal he is of imperfectly formed mind'" (296). Van Helsing and Mina's urge to classify and "type" Dracula's criminality, like Dr. Petrie's remarks on the nature of Fu-Manchu's degeneracy, reflects the imperial West's need to justify racial hierarchies with scientific evidence.

65. *The Mystery of Dr. Fu-Manchu* was serialized in 1911 and published in 1913, overlapping with the establishment of Greenwich Standard Time in 1912. That Petrie's expression of alienation coincides with Big Ben chimes reveals an affinity between the Fu-Manchu novels and canonical modernist fiction that explicitly critiques the dehumanizing cultural effects of mechanized time, such as Conrad's *The Secret Agent* (1907), Lawrence's *Women in Love* (1923), and Woolf's *Mrs. Dalloway* (1925).

66. Felix Driver's *Geography Militant: Cultures of Exploration and Empire* points out that at the turn of the century, "London was imagined as a miniature globe in itself. . . . The metaphor of the abyss turned the spectacle of exotic difference into something infinitely more threatening: a gaping chasm in the social landscape, undermining the very base of existing institutions" (182–3). For further discussion of London's racialized topography, see Simon Joyce, *Capital Offenses: Geographies of Class and Crime in Victorian London* and Judith Walkowitz, *City of Dreadful Delight*.

2. Race and Rupture

1. I am indebted to Richard Cork's *Art Beyond the Gallery in Early 20th Century England* (hereafter *ABG*), which not only offers a meticulous history of the Cabaret Theatre Club and the Cave of the Golden Calf but also contains illuminating formal analysis of the Cave's murals, paintings, and carvings. Cork's study is especially valuable for its reproductions of several now-lost original artworks and decorations from the Cave.

2. Madame Strindberg's idiosyncrasies are documented by Wyndham Lewis in *Rude Assignment* (1950) and C. R. W. Nevinson in *Paint and Prejudice* (1937); see also Barbara Belford, *Violet: The Story of the Irrepressible Violet Hunt and Her Circle of Lovers and Friends—Ford Madox Ford, H. G. Wells, Somerset Maugham, and Henry James*, 188–89, and Paul O'Keeffe, *Some Sort of Genius: A Life of Wyndham Lewis*, 112–13.

3. See Gluck's excellent study, *Popular Bohemia: Modernism and Urban Culture in Nineteenth-Century Paris*, 115–24.

4. For historical overviews of avant-garde activity in London, see David Peters Corbett, *The Modernity of English Art 1914–30*, Richard Cork, *Vorticism and Abstract Art in the First Machine Age*, vol. 1, *Origins and Development*, Anna Gruetzner-Robins, *Modern Art in Britain, 1910–1914*, Charles Harrison, *English Art and Modernism 1900–1939*, Peter Stansky, *On or about 1910: Early Bloomsbury and Its Intimate World*, and Lisa Tickner, *Modern Life and Modern Subjects: British Art in the Early Twentieth Century*.

5. Woolf, "Mr. Bennett and Mrs. Brown," 194. See Christopher Reed, "Forming Formalism: The Post-Impressionist Exhibition" for an overview of Roger Fry's ambitions for the London art world.

6. Originally in *Daily Chronicle*, March 20, 1912; quoted in Cork *ABC,* 63.

7. For detailed discussions of Marinetti's politics and their effect on London artists, see Paul Peppis, *Literature, Politics, and the Avant-Garde: Nation and Empire, 1901–1918,* Lawrence Rainey, "The Creation of the Avant-Garde: F. T. Marinetti and Ezra Pound," and Cork, *Vorticism,* 26–55.

8. "Preliminary Prospectus for the Cabaret Theatre Club and the Cave of the Golden Calf," Yale Center for British Art.

9. For detailed explanations of the origins of the rivalry between Wyndham Lewis and Roger Fry's Omega Workshops, see Quentin Bell and Stephen Chaplin, "The Ideal Home Rumpus." See also Cork, *Vorticism,* 92–5, and Judith Collins, *The Omega Workshops,* 54–62.

10. See Peppis, 96–132 for a discussion of the political commitments of *BLAST* 2.

11. "Kill John Bull with Art" was the title of an essay Lewis published in *Outlook* on July 18, 1914. See also Lewis, *Blasting and Bombardiering,* 40.

12. For histories and critical analyses of avant-garde salon culture, see Virginia Nicholson, *Among the Bohemians: Experiments in Living 1900–1939,* Janet Lyon, "Josephine Baker's Hothouse," and Jane Garrity, "Selling Culture to the 'Civilized': Bloomsbury, British *Vogue,* and the Marketing of National Identity." See Shari Benstock, *Women of the Left Bank: Paris, 1900–1940* for a history of the Parisian coterie modernism that preceded and influenced the coteries in London.

13. See Wees, *Vorticism and the English Avant-Garde,* 54–71, Cork, *ABC,* 205–6, and Nicholson, *Among the Bohemians,* 99–162.

14. The Cave was perhaps the most flamboyant of a new crop of clubs that had succeeded their staid nineteenth-century predecessors. New venues where men and women mingled freely into the night, such as the Crab Tree and the Studio Club, were rapidly supplanting older gentlemen's establishments like the Chelsea Arts Club and the London Sketch Club. The Cave's aggressive modernity opposed itself to the world of the longstanding Café Royal, a space once patronized by Oscar Wilde and Aubrey Beardsley but that now seemed to embody the very passéism that young artists sought to overturn. See Cork and Wees.

15. See Harold B. Segel, *Turn-of-the-Century Cabaret,* xiii–xxviii.

16. Exodus 32:1–35.

17. "Cabaret Theatre Club," Original brochure, May 1912, Yale Center for British Art.

18. *The Observer,* June 16, 1912. Quoted in Cork, *ABC,* 68.

19. Quoted from an anonymous newspaper clipping in Cork, *ABC,* 77.

20. *Ombre chinoise* was one of the most popular elements of French cabaret, especially at the Montmartre nightclub Le Chat Noir, where it was featured regularly on the program. See Appignanesi, 10–22 and Segel, 66–79. For Ford Madox Ford's recollection of his own shadow play, see *Return to Yesterday,* 410–11; see also Ford's fictionalized account of this play and the Cave of the Golden Calf in his 1923 novel, *The Marsden Case.*

21. For a scathing review of Katherine Mansfield's performance and of Mozart's *Bastien und Bastienne,* see John Playford, "Music and Musicians: Mozart in a Cabaret."

22. See Laura Winkiel, "Cabaret Modernism: Vorticism and Racial Spectacle," and Philip Hoare, *Oscar Wilde's Last Stand,* 6–12.

23. In the spring of 1914, Pound delivered a lecture on vorticism at Wyndham Lewis's newly established Rebel Art Centre on Great Ormond Street. The key ideas from this lecture found their way into Pound's "Vortex" manifesto in *BLAST;* the text of the original lecture appeared that September in the *Fortnightly Review,* and Pound later reproduced it in his historical-biographical tract, *Gaudier-Brzeska: A Memoir.*

24. Eliot's comment was made in his 1918 *Egoist* review of Lewis's vorticist novel *Tarr.*

25. Page numbers for West, "Indissoluble Matrimony" are the original page numbers from *BLAST.*

26. Studies of *BLAST*—e.g., Wees, Cork, *Vorticism,* and Peter Nicholls, *Modernisms*—seldom

mention West's "Indissoluble Matrimony"; one notable recent exception is Laura Winkiel's "Cabaret Modernism: Vorticism and Racial Spectacle."

27. See Victoria Glendinning, *Rebecca West: A Life*, 35–40.

28. Violet Hunt, Ford Madox Ford's lover, claims that she was responsible for including "Indissoluble Matrimony" in *BLAST:* "And I was instrumental in procuring for its pages the first short story of a young lady since better known. Rebecca West in her teens, with her tongue in her cheek, taking up the whole problem of man's life and making a delectable joke and parody of it! Good Spoof, indeed, but the public did not see it and, to her chagrin, insisted on regarding 'Indissoluble Matrimony' as a tragic experiment. Vehemently she protested against this attitude of the critics. In writing of the attempted suicide of the egregious Evadne, 'I was only,' she said, 'meaning to write a funny story about what were perfectly horrible situations'" (*I Have This to Say: The Story of My Flurried Years*, 216).

29. Relative to coeval avant-garde movements like imagism, expressionism, and symbolism, vorticism's lifespan and body of art were quite limited. Following *BLAST 2: The War Number* (1915), in which the Vortex became an explicitly political metaphor for England's battle against Germany, the vorticist movement in London dwindled. T. E. Hulme and Henri Gaudier-Brzeska, two of the movement's seminal figures, did not survive the war, and Ezra Pound and Wyndham Lewis had both turned their creative energies away from vorticism by 1920. Lewis's novel *Tarr* (published serially in Pound's *Egoist* between 1916 and 1917) and his 1919 pamphlet on urban design, *The Caliph's Design: Architects! Where Is Your Vortex?*, were his last large-scale vorticist projects. Pound organized an exhibition of English vorticist art in New York in 1916–17, and promoted the work of Gaudier-Brzeska in a series of articles and reviews, but finally moved to Paris in 1919, leaving London and vorticism behind. In 1930, a character in Evelyn Waugh's comic novel *Vile Bodies* mailed party invitations that borrowed the "Blasts" and "Blesses" from *BLAST*, but vorticism itself was by then long defunct. Rebecca West's "Indissoluble Matrimony," therefore, was the earliest piece of published fiction in an aesthetic movement that only lasted about five years. On the end of vorticism in London, see Wees, 206–12, and O'Keeffe, 139–75.

30. See Marcus's "Editor's Introduction" in *The Young Rebecca: Writings of Rebecca West 1911–17.*

31. For discussions on how Lewis and the vorticists defined the English avant-garde in opposition to continental European avant-gardism, see Rainey, "The Creation of the Avant-Garde," Nicholls, 165–92, and Wees, 103–18. For accounts of *BLAST*'s self-promotion, see Morrisson, *The Public Face of Modernism: Little Magazines, Audiences, and Reception, 1905–1920*, 116–32, and Aaron Jaffe, *Modernism and the Culture of Celebrity*, 179–94. See also Alan Robinson, *Symbol to Vortex: Poetry, Painting and Ideas, 1885–1914* and Christopher Butler, *Early Modernism: Literature, Music and Painting in Europe 1900–1916*.

32. *BLAST*'s conceptions of race have received startlingly little critical attention. Art historians such as Cork and Tickner touch on racial issues in passing, but the general critical tendency—exemplified by Rainey, Nicholls, and Levenson—has been to focus on questions of national identity. Even works such as Jonathan Black's *Blasting the Future! Vorticism in Britain 1910–1920* (a collection of critical essays published to accompany exhibitions in London and Manchester in 2004) and Miranda Hickman's 2005 study, *The Geometry of Modernism: The Vorticist Idiom in Lewis, Pound, H. D., and Yeats*, which treat *BLAST*'s history and aesthetic commitments in lavishly illustrated detail, overlook the question of race entirely.

33. The best-known of these aesthetic histories are by William Wees, whose *Vorticism and the English Avant-Garde* extensively details Worringer and Hulme's role in establishing vorticism's goals, and by Michael Levenson, whose *A Genealogy of Modernism: A Study of English Literary Doctrine, 1908–1922* devotes several chapters to the cultural influences on the prewar London avant-garde. See also Vincent Sherry, *Ezra Pound, Wyndham Lewis, and Radical Modernism,*

Jo Anna Isaak, *The Ruin of Representation in Modernist Art and Texts,* and Timothy Materer, *Vortex: Pound, Eliot, and Lewis.*

34. Worringer articulates these ideas in the second essay of *Abstraction and Empathy,* "Naturalism and Style."

35. Edward Comentale and Andrzej Gasiorek's collection *T. E. Hulme and the Question of Modernism* offers a comprehensive treatment of Hulme's career. See also Levenson, 37–47.

36. For discussions of modernism's investment in primitivism, see Sieglinde Lemke, *Primitivist Modernism: Black Culture and the Origins of Transatlantic Modernism,* Colin Rhodes, *Primitivism and Modern Art,* Elazar Barkan and Ronald Bush, *Prehistories of the Future: The Primitivist Project and the Culture of Modernism,* William Rubin, ed., *"Primitivism" in 20th Century Art: Affinity of the Tribal and the Modern,* Mark Antliff and Patricia Leighten, "Primitive." See also Jack Flam, introduction to *Primitivism and Twentieth-Century Art: A Documentary History.*

37. Despite T. E. Hulme's influence over Lewis and the vorticists, he is conspicuously absent from the pages of *BLAST.* Apparently jealous of Hulme's attentions to Jacob Epstein, the vorticist sculptor whose work *Rock Drill* definitively employed primitive form to capture the hard-edged spirit of the modern machine age, Wyndham Lewis cut himself off from Hulme and neither credited him nor included his writings in *BLAST.* Additionally, the artist-patron Kate Lechmere, whose money enabled Lewis to open the Rebel Art Centre, betrayed Lewis with Hulme. William Wees furnishes the amusing anecdote that when "Lewis first learned that Kate Lechmere was seeing Hulme, he rushed to Frith Street and attacked Hulme, who dragged Lewis out to the street and hung him upside down by his trouser cuffs on the railing of Soho Square" (84–5).

38. For studies that address blackness, women, and the artistic discourses of primitivism, see Tyler Stovall, *Paris Noir: African-Americans in the City of Light,* Jody Blake, *Le Tumulte Noir: Modernist Art and Popular Entertainment in Jazz-Age Paris, 1900–1930,* Petrine Archer-Straw, *Negrophilia: Avant-Garde Paris and Black Culture in the 1920s,* and Nancy Nenno, "Femininity, the Primitive, and Modern Urban Space: Josephine Baker in Berlin."

39. See Sander Gilman's influential essay "Black Bodies, White Bodies: Toward an Iconography of Female Sexuality in Late Nineteenth-Century Art, Medicine, and Literature," and Torgovnick, *Gone Primitive,* 85–104.

40. See Nevinson, 78–81, and Wees, 103–18.

41. See also Misha Kavka, "Men in (Shell) Shock: Masculinity, Trauma, and Psychoanalysis in Rebecca West's *The Return of the Soldier.*"

42. See Jane Marcus, *Suffrage and the Pankhursts.*

43. See Bonnie Kime Scott, "Rebecca West," and Patrick Collier, "Journalism Meets Modernism," for pithy accounts of West's feminism and its expression in journalism, literature, and criticism.

44. For illuminating discussions on the suffragette-vorticist relationship, see Janet Lyon, *Manifestoes: Provocations of the Modern,* 92–123 and Lisa Tickner, "Men's Work? Masculinity and Modernism."

45. See Tickner, *The Spectacle of Women* for journalistic and artistic representations of these "types" of women.

46. West herself became a mother immediately after the publication of *BLAST:* Anthony Panther Wells, the illegitimate child of West and H. G. Wells, was born on the watershed date August 4, 1914. In a 1915 letter to her friend Carrie Townshend, West quipped, "I have just seen about *Blast* in the *Times Literary Supplement.* It is described as a Manifesto of the Vorticists. Am I a Vorticist? I am sure it can't be good for Anthony if I am" (*Letters,* 23). Like West's letter, "Indissoluble Matrimony" mocks the cultural assumption that women's militancy, whether political or artistic, transformed them into unsuitable mothers.

47. The exact date of *The Good Soldier*'s completion remains unclear. Ford claimed that he

wrote the entire novel after his fortieth birthday in the early summer of 1914; however, scholars have been unable to verify whether Ford's descriptions of the novel's composition are corroborated by the anecdotal evidence provided by Richard Aldington, one of Ford's three amanuenses for *The Good Soldier*, or by Violet Hunt, Ford's lover, or from other evidence of the novel's printing at John Lane. The larger question raised by this uncertainty, of course, is whether Ford's multiple references to August 4 in the novel were prescient or merely coincidental, and if he had included them before or after England declared war on Germany on August 4, 1914. See Martin Stannard, "A Note on the Text," 180–87, and Arthur Mizener, *The Saddest Story: A Biography of Ford Madox Ford*, 565 n. 21. For the purposes of my argument, I am following the dates of print publication: the first few chapters were published in *BLAST* on June 4, 1914, and the entire novel appeared in print on March 15, 1915, and these dates sufficiently prove that this text encompasses a prewar moment as well as the immediacy of the war itself.

48. On the seeming anomalousness of "The Saddest Story" in *BLAST*, see Ann Barr Snitow, *Ford Madox Ford and the Voice of Uncertainty*, 161–63, Mizener, 247, and Stannard, "A Note on the Text."

49. Ford published *Henry James: A Critical Study* in 1913, and his collaborative work with Joseph Conrad yielded three novels: *The Inheritors* (1901), *Romance* (1903), and *The Nature of Crime* (1909). In 1924, he published *Joseph Conrad: A Personal Remembrance*, a work that praises Conrad's literary achievements through a characteristic Fordian mixture of personal anecdote and critical analysis.

50. The letter was first published in the second U.S. edition in 1927 (New York: Albert & Charles Boni) and then in the second UK edition in 1928 (London: John Lane, The Bodley Head Ltd.).

51. See Michael Levenson's *A Genealogy of Modernism: A Study of English Literary Doctrine 1908–1922* for an account of Ford Madox Ford's role as a transitional figure from the Victorian literary era to the early modernist period.

52. In *The March of Literature*, Ford elaborates on the shift from the old to the new, describing a conversation he had with an Ezra-Pound-esque "young lion" who pronounced, "'Old fogeys like you and Conrad and Henry James go to unending troubles to kid the public into the idea that you provide them with vicarious experience. You efface yourselves like ostriches, never let yourself appear through a whole long, blessed story, go to enormous trouble to get in atmospheres, to invent plausible narrators—old colonels, ships' captains, priests, surgeons —what do I know all . . . oh, yes, "above all to make you *see*." . . . What the public wants is to see monstrous clever fellows'—and here he slapped himself on the cheek—'monstrous clever fellows like *me*. . . . You're all done with, I tell you. To me the far-flung future . . .'" (583).

53. See Mark Morrisson, *The Public Face of Modernism*, 17–53.

54. See Rita Felski, *The Gender of Modernity*, 35–60, for a discussion of modern nostalgia for the feminine; see Nicholas Brown, *Utopian Generations: The Political Horizon of Twentieth-Century Literature*, 83–103, for an insightful discussion of nostalgia in *The Good Soldier*.

55. Wyndham Lewis, introduction to *Wyndham Lewis and Vorticism: A Tate Gallery Exhibition Circulated by the Arts Council*.

56. Page numbers for Mansfield, "Je Ne Parle Pas Français" are from the edition edited by Vincent O'Sullivan.

57. For discussions of colonial politics in Katherine Mansfield's New Zealand writings, see Vincent O'Sullivan's introduction in *New Zealand Stories* and Suzanne Raitt's introduction to Mansfield's collection *Something Childish and Other Stories*.

58. "Je Ne Parle Pas Français" was first published in 1919 by John Middleton Murry and his brother Richard at the Heron Press in Hampstead. The original version, "printed for private circulation" (*Journal 1927*, x), was not the version published by Constable & Co. in 1920 when Michael Sadleir included "Je Ne Parle Pas Français" in *Bliss and Other Stories*. Sadleir tamed the sexual explicitness of Mansfield's original text and excised a number of passages

he deemed obscene, including the story's conclusion. Mansfield had ended her piece with the following exchange between Raoul and the café proprietress: "I must go. I must go. I reach down my coat and hat. Madame knows me. 'You haven't dined yet?' she smiles. 'No, not yet, Madame.' I'd rather like to dine with her. Even to sleep with her afterwards. Would she be pale like that all over? But no. She'd have large moles. They go with that kind of skin. And I can't bear them. They remind me somehow, disgustingly, of mushrooms" (144). Sadleir ended the story at "No, not yet, Madame," suppressing Raoul's remarks about sleeping with the café proprietress. For several decades, Sadleir's version stood as the standard edition of "Je Ne Parle Pas Français"; Jeffrey Meyers's introduction to the *Stories of Katherine Mansfield*, for example, applauds Sadleir's editorial decisions and criticizes Mansfield's "deliberately disgusting conclusion" that "hints at Raoul's homosexuality" (ix). Meyers insists, "The ending in the Constable edition is actually more subtle and effective than the original, which overemphasizes Raoul's cruelty and diminishes the sympathy we feel for the vulnerable Mouse." In 1984, Antony Alpers restored Mansfield's original text in *The Stories of Katherine Mansfield*, and in 2005, Vincent O'Sullivan also included the original text in the Norton Critical Edition of *Katherine Mansfield's Selected Short Stories*. I refer to Mansfield's uncut story rather than to the expurgated Constable version.

59. Reflecting on Mansfield's story "Bliss" in 1934, for example, T. S. Eliot damningly praised the author for having "handled perfectly the *minimum* material" in a manner that "would be called feminine," because "no story of any considerable structure could move as rapidly as Miss Mansfield's does" (*After Strange Gods*, 36).

60. J. W. N. Sullivan, "The Story-Writing Genius," and Malcolm Cowley, "'Page Dr Blum!': *Bliss.*"

61. The story's unhappy love triangle has been variously interpreted as a "narrative inspired by, about, hatred" (Bennett, 74), a tale that "expresses her profoundest adult fears and settles some personal scores" (Meyers, "Introduction," viii), a "story about inescapable victimisation and universal warping of desire" (Fullbrook, 94), and "a deeply subversive signal about [Mansfield's] own complex nature" (Tomalin, 170). Additional biographical readings of "Je Ne Parle Pas Français" appear in Cherry A. Hankin, *Katherine Mansfield and Her Confessional Stories*, and Jeffrey Meyers, *Katherine Mansfield: A Darker View*.

62. See Appignanesi, 74–83 for a discussion of the Lapin Agile.

63. Carco frames this anecdote with the remark that "something happened which was to be full of consequences for Cubism" (32). Art historians have long associated Pablo Picasso's early cubist works with his revelatory 1906 introduction to African art in the Trocadero Museum of Ethnology, and Carco's memoir suggests that the Senegalese painting of Max Jacob's brother had a similarly profound influence on Picasso's imagination.

64. It is interesting to note here that the sexualized relationship between an African woman and a French boy in "Je Ne Parle Pas Français" reverses a race discourse circulating through France during World War I. One powerful segment of the French infantry on the Western front was the *tirailleurs sénégalais*, or Senegalese riflemen, a group that numbered 190,000 by the summer of 1918. This enormous battalion of black soldiers inspired political cartoons, bawdy postcards, and vicious trench journalism about lascivious African men violating innocent white French women. Mansfield's story casts the black *woman* as the aggressor and the French male as her victim. See Annabelle Melzer's "Spectacles and Sexualities: The 'Mise-en-Scène' of the '*Tirailleur Sénégalais*' on the Western Front, 1914–1920," which recounts Parisian paranoia about Afro-French miscegenation during the war years.

65. For details about the editorial tussle between Mansfield and Sadleir, see *Letters*, 300–303, and Alpers, 559–61.

66. Although Michael Sadleir did eventually omit the "soft growl" passage from the version of "Je Ne Parle Pas Français" that he published in *Bliss and Other Stories*, Mansfield succeeded in retaining Raoul's comment that "there's always an African laundress."

67. Eliot, "The Love Song of J. Alfred Prufrock, line 73, and Pound, "Hugh Selwyn Mauberley," line 90.

68. See Rita Felski, *The Gender of Modernity*, 91–114, and Jessica Feldman, *Gender on the Divide*, 1–24.

3. Orienting Virginia Woolf

1. I use Woolf as a surname here although the author was unmarried in 1906 and her name was still Virginia Stephen. For the sake of convenience, I will use the name "Virginia Woolf" for the entire chapter.

2. It is interesting to note that Woolf's fleeting moments of cultural self-awareness in her 1906 Constantinople journals anticipate the lengthy, complex interrogations of English identity that shape her later writings. Woolf's depiction of the St. Sophia mosque, for example, hints not only at her description of the modern novel in *A Room of One's Own*, but also at the formalism she inaugurates in *Jacob's Room* and brings to perfection in *The Waves*: "St. Sophia, like a treble globe of bubbles frozen solid . . . fashioned in the shape of some fine substance, thin as glass, blown in plump curves; save that it is also as substantial as a Pyramid" (*PA*, 347). Then the Islamic custom of walking barefoot in Constantinople amuses Woolf but produces a defiant assertion of English superiority: "We paid our tribute to the oriental superstition graciously, & shuffled in through the doors with lively satisfaction in our toes; But then I left half my tribute at an early stage, & defiled the carpet with stout English boots" (349); Woolf's portrayal of Turkey and Turkish characters in *Orlando* reflects a similar mixture of respect and condescension. And finally, a Turkish prayer session creates the awareness, so central to *A Room of One's Own* and *Three Guineas*, of being excluded from practices or places: "The mystery of the sight, & the strangeness of the voice, made you feel yourself like one wrapped in a soft curtain; & the worshippers within are quite determined that you shall remain outside" (356).

3. Specifically, see Marcus, "Britannia," Kathy Phillips, *Virginia Woolf against Empire*, Andrea Lewis, "The Visual Politics of Gender in Virginia Woolf's *The Voyage Out*," Jaime Hovey, "'Kissing a Negress in the Dark': Englishness as a Masquerade in Woolf's *Orlando*," Janet Winston, "'Something Out of Harmony': *To the Lighthouse* and the Subject(s) of Empire," Michelle Cliff, "Virginia Woolf and the Imperial Gaze: A Glance Askance," Suzette Henke, "De/Colonizing the Subject in Virginia Woolf's *The Voyage Out*," Susan Hudson Fox, "Woolf's Austen/Boston Tea Party: The Revolt against Literary Empire in *Night and Day*," Patrick Brantlinger, "The Bloomsbury Faction Versus War and Empire," and Jane Garrity, *Step-Daughters of England: British Women Modernists and the National Imaginary*.

4. For critiques of Jane Marcus's reading of *The Waves*, see Mark Wollaeger, "Woolf, Postcards, and the Elision of Race: Colonizing Women in *The Voyage Out*," Patrick McGee, "The Politics of Modernist Form; Or, Who Rules *The Waves*?" and Laura Doyle, "Sublime Barbarians in the Narrative of Empire, or, Longinus at Sea in *The Waves*." Also see Marcus's 2004 defense of her argument in her study, *Hearts of Darkness: White Women Write Race*.

5. For notable exceptions, see Jed Esty, "Amnesia in the Fields: Late Modernism, Late Imperialism, and the English Pageant-Play," and Sonita Sarker, "*Three Guineas*, the In-corporated Intellectual, and Nostalgia for the Human."

6. See Lisa Tickner, *Modern Life & Modern Subjects: British Art in the Early Twentieth Century*, 48–77 and Michael Holroyd, "Augustus John, John Sampson and the Gypsies."

7. In his 1981 memoir *Conversations in Bloomsbury*, Mulk Raj Anand recalls discussing the androgynous deities of Hinduism with Woolf at the time that she was composing *Orlando*; see Anthea Arnold, "Fact or Fiction? An Indian Encounters Bloomsbury." See Hermione Lee, *Virginia Woolf*, 648–50, on Woolf and Ocampo's friendship, and see Patricia Laurence's *Lily*

Briscoe's Chinese Eyes: Bloomsbury, Modernism, and China for an extensive study of Ling Shuhua's ties to Bloomsbury.

8. In *Moments of Being*, Woolf re-creates the exotic ambience of Lady Ottoline Morrell's salons: "One remembers that drawing room full of people, the pale yellow and pinks of the brocades, the Italian chairs, the Persian rugs, the embroideries, the tassels, the scent, the pomegranates, the pugs, the pot-pourri and Ottoline bearing down upon one from afar in her white shawl with the great scarlet flowers on it" (200).

9. Adrian Stephen's short 1936 memoir, *The "Dreadnought" Hoax*, remarks that "Swahili is, I believe, spoken in some parts of East Africa. Whether it is spoken in Abyssinia or not I don't know, but we thought it might be as well for me to know a few phrases, and to that end we had bought a grammar from the Society for the Propagation of the Gospel" (33).

10. See Lyn Pykett, *Engendering Fictions: The English Novel in the Early Twentieth Century*, 97–98, Daniel Schwartz, *Reconfiguring Modernism: Explorations in the Relationship Between Modern Art and Modern Life*, 23–48, Randall Stevenson, *Modernist Fiction*, 58–81, Alex Zwerdling, *Virginia Woolf and the Real World*, 145–46.

11. See Woolf's *Roger Fry* (149–62) for a vivid description of critical and popular reactions to the postimpressionist exhibit.

12. The Bloomsbury group's involvement with the Ballets Russes was characterized by a fascination with the exotic and the Oriental. Clive Bell, Leonard Woolf, and Lytton Strachey frequently wrote about the Ballets Russes in *The Nation* and *The New Statesman*, connecting Diaghilev's cross-cultural innovations with what Lynn Garafola has called "the leftward leaning politics, formalism, and aesthetic concerns that formed Bloomsbury's loosely defined 'ideology'" (316). The painter Duncan Grant designed the sets and costumes for the Ballets Russes's production of *Togo, or, The Noble Savage*, which featured a cast of Africans and Mexicans dancing to jazz music and wearing African wigs (Anscombe, *Omega and After*, 111; Garafola, 114). The economist John Maynard Keynes married the Russian dancer Lydia Lopokova, bringing her into Bloomsbury social circles; Woolf would later call Lopokova her inspiration for the Italian character Lucrezia Warren-Smith in *Mrs. Dalloway*. See n. 25, below, and Peter Jacobs, "Quel Décor! Nijinsky Conquers Bloomsbury."

13. See Elleke Boehmer's perceptive discussion of Leonard Woolf's writings in *Empire, the National, and the Postcolonial, 1890–1920*, 169–214; see also Andrew McNeillie's "Leonard Woolf's *Empire and Commerce in Africa* revisited."

14. Woolf's anti-Semitism, always a contested subject, surfaces in her diaries and fiction. Her short story "Jews" (1909), for example, describes a "fat Jewess" with a "coarse palate" whose food "swam in oil and was nasty" (14); an unflattering diary entry from 1930 rails against Leonard's family and "how ugly, how nosey, how irreparably middle class they all are" (*Diary* III, 320); Marie Woolf, Leonard's mother, aggravates Virginia with her "pendulous cheeks & red nose & cheap earrings," spreading a "net of falsity" over everything (321); Eleanor Pargiter in *The Years* makes the vicious comment that "there'll be a line of grease round the bath" after "the Jew" Abrahamson finishes his ablutions (339). But such ill-blooded sentiments never interfered with Woolf's indignation at the brutal treatment of Jews in Europe and England. In 1939, she and Leonard went to great lengths to help Robert Spira, an Austrian Jewish refugee who had been interned on the Isle of Man; the Woolfs used their political connections to reunite Spira with his wife, Mela, and to get the couple visas to the United States. See "Letters from Virginia" and Hermione Lee, *Virginia Woolf*, 308–310.

15. The Hogarth Press published all of Woolf's work as well as Leonard's early novels, *The Village in the Jungle* and *The Wise Virgins*. In addition to literature, the Hogarth Press provided a platform for books addressing race and empire, by authors ranging from members of Parliament to subjects of colonized nations. A sample list of colonial biographies and autobiographies includes *Mrs. Eliza Fay, Original Letters from India; Avakkum: The Life of the Archpriest Avakkum by Himself*, translated by J. Harrison and H. Mirrless; *A Woman of India: Being the Life*

of Saroj Nalini by G. S. Dutt; and *An African Speaks for His People,* by Parmenas Githendu Mockerie. Political or historical analyses of race relations include *White Capital and Coloured Labour,* by Lord Olivier; *The Race Problem in Africa,* by Charles Buxton, MP; *India in Transition,* by D. Graham Pole; *The Case for West-Indian Self Government,* by C. L. R. James; and *Caste and Democracy,* by K. M. Panikkar.

16. A detailed history of English porcelain can be found in Hilary Young's *English Porcelain, 1745–95: Its Makers, Design, Marketing and Consumption.* See also David Battle, *Sotheby's Concise Encyclopedia of Porcelain.*

17. The Chinese had elaborate tea-drinking rituals and practices that were not imported into England as the tea leaves themselves were. Over the eighteenth and nineteenth centuries, the English ritualized tea drinking according to their class divisions, social occasions, and seasons of the year. The evolution of traditions like high tea, low tea, afternoon tea, strawberry tea, summer tea, and the tea party worked to strengthen the associations between tea drinking and Englishness. Like "China ware," tea drinking quickly lost any cultural connection to its Chinese origins.

18. For a historical overview of Britain's tea trade from the late seventeenth century through the twentieth century, see Forrest, *Tea for the British: The Social and Economic History of a Famous Trade.* See also Chow and Kramer, *All the Tea in China* and Campbell, *The Tea Book.*

19. See Nadine Beauthéac, "Tea Barons."

20. Three years before *To the Lighthouse* was published, Woolf visited the massive British Empire Exhibition at Wembley. Her 1924 essay "Thunder at Wembley" imagines a stormy end to the exhibition that anticipates the darkness of "Time Passes" and portends the end of empire itself: "Dust swirls down the avenues, hisses and hurries like erected cobras round the corners. Pagodas are dissolving in dust. Ferro-concrete is fallible. Colonies are perishing and dispersing in a spray of inconceivable beauty and terror which some malignant power illuminates. Ash and violence are the colours of its decay. From every quarter human beings come flying—clergymen, school children, invalids in bath-chairs. They fly with outstretched arms, and a vast sound of wailing rolls before them, but there is neither confusion nor dismay. Humanity is rushing to destruction, but humanity is accepting its doom. . . . The Empire is perishing; the bands are playing; the Exhibition is in ruins. For that is what comes of letting in the sky" (*"Thunder at Wembley,"* 410–11). See Scott Cohen, "Virginia Woolf, Wembley, and Imperial Monuments."

21. For further discussion of Fry as an advocate of avant-garde primitivism, see Torgovnick, 85–104 and Christopher Reed, *A Roger Fry Reader,* 232–48.

22. For illustrations and reproductions of Omega Workshops art, see *The Omega Workshops 1913–19: Decorative Arts of Bloomsbury,* Judith Collins, *The Omega Workshops,* Isabelle Anscombe, *Omega and After: Bloomsbury and the Decorative Arts,* Tony Bradshaw, *A Bloomsbury Canvas* and *The Bloomsbury Artists: Prints and Book Design,* Gillian Naylor, *Bloomsbury: Its Artists, Authors and Designers,* Richard Shone, *The Art of Bloomsbury: Roger Fry, Vanessa Bell and Duncan Grant,* and Richard Cork, *Art Beyond the Gallery in Early 20th Century England.*

23. The Omega Workshops also borrowed designs, colors, and forms from Diaghilev's Ballets Russes. The artists working with Roger Fry were, as Richard Cork puts it, "excited both by the exotic costumes and the abandoned movements of Diaghilev's dancers, whose example encouraged English painters to adopt a more liberated and unashamedly emphatic attitude towards the figures in their own work" (*ABG,* 144).

24. In 1944, the critic Raymond Mortimer praised Duncan Grant's work for its "references to Byzantine mosaics, to Matisse, to African sculpture, to early Italians" (9). Grant's work for Roger Fry and the Omega Workshops bore the evidence of his fascination with non-Western art and iconography, such as his marquetry tray featuring a veiled Oriental woman riding an elephant, his *Self-Portrait in Turban,* an oversized fabric collage titled *Caryatid,* a painting called *The Dancers,* and the famous mural *Bathing.* However, the paintings and sketches he executed for himself contain a more overtly transgressive (and relatively unknown) racial poetics. A

posthumously published collection of works called *Private: The Erotic Art of Duncan Grant* show-cases sexual, balletic images of black men coupled with white men. Race animates eros in Grant's biblical scenes, such as his "Descent from the Cross," where a white Jesus is borne aloft by two nude black men, and in revisions of classical mythology, such as his nude paintings of a white Hercules battling a black Diomede. Created with the "primitive vision" that Roger Fry so admired, Grant's clandestine black-white images add a striking sexual dimension to Fry's doctrines about race and form. See Richard Shone, "Duncan Grant: Designer and Decorator" and "The Myths and Fantasies of Duncan Grant."

25. See Winifred Gill, "Beads at the Omega" and Evelyn Silber, *Gaudier-Brzeska: Life and Art*, 121–23.

26. For further elaboration of this point, see Jane Goldman, *The Feminist Aesthetics of Virginia Woolf: Modernism, Post-Impressionism, and the Politics of the Visual* and Christopher Reed, "Through Formalism: Feminism and Virginia Woolf's Relation to Bloomsbury Aesthetics."

27. For lesbian readings of *Orlando*, see Sherron Knopp, "'If I Saw You Would You Kiss Me?': Sapphism and the Subversiveness of Virginia Woolf's *Orlando*," Catharine Stimpson, "Zero Degree Deviancy: The Lesbian Novel in English," Panthea Reid, *Art and Affection: A Life of Virginia Woolf*, 309–14, Suzanne Raitt, *Vita and Virginia: The Work and Friendship of V. Sackville-West and Virginia Woolf*, 17–40, Quentin Bell, *Virginia Woolf: A Biography*, vol. 2, 131–40, James King, *Virginia Woolf*, 398–430, Karyn Z. Sproles, *Desiring Women: The Partnership of Virginia Woolf and Vita Sackville-West*, 70–86, and Julia Briggs, *Virginia Woolf: An Inner Life*, 187–215.

28. In a 1990 reissue of *Passenger to Teheran*, Sackville-West's son Nigel Nicolson furnishes a new introduction in which he clarifies the opaque circumstances of her travel writing: "The author is eloquent about her adventures and reactions, and it would be easy to trace her route on a map, but she is reticent to the point of obscurity about her own identity, her companions on different parts of the journey and her motives for it. . . . She speaks of diplomatic parties without saying that her husband was HM's Counsellor in Teheran, of letter-writing without revealing that her chief correspondent was Virginia Woolf, and of her 'work' without adding that she was completing in Persia her long poem *The Land* which is still her greatest literary testament" (17).

29. For a detailed historical overview of Iran in the twentieth century, see Keddie.

30. In a letter from Luxor, where Sackville-West and her travel companions stopped en route to Persia, Sackville-West tackles the difficulty of communication through an astonishing catalogue of Egyptian culture: "The only way I can deal with Egypt is as Molly McCarthy did with Christmas: alphabetically. Amon, Americans, alabaster, Arabs; bromides, buffaloes, beggars, Bronx; camels, crocodiles, colossi, Cook's; donkeys, dust, dahabeeahs, dragomen, dervishes, desert; Egyptians, Evian; fezzes, fellaheen, feluccas, flies, fleas; Germans, goats, granite; hotels, hieroglyphics, hoopoes, Horus, hawks Isis, imshi, irrigation, ignorance; jibbahs; kites, Kinemas, Kodaks; lavatories, lotus, Levantines; mummies, mud, millionaires; Nubia, Nile; opthalmia, Osiris, obsidian, obelisks; palms, pyramids, parrokeets; quarries; Ramses, ruins; sunsets, sarcophagi, steamers, soux, sand, shadoofs, stinks, Sphinx; temples, tourists, trams, Tut-ankh-amen; Uganda; vultures, Virginia; water-bullocks, warts; Xerxes, Xenophon; yaout; zest (my own)" (DeSalvo and Leaska, 93). Woolf replied, "You are a crafty fox to write an alphabet letter, and so think you have solved the problem of dumbness" (95).

31. See the introduction of Pratt's *Imperial Eyes: Travel Writing and Transculturation* for a detailed discussion of the concept of the contact zone, which is comprised of "the space of colonial encounters, the space in which peoples geographically and historically separated come into contact with each other and establish ongoing relations, usually involving conditions of coercion, radical inequality, and intractable conflict" (6).

32. The original Latin read, "Nos patriae fines et dulcia linquimus arva." See DeSalvo and Leaska, 175 , n. 7.

33. Woolf's and Sackville-West's letters during the latter's travels through central Asia offer

a lively portrait of the two writers' intersecting literary spheres. They trade ideas about the creative process, their literary awards, and unexpected copies of Woolf's novels that turn up in Persian drawing rooms; their letters comment on literature by Marcel Proust, Edgar Rice Burroughs, D. H. Lawrence, Plutarch, Henry Fielding, André Gide, and William Cowper; and they gossip about the culture of modernism in London, discussing controversial literary criticism by John Middleton Murry, the quality of T. S. Eliot's poetry, conversations between E. M. Forster and Lytton Strachey, and articles in *Vogue* magazine.

34. James Elroy Flecker (1884–1915), a Georgian poet, was one of several English writers of his time fascinated by the Middle and Near East. Flecker's *Hassan*, published posthumously, belonged to a larger body of English literature drawn from Islamic cultures. In the late nineteenth century, many English writers translated or retold the Arabian Nights; notable among these were Robert Louis Stevenson's *New Arabian Nights* (1878), Sir Richard Burton's 16-volume *Arabian Nights* (1885–88), and Andrew Lang's *Arabian Nights' Entertainment* (1898). The popular novelist Marie Corelli enjoyed tremendous success with *The Sorrows of Satan* (1896), a tale set in a darkly romantic Eastern land. Flecker himself authored a collection of poems called *Golden Journey to Samarkand* (1913), and in the years after World War I, Kahlil Gibran's *The Prophet* (1923) and T. E. Lawrence's *Seven Pillars of Wisdom* (1935) were commercial successes in the English book market.

35. Appropriately, Sackville-West would compare the experience of reading *Orlando* in 1928 to "being alone in a dark room with a treasure chest full of rubies and nuggets and brocades" (DeSalvo and Leaska, 288).

36. Interestingly, in 1910, Woolf herself had written a small essay on Lady Hester Stanhope for the *Times Literary Supplement*, in which the Orient and its compliant "natives" provide a theater for an Englishwoman's self-consolidation. Driven to "near madness" ("Lady Hester Stanhope," 196) at being imprisoned in her Victorian parlor, Lady Hester decides that "English ways of life are made to suit timid herds, and that a remarkable person must seek a land less corrupted by hypocrisy, where nature prevails" (196–97). She travels (like Orlando) "in the trousers of a Turkish gentleman" (197) through Greece, Syria, Egypt, Turkey, and Lebanon, where she eventually buys a convent and dispenses medicine. But if she moves away from Victorian femininity, Woolf's Lady Hester Stanhope does not distance herself from Victorian imperialism: "Her influence at one time was vast, though vague; the children for twenty miles round Constantinople had heard her name. The apparition of this Englishwoman, with her large frame and her cadaverous face and her connexion with august personages in England, was itself a miracle; the natives thought her neither man nor woman, but a being apart" (197). Woolf's minibiography of Lady Hester overwrites Eastern geography to accommodate a spiritually impoverished but materially empowered British subject.

Twenty years later, Woolf cast a differently critical eye on the relationship between patriarchal repression at home and colonial activity abroad. In her foreword to the exhibition catalogue for a show titled "Recent Paintings by Vanessa Bell," Woolf notes the exceptionality of a woman's art show on Bond Street, pointing out that women artists in England had traditionally been restricted from painting nudes, because "for a woman to look upon nakedness with the eye of an artist, and not simply with the eye of mother, wife or mistress was corruptive of her innocency and destructive of her domesticity." Hence the fact, Woolf says acidly, "that every Victorian family has in its cupboard the skeleton of an aunt who was driven to convert the native because her father would have died rather than let her look upon a naked man" (foreword). Lady Hester Stanhope's feminist triumph is her famed reputation among the "natives" of central Asia, but the English woman artist "is driven to convert the native" when she is robbed of artistic channels.

37. For insightful readings of Woolf's work with the pastoral, see Susan Bazargan, "The Uses of the Land: Vita Sackville-West's Pastoral Writings and Virginia Woolf's *Orlando*" and Roger Hecht, "'I am Nature's Bride': *Orlando and the Female Pastoral*."

38. Ian Baucom's *Out of Place* articulates the importance of *lieux de mémoire* in the British imperial consciousness: "In these places, which can be either textual, monumental, or topographic, the past survives as a fetish of itself. *Lieux de memoire* are therefore cultic phenomena, objects of pilgrimage and veneration, the jealously guarded ruins of cultural ensembles possessed by a need to stop time or, better yet, to launch a voyage of return to the past" (19). See also Raymond Williams's foundational arguments about literary tropes of England-as-home in *The Country and the City.*

39. On models of national identity in this novel, see Erica Johnson, "Giving Up the Ghost: National and Literary Haunting in *Orlando.*"

40. Said argues that the cultural logic of Orientalism depends on a "flexible *positional* superiority, which puts the Westerner in a whole series of possible relationships with the Orient without ever losing him the relative upper hand" (*Orientalism,* 7).

41. *Orlando*'s narrator identifies himself as male on the second page of the novel: "Happy the mother who bears, happier still the biographer who records the life of such a one! Never need she vex herself, nor he invoke the help of novelist or poet" (14–15).

42. See Christina Froula, *Virginia Woolf and the Bloomsbury Avant-Garde: War, Civilization, Modernity,* 175–89, for a notable example of such a reading.

43. See Marjorie Garber, *Vested Interests: Cross-Dressing and Cultural Anxiety* for a discussion of *Orlando,* Turkish clothing, and English fashion in the late seventeenth and early eighteenth centuries.

44. In *Passenger to Teheran,* Vita Sackville-West describes sites in Teheran dedicated to Rustum, calling him the Persians' "favourite heroic character" (105) from the *Shahname.* Like *The Arabian Nights,* the *Shahname* occupied a prominent place in the nineteenth-century Western European fascination with Eastern mythologies and lore. The first English translation of the *Shahname* appeared in Calcutta in 1814, when it was published alongside the original Persian work. In 1853, Matthew Arnold wrote his now-famous poem, "Sohrab and Rustum: An Episode," which retells the tragic battle between father and son. Between the late nineteenth century and the early twentieth century, the *Shahname* had been fully translated into German, Italian, and French (Clinton, xiii–xxv). By naming her Gypsy leader Rustum, Woolf links *Orlando* with Eastern narratives about patriotism, monarchy, and national hierarchy, as well as with Western refashionings of Eastern lore.

45. I allude here to Benedict Anderson, who has persuasively demonstrated that modern nations are "imagined communities" that are "'modular,' capable of being transplanted, with varying degrees of self-consciousness, to a great variety of social terrains, to merge and be merged with a correspondingly wide variety of political and ideological constellations" (4). See the introduction of Anderson's *Imagined Communities: Reflections on the Origin and Spread of Nationalism.*

46. See Nigel Nicolson, *Portrait of a Marriage: Vita Sackville-West and Harold Nicolson,* and Victoria Glendinning, *Vita: A Biography of Vita Sackville-West.*

Conclusion

1. The "new modernist studies" gained a formal academic forum in 1994 with the founding of the journal *Modernism/modernity;* in 1998, the Modernist Studies Association held its inaugural conference.

2. See Ann Ardis, *New Women, New Novels: Feminism and Early Modernism,* Shari Benstock, *Women of the Left Bank,* Suzanne Clark, *Sentimental Modernism: Women Writers and the Revolution of the Word,* Jayne Marek, *Women Editing Modernism: "Little" Magazines and Literary History,* Gillian Hanscombe and Virginia Smyers, *Writing for Their Lives: The Modernist Women 1910–1940,* and Bridget Elliott and Jo-Ann Wallace, *Women Writers and Artists: Modernist (im)positionings.*

3. I am indebted to Douglas Mao and Rebecca Walkowitz for this phrase. See "The New Modernist Studies," 742.

4. See Laura Doyle and Laura Winkiel, eds., *Geomodernisms: Race, Modernism, Modernity*, and Melba Cuddy-Keane, "Modernism, Geopolitics, Globalization."

5. Simon Gikandi discusses the importance of transnational modernism in his "Preface: Modernism in the World," the lead piece in *Modernism/modernity*'s special 2006 issue "Modernism and Transnationalisms." Important studies of transnational modernism include Richard Begam and Michael Valdez Moses, eds., *Modernism and Colonialism: British and Irish Literature, 1899–1939*, Alice Gambrell, *Women Intellectuals, Modernism, and Difference: Transatlantic Culture, 1919–1945*, Anita Patterson, *Race, American Literature, and Transnational Modernisms*, Peter Brooker and Andrew Thacker, eds., *Geographies of Modernism: Literatures, Cultures, Spaces*, and Ann Ardis and Patrick Collier, eds., *Transatlantic Print Culture, 1890–1940: Emerging Media, Emerging Modernisms*.

6. See Mary Lou Emery, *Modernism, the Visual, and Caribbean Literature*, Patricia Laurence, *Lily Briscoe's Chinese Eyes: Bloomsbury, Modernism, and China*, Priya Joshi, *In Another Country: Colonialism, Culture, and the English Novel in India*, Joshua L. Miller, "The Gorgeous Laughter of Filipino Modernity: Carlos Bulosan's *The Laughter of My Father*," Anthony L. Geist and José B. Monléon, *Modernism and Its Margins: Reinscribing Cultural Modernity from Spain and Latin America*, Maren Linett, *Modernism, Feminism, and Jewishness*, and Werner Sollors, *Ethnic Modernism*.

7. See Janet Lyon, "Sickness and Decadence," Christopher GoGwilt, *The Fiction of Geopolitics: Afterimages of Culture, from Wilkie Collins to Alfred Hitchcock*, Peter Childs, *Modernism and Eugenics: Woolf, Eliot, Yeats, and the Culture of Degeneration*, Rebecca Walkowitz, *Cosmopolitan Style: Modernism beyond the Nation*, Jessica Berman, *Modernist Fiction, Cosmopolitanism, and the Politics of Community*, Kobena Mercer, ed., *Cosmopolitan Modernisms*, and Ryan Jerving, "Jazz Language and Ethnic Novelty." On T. S. Eliot and anti-Semitism, see the Special Section: Eliot and Anti-Semitism: The Ongoing Debate in *Modernism/modernity* 10, no. 1 (January 2003) and Eliot and Anti-Semitism: The Ongoing Debate II in *Modernism/modernity* 10, no. 3 (September 2003).

8. In a special 2008 issue of *PMLA* devoted to critical race theory and literary studies, the near absence of aesthetic considerations is striking. Shu-mei Shih's "Comparative Racialization: An Introduction" describes the current intellectual need to revisit "the worldliness of race" (1349), and the articles in the rest of the issue, accordingly, deal with the sociopolitical and anthropological realities of race, the workings of prejudice and discrimination, and the historical production of knowledge about race. See, for example, Etienne Balibar, "Racism Revisited: Sources, Relevance, and Aporias of a Modern Concept," Colleen Lye, "The Afro-Asian Analogy," Françoise Lionnet, "Continents and Archipelagoes: From E Pluribus Unum to Creolized Solidarities," and Imam Mersal, "Eliminating Diasporic Identities."

9. Simon Gikandi, "Picasso, Africa, and the Schemata of Difference."

10. See Laura Doyle, *Bordering on the Body: The Racial Matrix of Modern Fiction and Culture* and *Freedom's Empire: Race and the Rise of the Novel in Atlantic Modernity, 1640–1940*, Jed Esty, *A Shrinking Island: Modernism and National Culture in England*, Pericles Lewis, *Modernism, Nationalism, and the Novel*, Paul Peppis, *Literature, Politics, and the English Avant-Garde: Nation and Empire, 1901–1918*, and Laura Winkiel, *Modernism, Race, and Manifestoes*.

BIBLIOGRAPHY

Achebe, Chinua. "An Image of Africa: Racism in Conrad's *Heart of Darkness*." In *Heart of Darkness*, 4th ed., by Joseph Conrad, edited by Paul B. Armstrong, 336–49. New York: W. W. Norton, 2006.

Acton, Harold. *Memoirs of an Actor*. London: Methuen, 1948.

Adorno, Theodor W. "Parataxis: On Holderlin's Late Poetry." In *Notes to Literature*, vol. 2, edited by Rolf Tiedemann, translated by Sherry Weber Nicholsen. New York: Columbia University Press, 1992.

Alpers, Antony, ed. *The Stories of Katherine Mansfield*. Oxford: Oxford University Press, 1984.

Anderson, Benedict. *Imagined Communities: Reflections on the Origin and Spread of Nationalism*. London: Verso, 1991.

Annan, Noel. *Leslie Stephen: The Godless Victorian*. New York: Random House, 1984.

Anonymous review of Katherine Mansfield's *Stories*. *Times Literary Supplement*. March 2, 1946.

Anscombe, Isabelle. *Omega and After: Bloomsbury and the Decorative Arts*. New York: Thames and Hudson, 1981.

——. "The Context of the Omega." *Charleston Magazine*. Summer/Autumn 1991, 26–30.

Antliff, Mark, and Patricia Leighten. "Primitive." In *Critical Terms for Art History*, edited by Robert S. Nelson and Richard Shiff, 170–84. Chicago: University of Chicago Press, 1996.

Apollinaire, Guillaume. Program notes to *Parade* (May 18, 1917), 69.

Appignanesi, Lisa. *The Cabaret*. New Haven, CT: Yale University Press, 2004.

Ardis, Ann L. *New Women, New Novels: Feminism and Early Modernism*. New Brunswick, NJ: Rutgers University Press, 1991.

Ardis, Ann L., and Patrick Collier, eds. *Transatlantic Print Culture, 1880–1940: Emerging Media, Emerging Modernisms*. New York: Palgrave Macmillan, 2008.

Archer-Straw, Petrine. *Negrophilia: Avant-Garde Paris and Black Culture in the 1920s*. New York: Thames & Hudson, 2000.

Armstrong, Paul B. Introduction to *Heart of Darkness*, 4th ed., by Joseph Conrad, edited by Paul B. Armstrong, ix–xix. New York: W. W. Norton, 2006.

Arnold, Anthea. "Fact or Fiction? An Indian Encounters Bloomsbury." *Charleston Magazine*, Spring/Autumn 1995, 9–13.

Baker, Houston A., Jr. *Modernism and the Harlem Renaissance.* Chicago: University of Chicago Press, 1987.

Baldick, Chris. *Oxford English Literary History: The Modern Movement (1910–1940).* Oxford: Oxford University Press, 2006.

Balibar, Etienne. "Racism Revisited: Sources, Relevance, and Aporias of a Modern Concept." *PMLA* 123, no. 5 (October 2008): 1630–39.

Banton, Michael. *Racial Theories.* Cambridge: Cambridge University Press, 1998.

Barkan, Elazar, and Ronald Bush, eds. *Prehistories of the Future: The Primitivist Project and the Culture of Modernism.* Palo Alto, CA: Stanford University Press, 1995.

Battie, David, ed. *Sotheby's Concise Encyclopedia of Porcelain.* London: Conran Octopus, 1990.

Baucom, Ian. *Out of Place: Englishness, Empire, and the Locations of Identity.* Princeton, NJ: Princeton University Press, 1999.

Baudelaire, Charles. *The Painter of Modern Life and Other Essays.* 1863. Translated and edited by Jonathan Mayne. Reprint, London: Phaidon Press, 1964.

Bazargan, Susan. "The Uses of the Land: Vita Sackville-West's Pastoral Writings and Virginia Woolf's *Orlando.*" *Woolf Studies Annual* 5 (1999): 25–55.

Beauthéac, Nadine. "Tea Barons." In *The Book of Tea,* by Alain Stella, Gilles Brochard, Nadine Beauthéac, and Catherine Dozel, translated by Deke Dusinberre, 57–99. Paris: Flammarion, 1992.

Beckson, Karl. *London in the 1890s: A Cultural History.* New York: W. W. Norton, 1992.

Begam, Richard, and Michael Valdez Moses, eds. *Modernism and Colonialism: British and Irish Literature, 1899–1939.* Durham, NC: Duke University Press, 2007.

Behrendt, Patricia. *Oscar Wilde: Eros and Aesthetics.* London: Macmillan, 1991.

Belford, Barbara. *Violet: The Story of the Irrepressible Violet Hunt and Her Circle of Lovers and Friends—Ford Madox Ford, H. G. Wells, Somerset Maugham, and Henry James.* New York: Simon and Schuster, 1990.

Bell, Clive. *Art.* New York: Frederick A. Stokes, 1914.

——. "Negro Sculpture." In *Since Cézanne.* 113–21. London: Chatto & Windus, 1922.

Bell, Michael. "The Metaphysics of Modernism." In *The Cambridge Companion to Modernism,* edited by Michael Levenson, 9–32. Cambridge: Cambridge University Press, 1999.

Bell, Quentin. *Virginia Woolf: A Biography.* 2 vols. New York: Harcourt Brace Jovanovich, 1972.

Bell, Quentin, and Stephen Chaplin. "The Ideal Home Rumpus." *Apollo Magazine* (October 1964): 284–91.

Bennett, Andrew. *Katherine Mansfield.* Devon: Northcote House Publishers, 2004.

Benstock, Shari. *Women of the Left Bank: Paris, 1900–1940.* Austin: University of Texas Press, 1986.

Berman, Jessica. *Modernist Fiction, Cosmopolitanism, and the Politics of Community.* Cambridge: Cambridge University Press, 2001.

Berman, Marshall. *All That Is Solid Melts into Air: The Experience of Modernity.* New York: Simon and Schuster, 1982.

Bernasconi, Robert. "Who Invented the Concept of Race? Kant's Role in the Enlightenment Construction of Race." In *Race,* edited by Robert Bernasconi, 9–36. Oxford: Blackwell, 2001.

Berridge, Victoria, and Griffith Edwards. *Opium and the People: Opiate Use in Nineteenth-Century England.* New York: St. Martin's Press, 1981.

Bhabha, Homi. "How Newness Enters the World: Postmodern Space, Postcolonial Times and the Trials of Cultural Translation." In *The Location of Culture*, 212–35. London and New York: Routledge, 1994.

———. *The Location of Culture*. London and New York: Routledge, 1994.

Bishop, Edward. *A Chronology of Virginia Woolf*. London: Macmillan, 1989.

Black, Jonathan, ed. *Blasting the Future! Vorticism in Britain 1910–1920*. London: Philip Wilson Publishers, 2004.

Blake, Jody. *Le Tumulte Noir: Modernist Art and Popular Entertainment in Jazz-Age Paris, 1900–1930*. University Park: Pennsylvania State University Press, 1999.

Blake, William. "The Little Black Boy." In *The Complete Poetry and Prose of William Blake*, edited by David V. Erdman, 9. Berkeley: University of California Press, 1982.

Bloom, Clive. *Cult Fiction: Popular Reading and Pulp Theory*. New York: St. Martin's Press, 1996.

Boehmer, Elleke. *Colonial and Postcolonial Literature*. Oxford: Oxford University Press, 1995.

———. *Empire, the National, and the Postcolonial, 1890–1920*. Oxford: Oxford University Press, 2002.

Booth, Howard J., and Nigel Rigby. *Modernism and Empire: Writing and British Coloniality, 1890–1940*. Manchester: Manchester University Press, 2000.

Born, Richard A. *From BLAST to Pop: Aspects of British Modern Art, 1915–1965*. Chicago: The David and Alfred Smart Museum of Art, 1997.

Bradbury, Malcolm, and James McFarlane. "The Name and Nature of Modernism." In *Modernism: A Guide to European Literature 1890–1930*. 1976. Edited by Malcolm Bradbury and James McFarlane, 19–55. Reprint, London: Penguin Books, 1991.

Bradshaw, Tony, ed. *The Bloomsbury Artists: Prints and Book Design*. Aldershot, UK: Scolar Press, 1999.

———. *A Bloomsbury Canvas*. Aldershot, UK: Lund Humphries/Ashgate, 2001.

Brantlinger, Patrick. "The Bloomsbury Faction Versus War and Empire." In *Seeing Double: Revisioning Edwardian and Modernist Literature*, edited by Carol M. Kaplan and Anne B. Simpson, 149–67. New York: St. Martin's Press, 1996.

———. *Rule of Darkness: British Literature and Imperialism, 1830–1914*. Ithaca, NY: Cornell University Press, 1990.

Briggs, Julia. *Virginia Woolf: An Inner Life*. New York: Harvest Books, 2006.

Bristow, Joseph. "'A complex multiform creature'—Wilde's Sexual Identities." In *The Cambridge Companion to Oscar Wilde*, edited by Peter Raby, 195–218. Cambridge: Cambridge University Press, 1997.

———. *Empire Boys: Adventures in a Man's World*. London: Unwin Hyman, 1991.

Broken Blossoms; or, The Yellow Man and the Girl. Directed by D. W. Griffith. USA: D. W. Griffith Productions, 1919.

Brook, Peter. *Reading for the Plot: Design and Intention in Narrative*. Cambridge, MA: Harvard University Press, 1984.

Brooker, Peter, and Andrew Thacker, eds. *Geographies of Modernism: Literatures, Cultures, Spaces*. London: Routledge, 2005.

Brooks, Peter. *The Melodramatic Imagination*. New Haven, CT: Yale University Press, 1976.

Brown, Nicholas. *Utopian Generations: The Political Horizon of Twentieth-Century Literature*. Princeton, NJ: Princeton University Press, 2005.

Bürger, Peter. *The Theory of the Avant-Garde*. Translated by Mary Shaw. Minneapolis: University of Minnesota Press, 1984.

Butler, Christopher. *Early Modernism: Literature, Music and Painting in Europe 1900–1916*. Oxford: Oxford University Press, 1994.

"Cabaret Theatre Club." Original brochure. May 1912. Yale Center for British Art, New Haven, CT.

Calinescu, Matei. *Five Faces of Modernity: Modernism, Avant-Garde, Decadence, Kitsch, Postmodernism.* Durham, NC: Duke University Press, 1987.

Calloway, Stephen. "Wilde and the Dandyism of the Senses." In *The Cambridge Companion to Oscar Wilde,* edited by Peter Raby, 34–54. Cambridge: Cambridge University Press, 1997.

Campbell, Dawn. *The Tea Book.* Gretna, LA: Pelican Publishing Company, 1995.

Carco, Francis. *De Montmartre au Quartier Latin; or, The Last Bohemia: From Montmarte to the Latin Quarter.* Translated by Madeleine Boyd. New York: Henry Holt, 1928.

Charlesworth, Barbara. *Dark Passages: The Decadent Consciousness in Victorian Literature.* Madison: University of Wisconsin Press, 1965.

Chen, Tina. "Dissecting the 'Devil-Doctor': Stereotype and Sensationalism in Sax Rohmer's Fu Manchu." In *Re-Collecting Early Asian America,* edited by Josephine Lee, Imogene L. Lim, and Yuko Matsukawa, 218–37. Philadelphia: Temple University Press, 2002.

Cheng, Vincent J. *Joyce, Race, and Empire.* New York: Columbia University Press, 1995.

Childs, Peter. *Modernism and Eugenics: Woolf, Eliot, Yeats, and the Culture of Degeneration.* Cambridge: Cambridge University Press, 2001.

Choo, Ng Kwee. *The Chinese in London.* London: Oxford University Press, 1968.

Chow, Kit, and Ione Kramer. *All the Tea in China.* San Francisco: China Books and Periodicals, 1990.

Clark, Suzanne. *Sentimental Modernism: Women Writers and the Revolution of the Word.* Bloomington: Indiana University Press, 1991.

Cliff, Michelle. "Virginia Woolf and the Imperial Gaze: A Glance Askance." In *Virginia Woolf: Emerging Perspectives; Selected Papers from the Third Annual Conference on Virginia Woolf,* edited by Mark Hussey and Vara Neverow, 91–102. New York: Pace University Press, 1994.

Clifford, James. *The Predicament of Culture.* Cambridge, MA: Harvard University Press, 1988.

Clinton, Jerome W., trans. *The Tragedy of Sohrab and Rostam.* Seattle: University of Washington Press, 1987.

Cohen, Ed. *Talk on the Wilde Side: Toward a Genealogy of a Discourse on Male Sexualities.* London: Routledge, 1993.

Cohen, Paul A. *History in Three Keys: The Boxers as Event, Experience, and Myth.* New York: Columbia University Press, 1997.

Cohen, Scott. "Virginia Woolf, Wembley, and Imperial Monuments." *Modern Fiction Studies* 50, no. 1 (Spring 2004): 85–109.

Collier, Patrick. "Journalism Meets Modernism." In *Gender in Modernism: New Geographies, Complex Intersections,* edited by Bonnie Kime Scott, 186–224. Urbana: University of Illinois Press, 2007.

Collins, Judith. *The Omega Workshops.* Chicago: University of Chicago Press, 1984.

Comentale, Edward, and Andrzej Gasiorek, eds. *T. E. Hulme and the Question of Modernism.* London: Ashgate, 2006.

Conrad, Joseph. *Heart of Darkness.* 1899. Reprint, London: Penguin Books, 1995.

——. Preface to *Nigger of the "Narcissus."* 1897. In *Heart of Darkness,* 4th ed., by Joseph Conrad, edited by Paul B. Armstrong, 279–82. Reprint, New York: W. W. Norton, 2006.

Constable, Liz, Dennis Denisoff, and Matthew Potolsky, eds. *Perennial Decay: On the Aesthetics and Politics of Decadence.* Philadelphia: University of Pennsylvania Press, 1998.

Coombes, Annie E. *Reinventing Africa: Museums, Material Culture and Popular Imagination*. New Haven, CT: Yale University Press, 1994.

Corbett, David Peters. *The Modernity of English Art 1914–30*. Manchester: Manchester University Press, 1997.

Cork, Richard. *Art beyond the Gallery in Early 20th Century England*. New Haven, CT: Yale University Press, 1985.

———. *Vorticism and Abstract Art in the First Machine Age*. Vol. 1, *Origins and Development*. Berkeley: University of California Press, 1976.

Cowley, Malcolm. "'Page Dr. Blum!': *Bliss*." *The Dial* 71 (September 1921): 365.

Cowling, Mary. *The Artist as Anthropologist: The Representation of Type and Character in Victorian Art*. Cambridge: Cambridge University Press, 1989.

Craton, Michael. *Testing the Chains: Resistance to Slavery in the British West Indies*. Ithaca, NY: Cornell University Press, 1982.

Cuddy-Keane, Melba. "Modernism, Geopolitics, Globalization." *Modernism/modernity* 10.3 (2003): 539–58.

———. *Virginia Woolf, the Intellectual, and the Public Sphere*. Cambridge: Cambridge University Press, 2003.

Cvetkovich, Ann. *Mixed Feelings: Feminism, Mass Culture, and Victorian Sensationalism*. New Brunswick, NJ: Rutgers University Press, 1992.

Dangerfield, George. *The Strange Death of Liberal England*. New York: Capricorn Books, G. P. Putnam's Sons, 1935.

Davis, Coakley. *Oscar Wilde: The Importance of Being Irish*. Dublin: Town House, 1994.

Davis, Mary E. *Classic Chic: Music, Fashion, and Modernism*. Berkeley: University of California Press, 2006.

Dellamora, Richard. *Masculine Desire: The Sexual Politics of Victorian Aestheticism*. Chapel Hill: University of North Carolina Press, 1990.

DeSalvo, Louise, and Mitchell Leaska. *The Letters of Vita Sackville-West to Virginia Woolf*. New York: William Morrow and Company, 1985.

Dettmar, Kevin, and Stephen Watt. *Marketing Modernisms: Self-Promotion, Canonization, and Re-Reading*. Ann Arbor: University of Michigan Press, 1996.

Dollimore, Jonathan. *Sexual Dissidence: Augustine to Wilde, Freud to Foucault*. Oxford: Clarendon Press, 1991.

Doyle, Arthur Conan. *The Hound of Baskervilles*. New York: Grosset & Dunlap, 1902.

Doyle, Laura. *Bordering on the Body: The Racial Matrix of Modern Fiction and Culture*. Oxford: Oxford University Press, 1994.

———. *Freedom's Empire: Race and the Rise of the Novel in Atlantic Modernity, 1640–1940*. Durham: Duke University Press, 2008.

———. "Sublime Barbarians in the Narrative of Empire; or, Longinus at Sea in *The Waves*." *Modern Fiction Studies* 42, no. 2 (1996): 323–37.

Doyle, Laura, and Laura Winkiel, eds., *Geomodernisms: Race, Modernism, Modernity*. Bloomington: Indiana University Press, 2005.

Driver, Felix. *Geography Militant: Cultures of Exploration and Empire*. Oxford: Blackwell Publishers, 2001.

Eliot, T. S. *After Strange Gods: A Primer in Modern Heresy*. London: Faber and Faber, 1934.

———. "The Love Song of J. Alfred Prufrock." 1915. In *The Norton Anthology of English Literature*, 6th ed., vol. 2, edited by M. H. Abrams et al., 2140–43. New York: W. W. Norton, 1993.

———. Review of *Tarr* by Wyndham Lewis. *Egoist* 5.8 (1918) 105–6.

Elliott, Bridget, and Jo-Ann Wallace. *Women Artists and Writers: Modernist (im)positionings.* London and New York: Routledge, 1994.

Ellmann Richard, ed. *The Artist as Critic: Critical Writings of Oscar Wilde.* New York: Random House, 1968.

Emery, Mary Lou. *Modernism, the Visual, and Caribbean Literature.* Cambridge: Cambridge University Press, 2007.

———. "'Robbed of Meaning': The Work at the Center of *To the Lighthouse.*" *Modern Fiction Studies* 38, no. 1 (1992): 217–34.

Esty, Jed. "Amnesia in the Fields: Late Modernism, Late Imperialism, and the English Pageant-Play." *English Literary History* 69, no. 1 (Spring 2002): 245–76.

———. *A Shrinking Island: Modernism and National Culture in England.* Princeton, NJ: Princeton University Press, 2004.

Eysteinsson, Astradur. *The Concept of Modernism.* Ithaca, NY: Cornell University Press, 1990.

Eze, Emmanuel Chukwudi, ed. *Race and the Enlightenment: A Reader.* Cambridge: Blackwell Publishers, 1997.

Feldman, David. "Jews in London, 1880–1914." In *Patriotism: The Making and Unmaking of British National Identity,* vol. 2, *Minorities and Outsiders,* edited by Raphael Samuel, 207–25. London: Routledge, 1989.

Feldman, Jessica. *Gender on the Divide: the Dandy in Modernist Literature.* Ithaca, NY: Cornell University Press, 1993.

Felski, Rita. *The Gender of Modernity.* Cambridge, MA: Harvard University Press, 1995.

Firchow, Peter. *Envisioning Africa: Racism and Imperialism in Conrad's "Heart of Darkness."* Lexington: University of Kentucky Press, 1999.

Flam, Jack. Introduction to *Primitivism and Twentieth-Century Art: A Documentary History,* edited by J. Flam and M. Deutch, 1–22. Berkeley: University of California Press, 2003.

Flecker, James Elroy. *Hassan: The Story of Hassan of Bagdad, and How He Came to Make the Golden Journey to Samarkand.* New York: Alfred A. Knopf, 1922.

Floyd-Wilson, Mary. "'Clime, Complexion, and Degree': Racialism in Early Modern England." PhD diss., University of North Carolina, 1996.

Ford, Ford Madox. *The Critical Attitude.* 1911. Reprint, London: Duckworth, 1924.

———. Dedicatory letter to Stella Ford. 1927. In *The Good Soldier,* by Ford Madox Ford, xix–xxiv. New York: Vintage, 1989.

———. *The Good Soldier.* 1915. Reprint, New York: Vintage, 1989.

———. *Joseph Conrad.* London: Duckworth, 1924.

———. *The March of Literature: From Confucius' Day to Our Own.* New York: The Dial Press, 1938.

———. *Return to Yesterday: Reminiscences of James, Conrad, and Crane.* New York: Liveright, 1932.

Forrest, Denys. *Tea for the British: The Social and Economic History of a Famous Trade.* London: Chatto & Windus, 1973.

Forster, E. M. *A Passage to India.* 1924. Reprint, New York: Harcourt Brace Jovanovich, 1984.

Foucault, Michel. *The Order of Things: An Archaeology of the Human Sciences.* 1970. Reprint, New York: Vintage, 1994.

———. "What Is Enlightenment?" In *The Foucault Reader,* edited by Paul Rabinow, 32–50. New York: Pantheon Books, 1984.

Fox, Susan Hudson. "Woolf's Austen/Boston Tea Party: The Revolt against Literary Empire in *Night and Day.*" In *Virginia Woolf: Emerging Perspectives; Selected Papers from the*

Third Annual Conference on Virginia Woolf, edited by Mark Hussey and Vara Neverow, 259–65. New York: Pace University Press, 1994.

Freedman, Jonathan. *The Temple of Culture.* Oxford: Oxford University Press, 1992.

Froula, Christina. *Virginia Woolf and the Bloomsbury Avant-Garde: War, Civilization, Modernity.* New York: Columbia University Press, 2005.

Fry, Roger. Preface to the Omega Workshops Catalog. 1914. Reprinted in *The Roger Fry Reader,* edited by Christopher Reed, 201. Chicago: University of Chicago Press, 1996.

——. *Vision and Design.* 1920. Edited by J. B. Bullen. Reprint, New York: Dover, 1981.

Fryer, Peter. *Staying Power: Black People in Britain since 1504.* Atlantic Highlands, NJ: Humanities Press, 1984.

Fullbrook, Kate. *Katherine Mansfield.* Bloomington: Indiana University Press, 1986.

Gagnier, Regenia. *Idylls of the Marketplace: Oscar Wilde and the Victorian Public.* Palo Alto, CA: Stanford University Press, 1986.

Gambrell, Alice. *Women Intellectuals, Modernism, and Difference: Transatlantic Culture, 1919–1945.* Cambridge: Cambridge University Press, 1997.

Garafola, Lynn. *Diaghilev's Ballets Russes.* New York: Oxford University Press, 1989.

Garafola, Lynn, and Nancy Van Norman Baer, eds., *The Ballets Russes and Its World.* New Haven, CT: Yale University Press, 1999.

Garber, Marjorie. *Vested Interests: Cross-Dressing and Cultural Anxiety.* New York: Routledge, 1992.

Garrity, Jane. "Selling Culture to the 'Civilized': Bloomsbury, British *Vogue,* and the Marketing of National Identity." *Modernism/modernity* 6, no. 2 (1999): 29–58.

——. *Step-Daughters of England: British Women Modernists and the National Imaginary.* Manchester: Manchester University Press, 2003.

Gasiorek, Andrzej. "Ford's Modernism and the Question of Tradition." *English Literature in Transition* 44, no. 1 (2001): 3–27.

Gates, Henry Louis, Jr., ed. *"Race," Writing, and Difference.* Chicago: University of Chicago Press, 1986.

Gay, Peter. *Modernism: The Lure of Heresy from Baudelaire to Beckett and Beyond.* New York: W. W. Norton, 2007.

Geist, Anthony L., and José B. Monléon. *Modernism and Its Margins: Reinscribing Cultural Modernity from Spain to Latin America.* New York: Routledge, 1999.

Gerzina, Gretchen, ed., *Black Victorians, Black Victoriana.* New Brunswick, NJ: Rutgers University Press, 2003.

Giddens, Anthony. *The Consequences of Modernity.* Palo Alto, CA: Stanford University Press, 1990.

Giddens, Anthony, and Christopher Pierson. *Conversations with Anthony Giddens: Making Sense of Modernity.* Palo Alto, CA: Stanford University Press, 1998.

Gikandi, Simon. *Maps of Englishness: Writing Identity in the Culture of Colonialism.* New York: Columbia University Press, 1996.

——. "Picasso, Africa, and the Schemata of Difference." *Modernism/modernity* 10, no. 3 (September 2003): 455–80.

——. "Preface: Modernism in the World," *Modernism/modernity* 13, no. 3 (September 2006): 419–24.

Gilbert, Sandra, and Susan Gubar. *No Man's Land: The Place of the Woman Writer in the Twentieth Century.* Vol. 2, *Sexchanges.* New Haven, CT: Yale University Press, 1989.

Gill, Winifred. "Beads at the Omega." *Charleston Magazine,* Winter/Spring 1993–1994, 33–4.

Gillespie, Michael Patrick. "A Note on the Texts." In *The Picture of Dorian Gray*, 2nd ed., by Oscar Wilde, xv. New York: W. W. Norton, 2007.

Gilman, Sander. "Black Bodies, White Bodies: Toward an Iconography of Female Sexuality in Late Nineteenth-Century Art, Medicine, and Literature." In *"Race," Writing, and Difference*, edited by Henry Louis Gates, Jr., 223–61. Chicago: University of Chicago Press, 1986.

Gilroy, Paul. *The Black Atlantic: Modernity and Double Consciousness.* Cambridge, MA: Harvard University Press, 1993.

Glendinning, Victoria. *Rebecca West: A Life.* New York: Ballantine Books, 1987.

———. *Vita: A Biography of Vita Sackville-West.* New York: Quill, 1983.

Gluck, Mary. *Popular Bohemia: Modernism and Urban Culture in Nineteenth-Century Paris.* Cambridge, MA: Harvard University Press, 2005.

Gobineau, Arthur. *The Inequality of Human Races.* 1853. Translated by Adrian Collins. Reprint, New York: Howard Fertig, 1967.

GoGwilt, Christopher. *The Fiction of Geopolitics: Afterimages of Culture, from Wilkie Collins to Alfred Hitchcock.* Palo Alto, CA: Stanford University Press, 2000.

———. *The Invention of the West: Joseph Conrad and the Double-Mapping of Europe and Empire.* Palo Alto, CA: Stanford University Press, 1995.

Goldman, Jane. *The Feminist Aesthetics of Virginia Woolf: Modernism, Post-Impressionism, and the Politics of the Visual.* Cambridge: Cambridge University Press, 1998.

Goldman, Merle, and Leo Ou-Fan Lee. *An Intellectual History of Modern China.* Cambridge: Cambridge University Press, 2002.

Gould, Stephen Jay. *The Mismeasure of Man.* New York: W. W. Norton, 1981.

Greenslade, William P. *Degeneration, Culture, and the Novel: 1880–1940.* Cambridge: Cambridge University Press, 1994.

Gruetzner-Robins, Anna. *Modern Art in Britain, 1910–1914.* London: Barbican Art Gallery, 1997.

Guerard, Albert. *Conrad the Novelist.* Cambridge, MA: Harvard University Press, 1958.

Haller, John S. *Outcasts from Evolution: Scientific Attitudes of Racial Inferiority, 1859–1900.* Carbondale: Southern Illinois University Press, 1995.

Hankin, Cherry A., ed. *Katherine Mansfield and Her Confessional Stories.* New York: St. Martin's Press, 1983.

———. *Letters Between Katherine Mansfield and John Middleton Murry.* New York: New Amsterdam Books, 1991.

Hannaford, Ivan. *Race: The History of an Idea in the West.* Baltimore: Johns Hopkins University Press, 1996.

Hanscombe, Gillian, and Virginia Smyers. *Writing for Their Lives: The Modernist Women, 1910–1940.* London: Women's Press, 1987.

Harrison, Charles. *English Art and Modernism 1900–1939.* Bloomington: Indiana University Press, 1981.

———. "Modernism." In *Critical Terms for Art History*, edited by Robert S. Nelson and Richard Shiff, 142–55. Chicago: University of Chicago Press, 1996.

Head, Dominic. *The Modernist Short Story: A Study in Theory and Practice.* Cambridge: Cambridge University Press, 1992.

Hecht, Roger. "'I am Nature's Bride': *Orlando* and the Female Pastoral." In *Re: Reading, Re: Writing, Re: Teaching Virginia Woolf*, edited by Eileen Barrett, Patricia Cramer, and Paul Connolly, 22–28. New York: Pace University Press, 1995.

Henke, Suzette. "De/Colonizing the Subject in Virginia Woolf's *The Voyage Out*: Rachel Vinrace as *La Mysterique*." In *Virginia Woolf: Emerging Perspectives; Selected Papers from the*

Third Annual Conference on Virginia Woolf, edited by Mark Hussey and Vara Neverow, 103–8. New York: Pace University Press, 1994.

Hickman, Miranda. *The Geometry of Modernism: The Vorticist Idiom in Lewis, Pound, H. D., and Yeats.* Austin: University of Texas Press, 2005.

Hoare, Philip. *Oscar Wilde's Last Stand: Decadence, Conspiracy, and the Most Outrageous Trial of the Century.* New York: Arcade Publishing, 1998.

Holmes, Colin. *John Bull's Island: Immigration & British Society, 1871–1971.* London: Macmillan Education, 1988.

Holroyd, Michael. "Augustus John, John Sampson and the Gypsies." *Charleston Magazine,* Autumn/Winter 1996, 36–40.

Hovey, Jaime. "'Kissing a Negress in the Dark': Englishness as a Masquerade in Woolf's *Orlando.*" *PMLA* 112, no. 3 (1997): 393–404.

Howe, Irving. "Introduction: The Idea of the Modern." In *The Idea of the Modern in Literature and the Arts,* edited by Irving Howe, 11–40. New York: Horizon Press, 1967.

Hulme, T. E. *Speculations: Essays on Humanism and the Philosophy of Art.* Edited by Herbert Read. London: Routledge & Kegan Paul, 1949.

Hunt, Violet. *I Have This to Say: The Story of My Flurried Years.* New York: Boni and Liveright, 1926.

Ingles, Elisabeth. *Léon Bakst: The Art of Theatre and Dance.* London: Parkstone Press, 2000.

Isaak, Jo Anna. *The Ruin of Representation in Modernist Art and Texts.* Ann Arbor: UMI Research Press, 1982.

Jacobs, Peter. "'Quel Décor!' Nijinsky Conquers Bloomsbury." *Charleston Magazine,* Spring/Summer 1994, 15–19.

Jaffe, Aaron. *Modernism and the Culture of Celebrity.* Cambridge: Cambridge University Press, 2005.

Jameson, Fredric. "Modernism and Imperialism." In *Nationalism, Colonialism, and Literature,* edited by Terry Eagleton, Fredric Jameson, and Edward Said, 43–66. Minneapolis: University of Minnesota Press, 1990.

———. *The Political Unconscious: Narrative as a Socially Symbolic Act.* Ithaca, NY: Cornell University Press, 1981.

———. *A Singular Modernity: Essays on the Ontology of the Present.* London: Verso, 2002.

JanMohamed, Abdul. "The Economy of Manichean Allegory: The Function of Racial Difference in Colonial Literature." In *"Race," Writing, and Difference,* edited by Henry Louis Gates, Jr., 78–106. Chicago: University of Chicago Press, 1986.

Jerving, Ryan. "Jazz Language and Ethnic Novelty." *Modernism/modernity* 10, no. 2 (April 2003): 239–68.

Johnson, Erica. "Giving Up the Ghost: National and Literary Haunting in *Orlando.*" *Modern Fiction Studies* 50, no. 1 (Spring 2004): 110–28.

Joshi, Priya. *In Another Country: Colonialism, Culture, and the English Novel in India.* New York: Columbia University Press, 2002.

Joyce, James. *A Portrait of the Artist as a Young Man.* 1916. Reprint, Oxford: Oxford University Press, 2000.

———. *Ulysses.* 1922. Reprint, New York: Vintage, 1986.

Joyce, Simon. *Capital Offenses: Geographies of Class and Crime in Victorian London.* Charlottesville: University of Virginia Press, 2003.

———. "Sexual Politics and the Aesthetics of Crime: Oscar Wilde in the Nineties." *English Literary History* 12, no. 1 (Summer 2002): 501–23.

Kalliney, Peter. *Cities of Affluence and Anger: A Literary Geography of Modern Englishness.* Charlottesville: University of Virginia Press, 2006.

Kaplan, Sydney Janet. *Katherine Mansfield and the Origins of Modernist Fiction*. Ithaca, NY: Cornell University Press, 1991.

Katz, Tamar. *Impressionist Subjects: Gender, Interiority, and Modernist Fiction in England*. Champaign: University of Illinois Press, 2000.

Kavka, Misha. "Men in (Shell) Shock: Masculinity, Trauma, and Psychoanalysis in Rebecca West's *The Return of the Soldier*." *Studies in 20th Century Literature* 22, no. 1 (1998): 151–71.

Keddie, Nikki R. *Roots of Revolution: An Interpretive History of Modern Iran*. New Haven, CT: Yale University Press, 1981.

Keown-Boyd, Henry. *The Fists of Righteous Harmony: A History of the Boxer Uprising in China in the Year 1900*. London: Leo Cooper, 1991.

Kidd, Colin. *The Forging of Races: Race and Scripture in the Protestant Atlantic World, 1600–2000*. Cambridge: Cambridge University Press, 2006.

Kiernan, V. G. *The Lords of Human Kind*. Boston: Little, Brown and Company, 1969.

Kimbrough, Robert. Introduction to *Heart of Darkness*, 3rd ed., by Joseph Conrad, ix–xvii. New York: W. W. Norton, 1988.

King, James. *Virginia Woolf*. London: Hamish Hamilton, 1994.

Kipling, Rudyard. "The White Man's Burden." In *Rudyard Kipling's Verse*. 321–22. New York: Doubleday, 1940.

Knopp, Sherron. "'If I Saw You Would You Kiss Me?': Sapphism and the Subversiveness of Virginia Woolf's *Orlando*." *PMLA* 103 (1988): 24–34.

Knox, Robert. *The Races of Men: A Fragment*. 1850. Reprint, Miami: Mnemosyne Publishing, 1969.

Laurence, Patricia. *Lily Briscoe's Chinese Eyes: Bloomsbury, Modernism, and China*. Columbia: University of South Carolina Press, 2003.

Lawrence, D. H. *Women in Love*. 1920. Reprint, London: Penguin Books, 2007.

Lawrence, Karen. "Orlando's Voyage Out." *Modern Fiction Studies* 38, no. 1 (1992): 253–75.

Lee, Hermione. "*To the Lighthouse*: 'Making Shapes Square Up.'" In *Virginia Woolf: Critical Assessments*, edited by Eleanor McNees, 735–55. Mountfield, UK: Helm Information, 1994.

———. *Virginia Woolf*. New York: Alfred A. Knopf, 1997.

Lee, Robert G. *Orientals*. Philadelphia: Temple University Press, 1999.

Lemke, Sieglinde. *Primitivist Modernism: Black Culture and the Origins of Transatlantic Modernism*. Oxford: Oxford University Press, 1998.

Levenson, Michael, ed. *The Cambridge Companion to Modernism*. Cambridge: Cambridge University Press, 1999.

———. *A Genealogy of Modernism: A Study of English Literary Doctrine, 1908–1922*. Cambridge: Cambridge University Press, 1984.

Lewis, Andrea. "The Visual Politics of Gender in Virginia Woolf's *The Voyage Out*." *Woolf Studies Annual* 1 (1995): 106–19.

Lewis, Pericles, ed. *The Cambridge Introduction to Modernism*. Cambridge: Cambridge University Press, 2007.

———. *Modernism, Nationalism, and the Novel*. Cambridge: Cambridge University Press, 2000.

Lewis, Wyndham, ed. *BLAST 1*. 1914. Reprint, Santa Barbara: Black Sparrow Press, 1981.

———. *Blasting and Bombardiering*. London: Eyre & Spottiswoode, 1937.

———. Introduction to *Wyndham Lewis and Vorticism: A Tate Gallery Exhibition Circulated by the Arts Council*. 1956. Yale Center for British Art, New Haven, CT.

———. "Kill John Bull with Art." *Outlook* xxxiv, July 18, 1914.

———. *Rude Assignment: A Narrative of My Career Up-to-date.* London: Hutchinson, 1950.

Linett, Maren. *Modernism, Feminism, and Jewishness.* Cambridge: Cambridge University Press, 2007.

Lionnet, Françoise. "Continents and Archipelagoes: From E Pluribus Unum to Creolized Solidarities," Special Issue, *PMLA* 123, no. 5 (October 2008): 1503–15.

Lorimer, Douglas. *Colour, Class and the Victorians: English Attitudes to the Negro in the Mid-nineteenth Century.* New York: Holmes and Meier Publishers, 1978.

Lovejoy, Arthur O. *The Great Chain of Being: A Study of the History of an Idea.* Cambridge, MA: Harvard University Press, 1936.

Lunn, Kenneth, ed. *Hosts, Immigrants, and Minorities: Historical Responses to Newcomers in British Society.* Kent: Wm. Dawson & Sons, 1980.

Lye, Colleen. "The Afro-Asian Analogy." Special Issue, *PMLA* 123, no. 5 (October 2008): 1732–36.

Lyon, Janet. "Gadže Modernism." *Modernism/modernity* 11, no. 3 (2004): 517–38.

———. "Josephine Baker's Hothouse." In *Modernism, Inc.,* edited by Jani Scandura and Michael Thurston, 29–47. New York: New York University Press, 2001.

———. *Manifestoes: Provocations of the Modern.* Ithaca, NY: Cornell University Press, 1999.

———. "Sickness and Decadence." Paper presented at the annual meeting of the Modernist Studies Association VII. Chicago, 2005.

Lyon, John. Introduction to *Heart of Darkness,* by Joseph Conrad. London: Penguin Books, 1995.

MacKenzie, John. *Propaganda and Empire: The Manipulation of British Public Opinion 1880–1960.* Manchester: Manchester University Press, 1986.

Mansfield, Katherine. "Je Ne Parle Pas Français." 1919. In *Katherine Mansfield's Selected Stories.* Edited by Vincent O'Sullivan. 121–44. New York: W. W. Norton, 2006.

———. *Journal of Katherine Mansfield.* Edited by John Middleton Murry. New York: Alfred A. Knopf, 1927.

———. *The Journal of Katherine Mansfield.* Edited by John Middleton Murry. London: Constable, 1954.

———. *Something Childish and Other Stories.* Edited and introduced by Suzanne Raitt. London: Penguin Books, 1996.

———. *Stories.* Introduction by Jeffrey Meyers. New York: Vintage Classics, 1991.

Mao, Douglas, and Rebecca L. Walkowitz. *Bad Modernisms.* Durham, NC: Duke University Press, 2006.

———. "The New Modernist Studies." *PMLA* 123, no. 3 (May 2008): 737–48.

Marchetti, Gina. *Romance and the "Yellow Peril": Race, Sex, and Discursive Strategies in Hollywood Fiction.* Berkeley: University of California Press, 1994.

Marek, Jayne. *Women Editing Modernism: "Little" Magazines & Literary History.* Lexington: University Press of Kentucky, 1995.

Marcus, Jane. "Britannia Rules *The Waves.*" In *Decolonizing Tradition,* edited by Karen Lawrence, 136–62. Urbana: University of Illinois Press, 1992.

———. Editor's Introduction to *The Young Rebecca: Writings of Rebecca West, 1911–17,* Selected and edited by Jane Marcus, 265–66. Bloomington: Indiana University Press, 1982.

———. *Hearts of Darkness: White Women Write Race.* New Brunswick, NJ: Rutgers University Press, 2004.

———, ed. *Suffrage and the Pankhursts.* London: Routledge & Kegan Paul, 1987.

Marinetti, F. T. "Founding and Manifesto of Futurism." In *Modernism: An Anthology,* edited by Lawrence Rainey, 3–6. Oxford: Blackwell, 2005.

Marx, John. *The Modernist Novel and the Decline of Empire*. Cambridge: Cambridge University Press, 2006.

Materer, Timothy. *Vortex: Pound, Eliot, and Lewis*. Ithaca, NY: Cornell University Press, 1979.

Matz, Jesse. *Literary Impressionism and Modernist Aesthetics*. Cambridge: Cambridge University Press, 2001.

May, J. P. "The Chinese in Britain, 1860–1914." In *Immigrants and Minorities in British Society*, edited by Colin Holmes, 111–24. London: George Allen & Unwin, 1978.

McGee, Patrick. "The Politics of Modernist Form; Or, Who Rules *The Waves*?" *Modern Fiction Studies* 38, no. 2 (1992): 631–50.

McIntire, Gabrielle. "The Women Do Not Travel: Gender, Difference, and Incommensurability in Conrad's *Heart of Darkness*." *Modern Fiction Studies* 42, no. 2. (Summer 2002): 257–84.

McNeillie, Andrew. "Leonard Woolf's *Empire and Commerce in Africa* Revisited." *Charleston Magazine*, Spring/Summer 2001, 52–4.

Melzer, Annabelle. "Spectacles and Sexualities: The 'Mise-en-Scène' of the '*Tirailleur Sénégalais*' on the Western Front, 1914–1920." In *Borderlines: Genders and Identities in War and Peace, 1870–1930*, edited by Billie Melman, 213–44. New York: Routledge, 1998.

Mercer, Kobena, ed. *Cosmopolitan Modernisms*. Cambridge, MA: MIT Press, 2005.

Mersal, Imam. "Eliminating Diasporic Identities." Special Issue, *PMLA* 123, no. 5 (October 2008): 1581–89.

Meyers, Jeffrey. Introduction to *Stories*, by Katherine Mansfield. New York: Vintage Classics, 1991. vii–xiv.

——. *Katherine Mansfield: A Biography*. New York: New Directions Publishing Corporation, 1978.

——. *Katherine Mansfield: A Darker View*. New York: Cooper Square Press, 2002.

Miller, Joshua L. "The Gorgeous Laughter of Filipino Modernity: Carlos Bulosan's *The Laughter of My Father*." In *Bad Modernisms*, edited by Douglas Mao and Rebecca L. Walkowitz, 238–68. Durham, NC: Duke University Press, 2006.

Mizener, Arthur. *The Saddest Story: A Biography of Ford Madox Ford*. London: Bodley Head, 1971.

Moers, Ellen. *The Dandy: Brummel to Beerbohm*. Lincoln: University of Nebraska Press, 1978.

Montesquieu, Charles. *On the Spirit of the Laws*. 1748. Translated by Thomas Nugent. Reprint, London: J. Collingwood, 1823.

Moore, Alan, and Kevin O'Neill. *The League of Extraordinary Gentlemen*. La Jolla, CA: America's Best Comics, 2000.

Moretti, Franco. *A Way in the World: The Bildungsroman in European Culture*. London: Verso, 2003.

Morrisson, Mark S. *The Public Face of Modernism: Little Magazines, Audiences, and Reception, 1905–1920*. Madison: University of Wisconsin Press, 2001.

Mortimer, Raymond. *Duncan Grant*. Hammondsworth, UK: Penguin Books, 1944.

Nava, Mica, and Alan O'Shea, eds. *Modern Times: Reflections on a Century of English Modernity*. London: Routledge, 1996.

Naylor, Gillian. *Bloomsbury: Its Artists, Authors and Designers*. Boston: Little, Brown and Company, 1990.

Nead, Lynda. *Victorian Babylon: People, Streets and Images in Nineteenth-Century London*. New Haven, CT: Yale University Press, 2005.

Nenno, Nancy. "Femininity, the Primitive, and Modern Urban Space: Josephine Baker in Berlin." In *Women in the Metropolis: Gender and Modernity in Weimar Culture*, edited by Katharina von Ankum, 145–161. Weimar and Now, no. 11. Berkeley: University of California Press, 1997.

Nevinson, C. R. W. *Paint and Prejudice*. New York: Harcourt, Brace, 1937.

Nicholls, Peter. *Modernisms*. Berkeley: University of California Press, 1995.

Nicholson, Virginia. *Among the Bohemians: Experiments in Living 1900–1939*. London: Viking, 2002.

Nicolson, Nigel. Introduction to *Passenger to Teheran*, by Vita Sackville-West, edited by Nigel Nicolson, 17–24. New York: Moyer Bell, 1990.

——. *Portrait of a Marriage: Vita Sackville-West and Harold Nicolson*. 1973. Reprint, Chicago: University of Chicago Press, 1998.

Nordau, Max. *Degeneration*. 1895. Translated by George L. Mosse. Reprint, Lincoln: University of Nebraska Press, 1993.

North, Julian. "The Opium-Eater As Criminal in Victorian Writing." In *Writing and Victorianism*, edited by J. B. Bullen, 120–36. London: Longman, 1997.

North, Michael. *The Dialect of Modernism: Race, Language, and Twentieth-Century Literature*. New York: Oxford University Press, 1994.

Nunokawa, Jeff. *Tame Passions of Wilde: The Styles of Manageable Desire*. Princeton, NJ: Princeton University Press, 2003.

Nussbaum, Felicity. *The Limits of the Human: Fictions of Anomaly, Race, and Gender in the Long Eighteenth Century*. Cambridge: Cambridge University Press, 2003.

O'Connor, Maureen. "*The Picture of Dorian Gray* as Irish National Tale." In *Writing Irishness in Nineteenth-Century British Culture*, edited by Neil McGraw, 194–209. Aldershot, UK: Ashgate, 2004.

O'Keeffe, Paul. *Some Sort of Genius: A Life of Wyndham Lewis*. London: Jonathan Cape, 2000.

The Omega Workshops 1913–19: Decorative Arts of Bloomsbury. London: The Publications Section, Crafts Council, 1984.

Orwell, George. *Burmese Days*. 1934. Reprint, New York: Harvest Books, 1974.

O'Sullivan, Vincent. Introduction to *New Zealand Stories*, by Katherine Mansfield. Auckland, NZ: Oxford University Press, 1997.

Panayi, Panikos. "Anti-Immigration Riots." In *Racial Violence in Britain 1840–1950*, edited by Panikos Panayi, 1–25. Leicester: Leicester University Press, 1993.

——. *Immigration, Ethnicity and Racism in Britain, 1815–1945*. Manchester: Manchester University Press, 1994.

Parry, Benita. "Conrad and England." In *Patriotism: The Making and Unmaking of British National Identity*. Vol. 3, *National Fictions*, edited by Raphael Samuel, 189–98. London and New York: Routledge, 1989.

——. "The Moment and Afterlife of *Heart of Darkness*." In *Conrad in the Twenty-First Century*, edited by Cora Kaplan, Peter Mallios, and Andrea White, 38–53. New York: Routledge, 2004.

Patterson, Anita. *Race, American Literature and Transnational Modernism*. Cambridge: Cambridge University Press, 2008.

Peppis, Paul. *Literature, Politics, and the English Avant-Garde: Nation and Empire, 1901–1918*. Cambridge: Cambridge University Press, 2000.

Phillips, Caryl. Introduction to *Heart of Darkness*, by Joseph Conrad. New York: Modern Library Classics, 1999.

Phillips, Kathy. *Virginia Woolf against Empire*. Knoxville: University of Tennessee Press, 1994.

Playford, John. "Music and Musicians: Mozart in a Cabaret." *The New Age*, July 3, 1913, 274.

Potolsky, Matthew. "Decadence, Nationalism, and the Logic of Canon Formation." *Modern Language Quarterly* 67 (2006): 213–44.

Pound, Ezra. *The Cantos of Ezra Pound*. 1972. Reprint, New York: New Directions, 1996.

———. *Gaudier-Brzeska: A Memoir*. 1916. Reprint, New York: New Directions, 1970.

———. "Hugh Selwyn Mauberley." 1920. Reprinted in *Modernism: An Anthology*, edited by Lawrence Rainey, 48–61. Oxford: Blackwell Publishing, 2005.

Pratt, Mary Louise. *Imperial Eyes: Travel Writing and Transculturation*. London: Routledge, 1992.

"Preliminary Prospectus for the Cabaret Theatre Club and the Cave of the Golden Calf." April 1912. Yale Center for British Art, New Haven, CT.

Pykett, Lyn. *Engendering Fictions: The English Novel in the Early Twentieth Century*. New York: St. Martin's Press, 1995.

Rainey, Lawrence. "The Creation of the Avant-Garde: F. T. Marinetti and Ezra Pound." *Modernism/modernity* 1, no. 3 (1994): 195–220.

Raitt, Suzanne. *Vita and Virginia: The Work and Friendship of V. Sackville-West and Virginia Woolf*. Oxford: Clarendon Press, 1993.

Reed, Christopher. "Forming Formalism: The Post-Impressionist Exhibits." In *A Roger Fry Reader*, edited by Christopher Reed, 48–60. Chicago: University of Chicago Press, 1996.

———. "Through Formalism: Feminism and Virginia Woolf's Relation to Bloomsbury Aesthetics." *Twentieth Century Literature* 38, no. 1 (1992): 20–43.

Reed, Christopher, ed. *A Roger Fry Reader*. Chicago: University of Chicago Press, 1996.

Reid, Panthea. *Art and Affection: A Life of Virginia Woolf*. Oxford: Oxford University Press, 1996.

Rhodes, Colin. *Primitivism and Modern Art*. London: Thames and Hudson, 1994.

Rhys, Jean. *Voyage in the Dark*. 1934. Reprint, New York: W. W. Norton, 1982.

Richards, Thomas. *The Imperial Archive: Knowledge and the Fantasy of Empire*. London: Verso, 1993.

Rigby, Nigel, and Howard Booth. *Modernism and Empire: Writing and British Coloniality, 1890–1940*. Manchester: Manchester University Press, 2000.

Riquelme, John Paul. "Oscar Wilde's Aesthetic Gothic: Walter Pater, Dark Enlightenment, and *The Picture of Dorian Gray*." *Modern Fiction Studies* 46, no. 3 (Fall 2000): 610–31.

Robinson, Alan. *Symbol to Vortex: Poetry, Painting and Ideas, 1885–1914*. New York: St. Martin's Press, 1985.

Rohmer, Sax. *The Devil Doctor*. 1916. Reprinted in *The Fu-Manchu Omnibus*. London: Allison & Busby, 1998.

———. *The Mystery of Dr. Fu-Manchu*. 1913. Reprinted in *The Fu-Manchu Omnibus*. London: Allison & Busby, 1998.

———. *The Si-Fan Mysteries*. 1917. Reprinted in *The Fu-Manchu Omnibus*. London: Allison & Busby, 1998.

Ross, Stephen. *Conrad and Empire*. Columbia: University of Missouri Press, 2004.

Rubin, William, ed. *"Primitivism" in 20th Century Art: Affinity of the Tribal and the Modern*. New York: Harry N. Abrams, 1988.

Sackville-West, Vita. *Passenger to Teheran*. New York: George H. Doran Company, 1927.

Said, Edward. *Beginnings: Intention and Method*. New York: Columbia University Press, 1975.

——. *Culture and Imperialism*. New York: Vintage Books, 1993.

——. *Orientalism*. New York: Vintage Books, 1979.

Sarker, Sonita. "*Three Guineas*, the In-corporated Intellectual, and Nostalgia for the Human." In *Virginia Woolf in the Age of Mechanical Reproduction*, edited by Pamela Caughie, 37–66. New York: Garland, 2000.

Sartre, Jean-Paul. Preface to *The Wretched of the Earth*, by Frantz Fanon, 7–31. New York: Grove Press, 1963.

Schneer, Jonathan. *London 1900*. New Haven, CT: Yale University Press, 1999.

Schuchard, Ronald. "Burbank with a Baedeker, Eliot with a Cigar: American Intellectuals, Anti-Semitism, and the Idea of Culture." *Modernism/modernity* 10, no. 1 (2003): 1–26.

Schwartz, Daniel R. *Reconfiguring Modernism: Explorations in the Relationship between Modern Art and Modern Life*. New York: St. Martin's Press, 1997.

Scott, Bonnie Kime, ed. *Gender in Modernism: New Geographies, Complex Intersections*. Urbana: University of Illinois Press, 2007.

——, ed. *The Gender of Modernism: A Critical Anthology*. Bloomington: Indiana University Press, 1990.

——. "Introduction: A Retro-Perspective on Gender in Modernism." In *Gender in Modernism: New Geographies, Complex Intersections*, edited by Bonnie Kime Scott, 1–22. Urbana: University of Illinois Press, 2007.

——. "Rebecca West." In *The Gender of Modernism: A Critical Anthology*, edited by Bonnie Kime Scott, 560–69. Bloomington: Indiana University Press, 1990.

——. *Refiguring Modernism*. 2 vols. Bloomington: Indiana University Press, 1995.

Sedgwick, Eve. *Epistemology of the Closet*. Berkeley: University of California Press, 1991.

Segel, Harold B. *Turn-of-the-Century Cabaret*. New York: Columbia University Press, 1987.

Seshagiri, Urmila. "Modernist Ashes, Postcolonial Phoenix: Jean Rhys and the Evolution of the English Novel in the Twentieth Century." *Modernism/modernity* 13, no. 3 (September 2006): 487–505.

Sharpe, Jenny. *Allegories of Empire: The Figure of Woman in the Colonial Text*. Minneapolis: University of Minnesota Press, 1993.

Sharpley-Whiting, T. Denean. *Black Venus: Sexualized Savages, Primal Fear, and Primitive Narratives in French*. Durham, NC: Duke University Press, 1999.

Sherry, Vincent. *Ezra Pound, Wyndham Lewis, and Radical Modernism*. Oxford: Oxford University Press, 1993.

Shih, Shu-mei. "Comparative Racialization: An Introduction." Special Issue, *PMLA* 123, no. 5 (October 2008): 1347–62.

Shone, Richard. *The Art of Bloomsbury: Roger Fry, Vanessa Bell and Duncan Grant*. London: Tate Gallery Publishing, 1999.

——. "Duncan Grant: Designer and Decorator." In *A Bloomsbury Canvas*, edited by Tony Bradshaw, 22–25. Aldershot, UK: Lund Humphries/Ashgate, 2001.

——. "The Myths and Fantasies of Duncan Grant." In *A Bloomsbury Canvas*, edited by Tony Bradshaw, 74–5. Aldershot, UK: Lund Humphries/Ashgate, 2001.

Showalter, Elaine. *The Female Malady: Women, Madness, and English Culture, 1830–1980*. New York: Penguin Books, 1985.

Silber, Evelyn. *Gaudier-Brzeska: Life and Art*. London: Thames and Hudson, 1996.

Simmel, Georg. "The Metropolis and Mental Life." In *Georg Simmel On Individuality and*

Social Forms, edited and with an introduction by Donald N. Levine, 324–49. Chicago: University of Chicago Press, 1971.

Sinfield, Alan. *The Wilde Century: Effeminacy, Oscar Wilde, and the Queer Moment.* London: Cassell, 1994.

Sitwell, Osbert. *Great Morning.: Being the Third Volume of Left Hand, Right Hand! An Autobiography.* London: Macmillan, 1948.

Smith, Angela. *Katherine Mansfield and Virginia Woolf: A Public of Two.* Oxford: Oxford University Press, 1998.

Snitow, Ann Barr. *Ford Madox Ford and the Voice of Uncertainty.* Baton Rouge: Louisiana State University Press, 1984.

Sollors, Werner. *Ethnic Modernism.* Cambridge, MA: Harvard University Press, 2008.

Spalding, Frances. *Roger Fry: Art and Life.* Berkeley: University of California Press, 1980.

"Specialists in Crime." *Vanity Fair,* September 1930, 56.

Sproles, Karyn Z. *Desiring Women: The Partnership of Virginia Woolf and Vita Sackville-West.* Toronto: University of Toronto Press, 2006.

Spurr, David. *The Rhetoric of Empire: Colonial Discourse in Journalism, Travel Writing, and Imperial Administration.* Durham, NC: Duke University Press, 1993.

Stableford, Brian. *Scientific Romance in Britain 1890–1950.* New York: St. Martin's Press, 1985.

Stannard, Martin. "A Note on the Text." In *The Good Soldier,* by Ford Madox Ford, edited by Martin Stannard, 179–93. New York: W. W. Norton, 1995.

Stansky, Peter. *On or about 1910: Early Bloomsbury and Its Intimate World.* Cambridge, MA: Harvard University Press, 1997.

Stepan, Nancy. *The Idea of Race in Science: Great Britain, 1800–1960.* Hamden, CT: Archon Books, 1982.

Stephen, Adrian. *The "Dreadnought" Hoax.* 1936. Reprint, London: Hogarth Press, 1983.

Stevenson, Randall. *Modernist Fiction.* Lexington: University of Kentucky Press, 1992.

Stimpson, Catharine. "Zero Degree Deviancy: The Lesbian Novel in English." In *Writing and Sexual Difference,* edited by Elizabeth Abel, 243–59. Chicago: University of Chicago Press, 1982.

Stocking, George. *Race, Culture, and Evolution: Essays in the History of Anthropology.* Chicago: University of Chicago Press, 1982.

——. *Victorian Anthropology.* New York: Free Press, 1987.

Stoker, Bram. *Dracula.* 1897. Edited by Nina Auerbach. Reprint, New York: W. W. Norton, 1997.

Stovall, Tyler. *Paris Noir: African-Americans in the City of Light.* New York: Houghton Mifflin, 1996.

Suleri, Sara. *The Rhetoric of English India.* Chicago: University of Chicago Press, 1992.

Sullivan, J. W. N. "The Story-Writing Genius." *The Athenaeum,* April 2, 1920, 447.

Tickner, Lisa. "Men's Work? Masculinity and Modernism." *Differences* 4, no. 3 (Spring 1993): 1–37.

——. *Modern Life & Modern Subjects: British Art in the Early Twentieth Century.* New Haven, CT: Yale University Press, 2000.

——. *The Spectacle of Women: Imagery of the Suffrage Campaign 1907–1914.* London: Chatto and Windus, 1987.

Tomalin, Claire. *Katherine Mansfield: A Secret Life.* New York: St. Martin's Press, 1987.

Torgovnick, Marianna. *Gone Primitive: Savage Intellects, Modern Lives.* Chicago: University of Chicago Press, 1990.

Turnbaugh, Douglas Blair, ed. *Private: The Erotic Art of Duncan Grant, 1885–1978.* London: Gay Men's Press, 1989.

Van Ash, Cay, and Elizabeth Sax Rohmer. *Master of Villainy: A Biography of Sax Rohmer.* Bowling Green, OH: Bowling Green University Popular Press, 1972.

Visram, Rozina. *Asians in Britain: 400 Years of History.* London and Sterling, VA: Pluto Press, 2002.

Walkowitz, Judith. *City of Dreadful Delight: Narratives of Sexual Danger in Late-Victorian London.* Chicago: University of Chicago Press, 1992.

Walkowitz, Rebecca. *Cosmopolitan Style: Modernism Beyond the Nation.* New York: Columbia University Press, 2006.

Walvin, James. *Passage to Britain: Immigration in British History and Politics.* Hammondsworth, UK: Penguin Books, 1984.

Watson, Colin. *Snobbery with Violence: English Crime Stories and Their Audience.* London: Eyre Methuen, 1971.

Watson, James. "The Chinese: Hong Kong Villagers in the British Catering Trade." In *Between Two Cultures: Migrants and Minorities in Britain,* edited by James Watson, 181–213. Oxford: Basil Blackwell, 1977.

Watt, Ian. *Conrad in the Nineteenth Century.* Berkeley: University of California Press, 1979.

Watts, Cedric. Introduction to *Heart of Darkness,* by Joseph Conrad. Oxford: Oxford University Press, 2002.

Wees, William. *Vorticism and the English Avant-Garde.* Toronto: University of Toronto Press, 1972.

West, Rebecca. "Indissoluble Matrimony." 1914. Reprinted in *BLAST 1,* by Wyndham Lewis, 98–117. Santa Barbara: Black Sparrow Press, 1981.

———. *Selected Letters of Rebecca West.* Edited, annotated, and introduced by Bonnie Kime Scott. New Haven, CT: Yale University Press, 2000.

Wey Gómez, Nicolás. *The Tropics of Empire: Why Columbus Sailed South to the Indies.* Cambridge, MA: MIT Press, 2008.

Wheeler, Roxann. *The Complexion of Race: Categories of Difference in Eighteenth-Century British Culture.* Philadelphia: University of Pennsylvania Press, 2000.

Whitworth, Michael, ed. *Modernism.* Oxford: Blackwell, 2007.

Wilde, Oscar. *The Picture of Dorian Gray.* 1891. Edited by Donald Lawler. Reprint, New York: W. W. Norton, 1988.

Williams, Raymond. *The Country and the City.* Oxford: Oxford University Press, 1973.

———. "Metropolitan Perceptions and the Emergence of Modernism." In *The Politics of Modernism,* edited by Tony Pinkney, 37–48. London: Verso, 1989.

———. "The Politics of the Avant-Garde." In *The Politics of Modernism,* edited by Tony Pinkney, 49–63. London: Verso, 1989.

Winkiel, Laura A. "Cabaret Modernism: Vorticism and Racial Spectacle." In *Geomodernisms: Race, Modernism, Modernity,* edited by Laura Doyle and Laura A. Winkiel, 206–226. Bloomington: Indiana University Press, 2005.

———. *Modernism, Race and Manifestoes.* Cambridge: Cambridge University Press, 2008.

Winston, Janet. "'Something Out of Harmony': *To the Lighthouse* and the Subject(s) of Empire." *Woolf Studies Annual* 2 (1996): 38–70.

Wollaeger, Mark. *Joseph Conrad and the Fictions of Skepticism.* Palo Alto CA: Stanford University Press, 1990.

———. "Woolf, Postcards, and the Elision of Race: Colonizing Women in *The Voyage Out.*" *Modernism/modernity* 8, no. 1 (January 2001): 43–75.

Wollen, Peter. *Raiding the Icebox: Reflections on Twentieth-Century Culture.* Bloomington: Indiana University Press, 1993.

Woolf, Virginia. *Between the Acts.* New York: Harcourt, Brace, 1941.

——. *Congenial Spirits: The Selected Letters of Virginia Woolf.* Edited by Joanne Trautmann Banks. New York: Harcourt Brace Jovanovich, 1989.

——. *The Diary of Virginia Woolf.* Edited by Anne Olivier Bell. 5 vols. New York: Harcourt Brace Jovanovich, 1977–1984.

——. "*Dreadnought* Notes." 1940. Reprinted in *The Platform of Time,* edited and introduced by S. P. Rosenbaum, 165–7. London: Hesperus Press Limited, 2007.

——. Foreword to *Recent Paintings by Vanessa Bell.* London Artists' Association. 1930.

——. Interview. 1910. Reprinted in *The Platform of Time,* edited and introduced by S. P. Rosenbaum, 168–69. London: Hesperus Press Limited, 2007.

——. "Jews." In *Carlyle's House and Other Stories,* edited by David Bradshaw, foreword by Doris Lessing, 14–15. London: Hesperus Press, 2003.

——. "Lady Hester Stanhope." 1910. Reprinted in *Books and Portraits: Some Further Selections from the Literary and Biographical Writings of Virginia Woolf,* edited by Mary Lyon, 195–200. New York: Harcourt Brace Jovanovich, 1977.

——. "Letters from Virginia." *Virginia Woolf Bulletin* 2 (July 1999): 4–12.

——. *The Letters of Virginia Woolf, Vol. 3: 1923–28.* Edited by Nigel Nicolson and Joanne Trautmann. New York: Harcourt Brace Jovanovich, 1977.

——. *The Letters of Virginia Woolf, Vol. 4: 1929–1931.* Edited by Nigel Nicolson and Joanne Trautmann. New York: Harcourt Brace Jovanovich, 1978.

——. "Modern Fiction." In *The Virginia Woolf Reader,* edited by Mitchell A. Leaska, 283–91. New York: Harcourt Brace Jovanovich, 1984.

——. *Moments of Being.* 1976. Edited by Jeanne Schulkind. Reprint, New York: Harcourt Brace Jovanovich, 1985.

——. "Mr. Bennett and Mrs. Brown." 1924. Reprinted in *The Virginia Woolf Reader,* edited by Mitchell A. Leaska, 192–212. New York: Harcourt Brace Jovanovich, 1984.

——. *Mrs. Dalloway.* 1925. Reprint, New York: Harcourt Brace Jovanovich, 1953.

——. *Orlando.* 1928. Reprint, New York: Harcourt Brace Jovanovich, 1956.

——. *A Passionate Apprentice: The Early Journals 1897–1909.* Edited by Mitchell A. Leaska. New York: Harcourt Brace Jovanovich, 1977.

——. *Roger Fry: A Biography.* 1940. Reprint, New York: Harcourt Brace Jovanovich, 1968.

——. *A Room of One's Own.* 1929. Reprint, New York: Harcourt Brace Jovanovich, 1989.

——. "Thunder at Wembley." 1924. Reprinted in *The Essays of Virginia Woolf,* Vol. 3. Edited by Andrew McNeillie. New York: Harvest Books, 1995.

——. *To the Lighthouse.* 1927. Reprint, New York: Harcourt Brace Jovanovich, 1955.

——. *The Waves.* 1931. Reprint, New York: Harcourt Brace Jovanovich, 1959.

——. *The Years.* 1937. Reprint, New York: Houghton Mifflin Harcourt, 1969.

Worringer, Wilhelm. 1908. *Abstraction and Empathy.* Reprint, Chicago: Elephant Paperbacks, 1997.

Wu, William. *The Yellow Peril: Chinese Americans in American Fiction 1850–1940.* Hamden, CT: Archon Books, 1982.

Xing, Jun. *Asian America through the Lens: History, Representations, and Identity.* Walnut Creek, CA: AltaMira Press, 1998.

Yeats, W. B. "The Second Coming." 1919. Reprinted in *The Yeats Reader,* edited by Richard J. Finneran, 80. New York: Scribner Poetry, 2002.

Yeh, Wen-Hsin. "Introduction: Interpreting Chinese Modernity." In *Becoming Chinese:*

Passages to Modernity and Beyond, edited by Wen-Hsin Yeh, 1–30. Berkeley: University of California Press, 2000.

Young, Hilary. *English Porcelain, 1745–95: Its Makers, Design, Marketing and Consumption.* London: Victoria & Albert Museum, 1999.

Young, Robert. *Colonial Desire: Hybridity in Theory, Culture and Race.* London and New York: Routledge, 1995.

Zwerdling, Alex. *Virginia Woolf and the Real World.* Berkeley: University of California Press, 1986.

INDEX

abstract (nonrepresentational) art, 80–81, 84–86, 88–89, 93–94

Achebe, Chinua, 42, 52, 53

Adorno, Theodor, 44, 200n10

the aesthetic: critical race theory and lack of attention to, 220n8; race as organizing category of, 6, 12, 29–30, 196; subordination of the social to, 42, 196. *See also* aestheticized forms of race; primitive aesthetics

aestheticized forms of race: the avant-garde arts and, 6–7; Ballets Russes and, 6; Conrad and, 30–31, 42, 44–49, 52–53, 205n41; filiation and affiliation and, 8–9; Ford and, 119–120, 122–123; and newness, 15, 30; Omega Workshops and, 158–159, 163; popular culture and, 7; and realism, abandonment of, 6, 35, 41; unreliability of race and, 8–9; Wilde and, 30–31, 42, 52–53; Woolf and, 144

Aldington, Richard, 81, 211–212n47

alienation, urban: Conrad and, 52; Mansfield and, 126, 130, 139; as modernist signature, 13, 54, 62; Rohmer and, 13, 62, 70, 71, 73, 208n65

Ancient Lights and Certain New Reflections (Ford), 114

Anderson, Benedict, 219n45

Anscombe, Isabelle, 159

anti-Semitism, 34–35, 115, 149, 203n29, 215n14

anxieties and modernism: and agency, 58; and disruptions of racial continuity, 8;

dissolution of objective certainties, 58–59; feminist militancy and, 108–109, *110*, 211n46; signature, 13, 54. *See also* degeneration; scientific racism

Apollinaire, Guillaume, 4, 128

Appignanesi, Lisa, 82, 86

L'Après-midi d'un faune (Ballets Russes), 5

Arabian Nights, 72, 172, 218n34

Arnold, Matthew, 219n44

art and life boundary, 5, 125, 128, 134

art object, status of, 30, 32, 129–130, 134–135, 138, 194

"At the Bay" (Mansfield), 125

autotelic art, 111, 142, 155, 166

avant-garde: and break with the past, 80–81; hybridity and, 79; and newness, 77–78, 88; period of, 77; and primitive aesthetics, 13–14, 81; social-professional climate, 81. See also *BLAST;* Cave of the Golden Calf; Ford, Ford Madox; Fry, Roger; Lewis, Wyndham; Mansfield, Katherine; modernism; Omega Workshops; shock tactics

Bakst, Léon, 1, *2–3*, 5, 192, *193*

Balanchine, George, 5

Baldick, Chris, 200n12

Ballets Russes, 1–6, *2–4*, 84, 148, 192, *193*, 215n12, 216n23

Barnes, Djuna, 194

Baucom, Ian, 219n38

Baudelaire, Charles, 34, 62, 70, 114, 200n10

Beardsley, Aubrey, 209n14